D1351329

Pricing Convertible Bonds

OTHER TITLES IN THE WILEY TRADING ADVANTAGE SERIES

New Market Timing Techniques: Innovative Studies in Market Rhythm and Price Exhaustion
Thomas Denmark

Gaming the Market: Applying Game Theory to Create Winning Trading Strategies
Ron Shelton

Trading on Expectations: Strategies to Pinpoint Trading Ranges, Trends, and Reversals
Brendan Moynihan

Fundamental Analysis
Jack D. Schwager

Technical Analysis
Jack D. Schwager

Managed Trading, Myths and Truths
Jack D. Schwager

McMillan on Options
Lawrence G. McMillan

The Option Advisor, Wealth-Building Techniques Using Equity and Index Options
Bernie G. Schaeffer

PRICING CONVERTIBLE BONDS

Kevin B. Connolly

John Wiley & Sons
Chichester • New York • Weinheim • Brisbane • Singapore • Toronto

Copyright © 1998 by   John Wiley & Sons Ltd,
Baffins Lane, Chichester,
West Sussex PO19 1UD, England

National   01243 779777
International (+44) 1243 779777
e-mail (for orders and customer service enquiries): cs-books@wiley.co.uk
Visit our home page on http://www.wiley.co.uk
or http://www.wiley.com

Reprinted February 2000

Other Wiley Editorial Offices

John Wiley & Sons, Inc., 605 Third Avenue,
New York, NY 10158-0012, USA

WILEY-VCH Verlag GmbH, Pappelallee 3
D-69469 Weinheim, Germany

Jacaranda Wiley Ltd, 33 Park Road, Milton,
Queensland 4064, Australia

John Wiley & Sons (Asia) Pte Ltd, 2 Clementi Loop #02-01,
Jin Xing Distripark, Singapore 129809

John Wiley & Sons (Canada) Ltd, 22 Worcester Road,
Rexdale, Ontario M9W 1L1, Canada

Library of Congress Cataloging-in-Publication Data

Connolly, Kevin B.
    Pricing convertible bonds/Kevin B. Connolly.
       p. cm. – (Wiley series in financial engineering)
    Includes index.
    ISBN 0–471–97872–8
    1. Convertible bonds. 2. Convertible preferred stocks. 3. Option
(Contract) I. Title. II. Series.
HG4651.C6946 1998   98–19146
332.63′23–dc21   CIP

British Library Cataloguing in Publication Data

A catalogue record for this book is available from the British Library

ISBN 0–471–97872–8

Typeset in 10/12pt Times by MHL Typsetting, Coventry.
Printed and bound in Great Britain by Biddles Ltd, Guildford and King's Lynn
This book is printed on acid-free paper responsibly manufactured from sustainable forestry, for which at least two trees are planted for each one used for paper production.

Contents

Preface

There are few works on the subject of pricing convertible bonds. Most books discussing derivative products cover all the aspects of pricing futures and options in minute detail. But convertible bonds (CBs), along with warrants, are usually mentioned as an afterthought in later chapters. There has been a profusion of academic literature on the pricing and efficiency of the futures and options markets, but very little on CBs. And this is strange in that the convertible bond market is one of the last sources of genuinely risk-free returns in the field of derivative products. The convertible bond market has supplied and continues to supply risk-free revenues on a huge scale and, for identical reasons, provides very good value to equity market players with a low capacity for risk. So why the lack of literature and why are risk-free returns still available?

One reason is the lack of a standard contract. Exchange traded options have standard exercise prices, standard numbers of shares per contract and standard expiry dates. Each CB that comes to the market will have a unique non-standard expiry date. To make matters worse, most CBs pay a coupon and of course, this will also be unique to the particular issue.

Another reason is that many of the instruments are not exchange traded. Exchanges attempt to provide an efficient price discovery mechanism. With no official closing prices, many of the more traditional players are unwilling to participate.

Probably the main reason for the continued profit opportunities in the CB market is the sheer complexity of the instruments. All listed exchange traded derivatives have a very simple structure. Almost all have one point of price discontinuity in the future. On expiry, call and put options are worth the intrinsic value or nothing, depending on the price of the underlying share and the options' exercise price. This one point of discontinuity makes the valuation (mathematical or intuitive) relatively easy. With CBs, this is most definitely not the case. Although CBs have an embedded call option on the underlying equity, they are also subject to being recalled and so by definition have an embedded short-call feature. Many CBs are convertible into equity priced in one currency, but redeemable into a lump cash sum denominated in another currency, and this obviously gives rise to a foreign exchange complication. Many CBs also have a feature that allows the holder to sell the instrument back to the issuer at a fixed price before expiry and so have an embedded long-put option. Finally, many CBs coming to the market now have what are known as refix clauses. These refix clauses have the effect of (possibly) altering the original terms of the CB — usually, but not always, to the advantage of the holder. All these complications make the traditional exchange traded put and call participant shy away from dealing in CBs. This may be the very reason that profitable opportunities still exist. This will be the first book to address the complex issue of pricing convertible bonds correctly. The outline of the book is as follows.

Chapter 1 introduces the three basic investment vehicles discussed in this book: bonds, equities and CBs. Also introduced are the concepts of shorting, gearing up a risk-free investment and the ideas behind arbitrage and hedge trading. CB models are complex and require a considerable number of calculations. Even the simplest model therefore will require the use of a computer. However, we show in Chapter 2 that you do not have to be a computer programmer to price a CB — you just have to be able to use a spreadsheet. Most readers will be familiar with the use of spreadsheets and Chapter 2 reviews some of the more complex aspects of the Microsoft Excel spreadsheet software that will be used throughout the book. The expressions 'risk' and 'return' are often used without a rigorous understanding of the terms and how they are calculated. Chapter 3 addresses these issues and describes how to get from an historical sequence of prices to the standard estimates of risk and return. The concepts of expectation and volatility are also explained. Practitioners use the binomial model to explain the standard share price generation process underlying most derivative products, often without really understanding its implications. This is dealt with in Chapter 4, starting with the simple additive one-step model and gradually developing on to the multi-step multiplicative model. Chapter 4 also gives examples of stock price generating processes with non-independent price changes and explains the implications for risk and return estimation.

Chapter 5 is the main core of the book — the CB pricing model. The model depends on a simple two-way-bet construct involving two entities. In the context of this book, the two entities are a share and a CB riding on the back of the share. General mathematical expressions involving the values of two perfectly correlated entities are derived. What falls out of this construct is the fair price of a CB and, more importantly, a fair price that does not involve probability issues. The one-period two-way-bet model is then expanded to two periods, then three, and eventually to a general n-period model. Interest rate and coupon payment complications are then introduced. Chapter 5 ends with a model that describes, remarkably accurately, how CB prices vary in reality — a model that basically turns out to be a series of small straight-line equations that graphically look very much like a smooth curve.

Chapter 6 introduces into the model several of the problems that make pricing

CBs even more complex: Problems such as (1) the underlying equity often pays non-trivial dividends, (2) the issuer invariably has a right to call the bond back, (3) some CBs have an embedded put option, (4) using more than one interest rate and (5) foreign exchange issues with non-domestic CBs.

Almost as important as pricing a CB is estimating how the price will change when something else changes. CBs are affected by interest rates, share prices and the volatility of share prices. Chapter 7 deals with the calculation of these CB price sensitivities and shows, using unique contour diagrams, how these sensitivities vary as time passes. Chapter 7 also addresses the important issue of how price sensitivities vary over time.

Chapter 8 discusses the old fashioned simplistic description of a CB as a warrant plus bond and why some practitioners still (incorrectly) value the instruments this way. Only in very special circumstances can a CB be valued as a bond and warrant and in these special circumstances, a particularly simple closed form pricing model exists — the Black and Scholes Model. Chapter 8 also uses the example of an investment trust warrant to address the issue of dilution.

Refix clauses alter the terms of a CB. These features, originally introduced to the Japanese Warrant Market in 1991, were an attempt by the issuers to make the products more attractive. They have become increasingly popular in the CB market and their inclusion is dealt with in Chapter 9.

It is assumed that the interested reader will eventually want to build up his or her own CB pricing software. The Appendix gives in more detail most of the models and examples used throughout the book. The Appendix can also be used as a guide to the software on the disk supplied with this book. The reader is shown how to build up from the basic one-period model to a ten-period model. The final model has a dividend-paying share, coupons, a call provision and a bond put. A non-domestic CB example is given and examples of price sensitivity are shown.

The disk supplied with this book will assist the interested reader to build up his or her own CB pricing software. It should be pointed out that at the time of writing, proprietary CB software retails at about £11,000 per copy.

1
Introduction

Convertible bonds (CBs) are investment vehicles that are part bond and part equity. This duality makes CBs interesting to a wide variety of investors. Some investors are interested only in the bond part and some only in the equity part, but most get involved because the instruments can be bond one day and equity another. The purpose of this book is to attempt to explain, via a mathematical model, this unusual behaviour. Before we get into the complications of price modelling, we outline the three basic investment vehicles of bonds, equity and CBs. We give a number of examples of how CB prices vary with respect to the underlying share price, volatility and interest rates. Many CBs are complicated by the presence of call and put provisions and some also are affected by the levels of certain foreign exchange rates. Brief examples of these complications along with the increasingly popular Refix Clauses are given. The CB market is now very much dominated by the large hedge traders and in order fully to appreciate the modelling process and how profits are extracted, it is necessary to understand concepts such as (1) shorting shares, (2) the futures and options markets, (3) gearing up low-risk investments and (4) static and dynamic arbitrage trading. This chapter briefly reviews these topics.

1.1 BONDS

Bonds are issued by governments, local authorities and corporations and are generally bought by investors, fund managers and speculators. Bonds are essentially loans from one party to another. Governments and corporations issue bonds usually to finance some large project such as the building of a dam or the construction of a new plant. The issuance or flotation of a bond represents the generation of an agreement between the bond issuer and the bondholder. The issuer agrees to pay the holder a fixed sum of money (the redemption proceeds or redemption price) at the end of a given period of time. In addition to the redemption proceeds, most bonds also pay a fixed coupon. Coupons are usually paid annually or semi-annually and are expressed as a percentage of the redemption price. A typical example would be a bond with a face value of, say, £100 maturing in ten years with an annual coupon of 5%. The buyer of such a bond would receive £5 a year for ten years and a final sum of £100. The price paid for such a bond will be dictated by, amongst other things, the current level of interest rates and this will be discussed in Chapter 5.

When someone buys a bond at issue he is essentially lending someone else (or some entity) a lump sum of money today in return for the promise of a stream of future payments and a final lump sum. If the original purchaser later sells on the bond to someone else and the maturity date is still some time in the future, then the seller is receiving a lump sum of cash and passing on to the new holder the promised sequence of futures payments. As a given bond is sold and bought over time, the parties exchange lump sums of cash and pass on the promised future payments to someone else. Eventually the maturity date will arrive and the final coupon and the final redemption price will be paid to the last person holding the bond. After this, the bond expires and is no more — all debts will have been repaid. When buying a bond it is quite easy to calculate the yield to maturity. Relatively simple mathematical expressions involving the coupons, the redemption price and the time to maturity give the yield. So when buying a bond you know for sure what your future income is going to be and you know for sure what final lump sum you will receive on the maturity date. This is why bonds are classed as low- or no-risk investments; that is the theory anyway.

Unfortunately, some issuers default and this is where the problems arise in trying to price some bonds and why classifying all bonds as risk free is nonsense. To be fair, most government-backed issues never fail. And the same can be said of most blue-chip corporations' issues. But some corporations do get into trouble and either default on a coupon or, worse still, the redemption proceeds. There exist a number of institutions that do nothing else but rate corporate bonds. Corporations that are considered to have a very low risk of default are rated AAA. Corporations considered to have a higher risk of default are rated AA. The rating scale goes all the way down to B−. From time to time ratings change. A corporation can be rated A− one day and the next BBB. Ratings are changed usually because of some event that affects the future likelihood of default.

When a corporation defaults on a coupon or redemption payment it is usually a very serious matter. The worst-case scenario is usually when a company goes into liquidation. In the event of a total meltdown the bondholders usually stand in front of any other creditor. This means that after the tax man gets his share, the bondholders stand first in line if there are any residual assets.

1.2 EQUITY

Owning equity or a share in a company is the same thing as having a stake in the company's fortunes. If the company does well then the price of the shares will increase. If the company does poorly then the price of the shares will fall. Unlike a corporate bond, which is a promise to pay a fixed stream of coupons plus a final lump sum, a share represents a sort of ownership. Holding one share in a company that has one million shares in issue means that you own one millionth of all the company's assets. Corporations usually pay dividends to shareholders but are not obliged to. Some corporations pay small or no dividends, preferring to plough profits back into building business. Everyone knows of the spectacular success of the Microsoft Corporation — a company that pays no dividend at all.

For obvious reasons, holding shares is considered to be more risky than holding bonds and this has been shown to be the case historically. Equity holders expect, and in the long run usually achieve, a higher return for taking on higher risk. In the event of bankruptcy, the equity holders are usually the last in line for any of the remaining assets.

1.3   CONVERTIBLE BONDS

CBs are interesting in that when they are issued no one really knows what sort of vehicle they will end up as — shares or bonds? Neither the issuing corporation nor the individual buying has any idea what is going to happen. What eventually happens depends on a number of factors. If the quoted share price rises significantly, the CBs could all be converted (once and for all) into shares. If the share price remains constant or falls, then the CBs could eventually be redeemed just like a regular straight bond. It is this feature that makes the instruments so unusual and seemingly difficult to price. The uncertainty of what is going to happen to the instruments in the future has a significant impact on the behaviour of the price today. The key feature of a CB that makes it a mixture of bond and equity is that the individual holding the instrument has an option; he can turn it into equity at any time or let it run to expiry and take a cash lump, just like a bond. The decision is his.

1.3.1   A Convertible Bond Example

To illustrate we consider the following imaginary CB from issue to maturity:

ABC Bank convertible bond

Nominal value:	£5,000
Conversion price:	£8.00
Conversion ratio:	625
Coupon:	0%
Underlying share price:	£7.80
Dividend yield of underlying share:	1%

Time to maturity:	1 year
Quoted market price at issue:	103

If we buy one of these CBs, what actually are we buying, what are we paying and what will eventually be our fate? First we address the issue of the quoted market price: 103. The way in which CB prices are quoted is a legacy from the straight bond market, i.e., everything is in terms of a percentage of the nominal value of the bond. So a price of 103 means that the price at issue is 103% of the nominal £5,000. Buying one of these CBs therefore entails spending £5,150. This particular issue has no coupon, which is unusual. We deliberately chose a zero coupon example because, as we will explain later, the presence of a coupon complicates the matter of the price paid. So in this example we simply pay up £5,150 and can, if we choose, wait for a year to pass.

Before we consider what happens in a year's time let us look in more detail at what we own. We have just paid £5,150 for a piece of paper that gives us certain options. The vehicle is a convertible bond and as such we could, if we wanted to, immediately convert the instrument into shares. If we did this the conversion ratio tells us the number of shares we will receive. So converting this bond will result in the generation of 625 shares. Where the shares come from we address later. For the present let us consider the situation if we convert. Our CB no longer exists. In its place we have 625 shares. The current market price of these shares is £7.80 each and so the total value is $625 \times 7.80 = £4,875$. We seem to have lost $5,150 - 4,875 = £275$ in the conversion process. Looking at the situation in another way, we seem to have paid £275 more than was really necessary to get the 625 shares. It is certainly true that we have paid more than the intrinsic value of the 625 shares, but there is of course a very good reason for this. To see why, we consider what the situation would be if we do not immediately convert but wait a year for maturity. On the final day of the instrument's life we have to make up our minds what to do with the CB, because tomorrow it will no longer exist — it will have expired. We consider two extreme scenarios, one with the final share price above the conversion price (£8.00) and one with it below.

1. On the final day the underlying share price is £10. Converting the CB will result in the generation of 625 shares valued at £10 a share, resulting in a total final value of $625 \times 10 = £6,250$.
2. On the final day the underlying share price is £2. Converting the CB into shares would result in a final value of $625 \times 2 = £1,250$. However, as the holder, we do not have to convert into shares, we can choose the redemption option and take the lump sum of £5,000 instead. In this situation we would obviously redeem rather than convert.

That is why with one year to go we invariably pay over the intrinsic value for the CB. There is always the chance that the share price will fall in the future and the option embedded in the CB gives us a get-out clause. The embedded option allows us to walk away from the risks of a significant fall in the share price but at the same time allows us to profit from a significant rise. The £275 up-front excess payment may seem large at first, but in fact may be small compared to the money lost if the share price were to fall significantly. The critical share price is the conversion price of £8.00. Above this it is optimal to convert and below it is optimal to redeem.

1.3.2 Convertible Bond Market Terminology

In the above example we referred to the CB price as 103 or £5,150 for the package, whereas the underlying shares were priced at £7.80 each. This can be all very confusing. It is best to think of CBs in one of two ways: either (1) as a package of a fixed number of shares or (2) on a per-share basis, i.e., break down the CB into a new imaginary CB with one share, and price it in the same terms as the share market. The CB market uses the former approach and furthermore, rather than quoting prices in pounds, expresses everything as a percentage of the nominal amount. The market also has its own standard terminology for the excess cash value of £275 and the intrinsic value. The excess value is known as the 'premium' and the intrinsic value is referred to as the 'parity'. The premium of a CB is generally not given in cash-value terms but as a percentage over the intrinsic value or parity. So in this particular example the premium of £275 would be reported as $100 \times 275/(625 \times 7.80) = 5.64\%$. Table 1.1 lists the standard CB parameters in (1) cash-value terms, (2) quoted-market terms and (3) on a per-share basis.

Throughout most of this book, CB model prices are calculated on a per-share basis. This is because it is easier to think of modelling the underlying share price first, and then the CB that runs on the back of the share price second. Shares are bought and sold in single units and so it is convenient to think of a CB in single share units as well. In our example the CB was issued at a quoted market price of

Table 1.1 ABC Bank convertible bond

	Cash value	Market quote in bond points	Value per share
Nominal value	£5,000	100.00	£8.00
Conversion price	£5,000	100.00	£8.00
Conversion ratio	625	—	—
Coupon	£0	0.00	£0.00
Parity	£4,875	97.50	£7.80
Price at issue	£5,150	103.00	£8.24
Premium	£275	5.50	£0.44
Premium (as a %)	5.64%	5.64%	5.64%

103. This translates to a package price of £5,150 for an instrument that can be converted into 625 shares and so if the CB has only one share it would be priced at 5150/625 = £8.24. The current share price is £7.80 and this represents a premium of 8.24 − 7.80 = £0.44 per share or 100 × 0.44/7.8 = 5.64%.

1.3.3 Convertible Bond Prices versus Share Prices

Exactly why the option to redeem or convert in one year's time should be worth paying a premium of 5.64% today will be addressed in detail in Chapter 5, but here we give a few examples of how the CB price will vary with respect to some of the most important variables. We first look at how the price varies as the underlying share price varies and this is shown in Figure 1.1.

This chart shows why some equity fund managers like CBs. At high share prices the CB price approaches the parity line. At high share prices the instruments behave almost exactly like a package of shares and so enjoy all or most of the benefits of a rising market. As the share price falls so does that of the CB but at a lower rate. At very low share prices the CB price flattens out to constant level. This is due to the fact that on expiry, with the share price low, the redemption rather than the conversion option would be invoked. So as share prices fall the bond feature gives the instrument some protection and there is a definite lower limit, known as the 'bond floor', below which the price (except in unusual circumstances) will not fall.

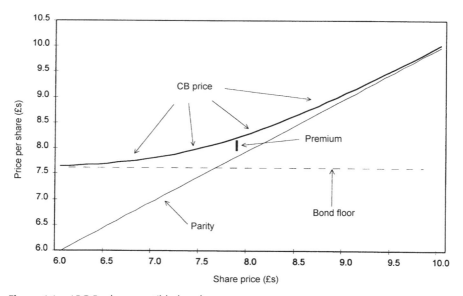

Figure 1.1   ABC Bank convertible bond

The equity fund manager thus has the benefits of being exposed to the share price rise but not the fall. The price he pays for this is the premium and this is also shown in Figure 1.1 as the vertical distance between the parity line and the CB price. The premium is a function of many factors such as share price, interest rates and time to maturity. Other things being equal, CBs have a low premium at high share prices and a high premium at low share prices. Also, as the maturity date approaches, the value of the embedded option decreases with a corresponding fall in premium.

1.3.4   Convertible Bond Prices with Different Share Price Volatility

An important factor in the pricing of CBs is the volatility of the underlying share. The strict definition of volatility and how it is estimated is dealt with in Chapter 3. However, for the moment, here we simply illustrate what the general effects are of share price volatility on CB price behaviour. Figure 1.2 shows how the prices of two CBs, identical in all respects, except that one is convertible into a share that historically exhibits low volatility, and the other is convertible into a share with high volatility.

Not surprisingly, volatility increases the price of a CB. A share with a higher volatility has a higher chance of ending up with a price significantly greater than the conversion price and so has the potential to be worth more. With a CB such as this one, that has only one year to expiry, the difference is most marked when the

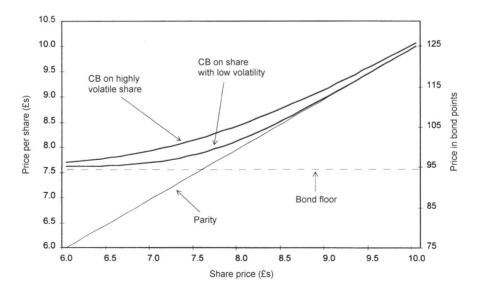

Figure 1.2   Convertible bonds on shares with different volatilities

share price is near the conversion price (£8.00). When the share price is very much higher or lower than this figure, the difference in the two price levels decreases. Although the two price curves in Figure 1.2 are different, they still exhibit the same characteristics of (1) approaching the parity line at high share prices and (2) approaching the same bond floor at low share prices. The real difference is in the curvature. Derivative traders have a special name for this curvature — they call it 'gamma'. The CB with the lower volatility has a greater degree of curvature when the share price is near £8.00 and there are special reasons for this which we will address in Chapter 7.

1.3.5   Convertible Bond Prices In Different Interest Rate Environments

In the ABC Bank example, if the share price on the maturity date is anywhere below the conversion price then the holder will choose to redeem and take his £5,000 or £8.00 per share. In this situation the holder will have (after the event) actually owned something that eventually turned out to pay a fixed sum of money — just like a bond. It will be no surprise therefore that a CB, like a straight bond, is sensitive to interest rates; other things being equal, bond prices fall when interest rates rise. Figure 1.3 shows the price of the ABC Bank CB under two different interest rate environments; one high and one low.

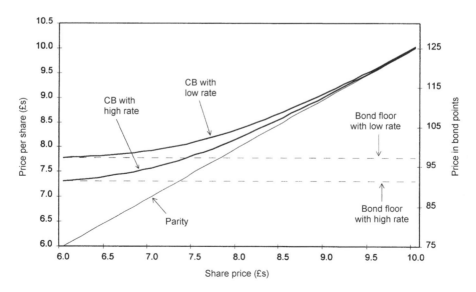

Figure 1.3   Convertible bonds with different interest rates

At high share prices, when the CB is trading like equity, it is almost completely independent of interest rate changes. But at low share prices, the dependence is just like that of a straight bond. This is the fascinating aspect of dealing in CBs. One day the instrument trades and feels just like straight shares; another day it trades and feels like a straight bond. If the share price is high enough, interest rates could double with absolutely no effect. If the share price is low enough, the instrument will not only be relatively insensitive to the changes in the share price but will be much more sensitive to interest rate changes. And the transition from the equity state to the bond state is gradual and smooth. At medium share price levels, the CB will be partially sensitive to share price changes and partially sensitive to interest rate changes — the degree depending on many factors such as volatility, coupon levels and share dividends. An investor must be aware of these complications. If an individual gets involved in a CB looking for some upside potential but wanting downside protection, he should realise that the bond floor he had bet on may drop to a lower level if interest rates rise.

1.3.6   The Effect of the Call Provision

Almost all CBs are issued with what are known as 'call provisions'. This is an extra option embedded in the instrument that gives the issuer the right to 'call back' the CB at some predesignated price. The problem with call provisions is that they are the issuer's option and not the CB holder's. This means that you may be in the situation of happily monitoring the price of your portfolio of CBs, banking the coupons as they come in and then suddenly one morning receiving a call notice. Almost invariably call notices are issued to induce the holder to convert. Suppose, in our ABC Bank CB example, the share price has risen to £10.00 (the CB will have risen to 125). And say that at this point we receive a call notice at 102 . This means that if we do nothing and ignore the call notice, the issuer has the right to tear up the agreement in the CB contract and send us a sum of money equivalent to 102 points, i.e., £5,100 or £8.16 per share. If we do nothing we will lose 23 points per bond (£1,150 or £1.84 per share) overnight. To circumvent this loss, we, along with all other CB holders, would immediately convert into shares. Since the CB was trading at no premium to the share price there would be no loss at all. The only difference would be that we now own shares and the CB no longer exists. Our situation would now be different in that there would no longer be the comforting bond floor — we are now at risk to a serious fall in the share price.

The call provision, however, is not such a serious negative as it might first appear. This is mainly because one often gets a fair degree of warning when an issuer's call is about to be triggered. Also, most call provisions can only be invoked subject to certain conditions, the most common one being that the share price must be at least 130% of the conversion price for a certain period (typically 30 days). Another common condition is that the call cannot be invoked for a certain period after the

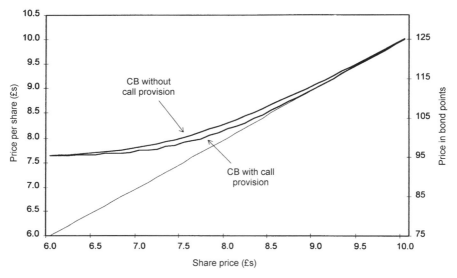

Figure 1.4   The influence of a call provision on ABC Bank convertible bond

instrument has been issued — say three to five years. Whatever the situation, it is obvious that the presence of a call provision will affect the CB price. Figure 1.4 shows two otherwise identical CBs; one with and one without a call provision. The call provision reduces the price of the CB. The call provision is a forever-present risk that the life of the CB may be terminated. You may start off buying a CB at issue thinking that you will enjoy ten years of coupons. But if the share price rises significantly you may be called and the instrument may be torn up after only one year. Call provisions mean that you have no idea how long a CB will exist.

1.3.7   The Effect of the Put Option

Some CBs have put options. These enable the holder to redeem early. The presence of a put option allows the holder to force the issuer to buy back the instrument much earlier than originally intended. These put options are obviously a positive feature and Figure 1.5 shows what effect one would have on our ABC Bank example. The put has most influence when share prices are low. And this makes sense. At low share prices the CB is more likely to be redeemed. The put gives the CB holder the opportunity to redeem early. In this example the redemption proceeds are £8 per share. The value today of the redemption proceeds is simply the discounted value of £8. If this CB is run to expiry, the discounting takes place over one year. If the put date is, say, only six months away, then the discounting takes place over six months. The value of £8 discounted over six months is higher than £8

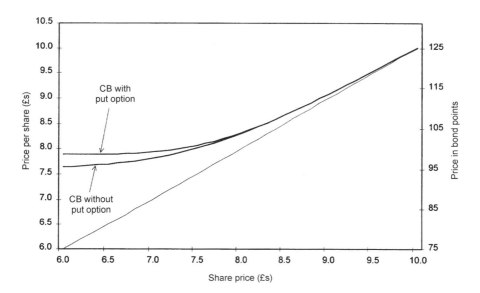

Figure 1.5   Influence of a put option on ABC Bank convertible bond

discounted over one year. The put option has the effect of reducing the time taken to receive the £8 and so has the effect of increasing the value of the CB today.

1.3.8   Foreign Exchange Effects in Non-Domestic Convertible Bonds

There are many CBs that are convertible into shares denominated in one currency but redeemable into a lump cash sum denominated in another. At the time of writing there are over 400 Euro CBs that fall into this category. A typical example is the Akebono Brake Swiss Franc CB. This instrument has a nominal value of 50,000 Swiss Francs and can be converted into 6,112 shares of Akebono brake stock. The prospectus states that the conversion price of this instrument is 605 Yen, *but this is not so*. To see why we have to look at what happened on the day of issue and what will happen on maturity. When issued, the Swiss Frank/Japanese Yen exchange rate was 73.95 Yen = 1 Swiss Franc and it is easy to see where the value of 50,000 Swiss Francs comes from. The Yen value of 6,112 shares at 605 is given by 6112 × 605 = 3,697,760 Yen. This quantity of Yen at an exchange rate of 73.95 translates into 3,697,760/73.95 = 50,000 Swiss Francs. But the exchange rate is constantly changing and therefore so is the conversion price. On expiry, someone holding one of these CBs will have to choose to convert or to redeem. If the holder converts he gets 6,112 shares. If the holder redeems he gets 50,000 Swiss Francs. The decision is complicated by the fact that the package of shares and the cash

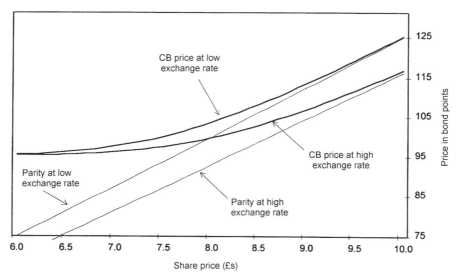

Figure 1.6   Influence of exchange rates on non-domestic convertible bond

lump sum are in different currencies. In the extremely unlikely event that the exchange rate is still 73.95; then the crucial deciding share price would still be 605 Yen. At this rate, it would make sense to convert if the share price were above 605 Yen and redeem below. At this rate the conversion price would indeed be 605 Yen. But what if the rate had changed to, say, 90 Yen per Swiss Franc? The crucial deciding share price would then be 736 Yen. At this new rate, the conversion price would thus be 736 Yen. Foreign exchange rates change every day. In fact they change every minute. So the fascinating aspect of this and all the other non-domestic CBs is that the conversion price is constantly changing and this has a profound effect on the price behaviour prior to expiry. Figure 1.6 shows just one example of the price behaviour of a non-domestic CB at two different levels of the foreign exchange rate.

1.3.9   The Effects of Refix Clauses on Convertible Bond Prices

By this stage the average reader would certainly agree that CBs are complicated instruments. All have an embedded equity call option. Almost all have an issuer's short-call provision of some sort. Some are puttable and all the non-domestic ones have the foreign exchange rate complication. But it gets worse. In the early 1990s Japanese corporations began to issue CBs with 'Refix Clauses'. These were designed to make the issues 'sweeter', i.e., more attractive to the investment community. In its simplest form, a refix clause alters the conversion ratio (or shares

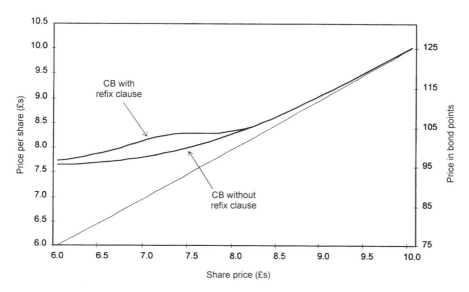

Figure 1.7   Influence of refix clause on convertible bond

per bond) and conversion price, subject to the share price level on certain days between issue and expiry. Suppose that on one of these days the share price has fallen by 20% from the price on issue, then the refix clause may have the effect of increasing the number of shares per bond by 20% and at the same time reducing the conversion price by 20%. So a CB that one moment was looking like ending up being redeemed may now, since the conversion price is lower, actually end up being converted. It is easy to see why refix clauses are attractive and add value as an investment package but, of course, like everything else, the added value usually has to be paid for up front in the form of a higher premium. Figure 1.7 shows two ABC Bank CBs; one with a refix feature and one without.

1.3.10   Concluding Remarks on CB Price Behaviour

The above is only a brief introduction to the basic characteristics of a CB. In the chapters that follow we discuss each feature in more detail and show how, using a relatively simple model, these complex instruments can be accurately priced.

1.4   NON-STANDARD INVESTMENT STRATEGIES

The ordinary investor usually thinks in terms of buying something first and then selling later, when hopefully, the price has risen. Most individuals think only in terms of capitalising on the price of something rising. Below we show that, in some markets, it is just as easy to profit from the price of something falling using a process known as 'shorting'. This section also explains how, by the use of gearing, small risk-free arbitrage profits can be magnified into large arbitrage profits.

1.4.1   The Concept of Going Long or Short

Crucial to the pricing of all equity derivatives is the ability to be able to short. Equity call options, warrants and CBs all decrease in price if the underlying share price falls. Fundamental to the idea of a fair price for a derivative is the idea of constructing a market-neutral portfolio of long one thing and short another. Although many readers will be familiar with these terms it is useful to expand on the definition of a long and short position. The most straightforward position is to be long. A long position is one that will be profitable if the price of something rises. Most individuals have a concept of being long — you simply buy something and hope the price rises and then sell. The profit will be the difference between the purchase and sale price. If the price falls you suffer a negative profit, i.e., a loss. It is easy to think of buying a stock or a given quantity of a commodity or even a given number of foreign currency units. Probably more abstract is the concept of going long a futures contract. However, the principle is the same. When you buy a futures contract you enter into an agreement that commits you to a long position. It does not really matter what is underlying the futures contract. All that matters is that you want the price to rise so that you can sell at a profit.

Initially, to the inexperienced, the concept of entering a short position can be confusing. In the jargon of the market place one 'sells short'. But how can you sell something you don't own? Let us forget this issue for the moment and just say that entering a short position will result in a profit if the price falls and a loss if the price rises. With futures contracts, shorting is quite straightforward if one forgets about the underlying financial instrument. Opening a short position is simply entering into a contract that guarantees a profit if the price falls and guarantees a loss if the price rises. A short position is closed out with a buy transaction. If the opening (selling) price is higher than the closing (buying) price then a profit results. One will have bought something low and sold high but in a back to front sense. Provided the purchase price is lower than the sale price, a profit will result. The fact that the transactions are carried out in the reverse time order to what one is usually accustomed to is really irrelevant, since nothing ever changes hands except contracts defining commitments.

Shorting something real like equity can be more complex. Typically one uses a technique known as 'borrowing'. Consider the following example. A certain share is trading in the market at £10 and an individual believes that in the near future the price will fall significantly. The individual whom we shall refer to as the shorter or 'Mr S', knows a fund manager, 'Mr FM', who has a large position in the shares and this position is likely to remain unchanged even if his prediction of a price fall proves true. Mr S approaches Mr FM and asks to borrow some shares for a certain period of time. Mr FM agrees in return for a deposit equal to the value of the shares, i.e., £10. Mr S deposits £10 cash with Mr FM and physically receives the stock which he then sells on into the market place. Mr S has sold the borrowed stock and so has received £10 cash from the buyer. The situation is now as follows.

Mr S: Mr S has placed a deposit of £10 cash with Mr FM, received £10 cash from the share buyer and so is cash neutral. He has, however, a commitment to Mr FM to return the shares to him on or before some time in the future. Since Mr S has no shares as such, he is essentially short. At some point in the future he will have to get (i.e., buy) the shares from the market to return to Mr FM.

Mr FM: Mr FM has a deposit of £10 cash sitting on deposit earning interest. He still is long of the shares since he has not actually sold any but just lent some to Mr S. So Mr FM is still long (via a contract with Mr S) and has the advantage of receiving additional income for his funds.

In practice the interest earned from the cash deposit is split between Mr FM and Mr S under what is known as a 'repo' agreement. We continue with this example and see what the outcome will be under the following two scenarios.

Scenario 1: The share price falls to £8. Mr S goes into the market and buys at £8 and delivers shares to Mr FM. Mr FM returns the deposit of £10 and the transaction is over. Mr FM still is long of the shares and has enjoyed additional income (or a fraction thereof). Mr S has bought the shares at £8 and sold at £10 realising a profit of £2.

Scenario 2: The share price rises to £12. Mr S goes into the market and buys at £12 and delivers to Mr FM. Mr FM returns the deposit of £10 and the transaction is over. Mr FM still is long of the shares and has enjoyed additional income (or a fraction thereof). Mr S has bought the shares at £12 and sold at £10 realising a loss of £2.

This all sounds very complicated but for most of the developed stock markets (excluding the UK) the process of stock borrowing is a very efficient business. Many participants, small and large, find it just as easy to go short as to go long.

1.4.2   Gearing up Investments

Most standard investment strategies usually involve buying something like a share at one price in the anticipation of selling at a higher price. Say a share is priced today at £10. Most individuals will be asked to put up the full value of £10. If the price were to increase to £12 then a profit of £2 or 20% could be had. Suppose we are convinced that this is in fact going to happen but we have only £1,000 at hand. The standard investment strategy is going to give us a profit of £200. Suppose we are so sure of a price rise that we manage to convince our friendly bank manager to lend us a further £2,000. We can now use our total sum of £3,000 to buy 300 shares. If we are right about the share price then selling all 3,000 shares at £12 will result in a profit of £600. So rather than making £200 we will have made £600 (less the bank interest charges). This is an example of using 'gearing' or 'leverage'. Borrowing money to increase exposure to an investment has the potential drastically to alter the absolute value of profits. In this example we say that the position is 'three times geared'. The resulting profit is correspondingly three times the profit of an ungeared investment. But, of course, we may get things wrong. What if the share price instead of rising, fell to £7? The loss of £3 per share translates into a geared loss of £900 — almost wiping out our original stake. Gearing up increases losses as well as profits.

Anyone involved in futures is, by definition, automatically geared. A typical stock index future like the UK's FTSE requires a deposit of only about 10%. Buying one FTSE contract at a level of 4,000 will require a deposit of only £4,000. One FTSE contract gives exposure equivalent to 10 times the index level. So being long one contract at 4,000 is equivalent to buying £40,000 worth of equity. And this is using a deposit of only £4,000. The investment is ten times geared.

Banks are in the business of lending money and in particular lending money to investors or speculators wishing to gear up. Because gearing can cause losses as well as profits, the gearing they offer depends on the riskiness of the underlying investment. If the strategy is very risky, such as speculating on futures or options, they may offer gearing of only two or three times. But some strategies are considered to have such a low risk that gearings of up to ten times are possible. When the exchange traded options market was in its infancy in the late 1970s and early 1980s there were two strategies known as 'conversions' and 'reversals' that had essentially zero risk. There was one well-known Dutch bank that was giving a gearing of 50 times on these strategies. This meant that the market participants who were making profits of, say, 1% to 2% were enjoying real profits of 50% to 100%. Small individual option market makers with only £100,000 were making staggering profits. Unfortunately, word got around and conversions and reversals now trade at exactly the right price.

The reason we mention gearing here is that it is used extensively by the hedging community to extract profits from CBs. There still exist today CBs that are trading at the wrong prices. There are strategies that can be employed by being long CBs and short shares that are very low risk indeed. At the time of writing many banks are offering gearing on such strategies of between 10 and 15 times. A CB price has to be wrong by only 3% for a geared strategy to extract profits of 30% to 45%.

1.4.3 Arbitrage — Static and Dynamic

Arbitrage is the generation of a riskless profit and so by definition should not exist. But it does. At the time of writing the arbitraging of CBs provides, and probably will continue to provide, an enormous income for the large hedge fund players. In an efficient world there should be no possibility for arbitrage. But there are many reasons why the possibilities still exist. There are two basic types of arbitrage — static and dynamic.

The static arbitrage is the most straightforward. Consider the situation of a certain share trading in two different market places. ICI, one of the world's largest chemical companies trades on the UK stock exchange and on the American Stock Exchange. The UK shares are quoted in pounds and the US shares in dollars. Clearly, they should both be worth the same. Calculating the dollar value of the sterling shares we should end up with the same price as those quoted in the US. And most of the time this will be the case. But there are occasions when the prices will differ slightly. When this happens certain market players buy shares in one market and sell shares in the other. The appropriate foreign exchange trade also has to be done. This activity will take place in very large size until it is no longer profitable — until the two prices are in equilibrium again. In the process an arbitrage profit will have been made, almost at no risk. There is of course a small risk. Invariably one side of the trade will have to be executed first. In the long run this sort of arbitrage activity keeps the two prices very close.

Another example of a static arbitrage is that involving zero or negative premium CBs. When the underlying share price of a CB is significantly higher than its conversion price the instrument often trades close to parity, i.e., with no premium. There are situations when, for one reason or another, the CBs fall to a slight discount to parity. This then presents a situation similar to the ICI example above. A CB at a discount is essentially offering the participant shares at a lower price than the market value. When this opportunity occurs, players enter the market, buying CBs and shorting shares on a 100% ratio. The CBs are then converted, producing shares that are used to cover the shorts. The profits are generated because shares are bought at one price and sold at another (higher) price. The possibility of this risk-free profit keeps most CBs trading at or slightly above the parity value. But opportunities continually present themselves. It is a matter of being patient and waiting for the right conditions.

Static arbitrages are not very difficult to understand. You do not have to be an intellectual giant to see why buying low and selling high makes a profit. A more sophisticated strategy involves constructing portfolios of longs and shorts that are continually adjusted. This strategy is known as dynamic arbitrage and its success is dependent on the existence of instruments with non-linear price profiles. Most derivatives have non-linear price profiles. Figure 1.2 illustrates how the price of a CB varies with respect to the underlying share — the relationship is curved or non-linear. The shape of the curve and the height above the parity line (the premium) depends on many things, but most importantly, on the volatility of the underlying share. There is a special reason why CBs on highly volatile shares should be more expensive. A dynamic arbitrage strategy known as the 'long volatility play' involves extracting profits out of a share's volatility. It is possible to construct a portfolio long of CBs and short shares that will profit from volatility. So shares that are highly volatile should have more expensive CBs. But this is not always the case.

We briefly outline the long volatility strategy and refer to Figure 1.8. The chart shows the component parts of a special portfolio. The portfolio has a long position in one CB and a short position in h shares, where h is what is known as the hedge ratio. The value of h is chosen such that the gradient of the profit-and-loss profiles would be identical if the portfolio were long a CB and long shares. Figure 1.8 illustrates what happens to the overall portfolio value if the underlying share price rises or falls. Consider first the situation if the share price rises significantly. We are short the shares so we would suffer a loss represented by the vertical distance between the straight line and the horizontal axis. The higher the share price rises, the larger the losses. But remember that we are long the CB and this will increase in price as the share price increases. As the share price increases we make a profit on the CB portion of the portfolio. Because the CB price profile curves away from the straight line representing the share price, the profits exceed the losses. Now consider the situation if the share price were to fall significantly. We are short shares so we would enjoy a profit represented by the vertical distance between the straight line and the horizontal axis. We are long the CB and so suffer a loss. But because the CB price curves away from the share price straight line the losses are smaller than the profits and so a net profit results. The overall profit profile is shown in the lower panel. So the portfolio makes a profit if the share price rises or falls and the more significant the move, the larger the profit. If the share underlying the CB is highly volatile, then these volatility profits can be quite large.

There is a catch of course. What Figure 1.8 does not show is what happens if the share price does not move. As time passes the premium (and hence price) of the CB will gradually fall. As time passes the curved price of the CB will begin gradually to collapse towards the parity line. As time passes the CB loses time value and these losses will have an impact on the overall profitability of the trade. If a CB is priced correctly then the profits enjoyed by volatility trading will exactly offset the losses due to time. The trick is to find a CB with a low premium but with a highly volatile share. In this way, the premium decay losses will be small and the volatility trading profits will be high. Most hedge traders now look at the price of a CB purely in volatility terms. In later chapters we will show that it is possible to infer from a CB price, the expected future volatility — the *implied* volatility. If it is possible to buy a CB at a low implied volatility of, say, 10%, knowing that in reality we will enjoy an actual future volatility of, say, 20%, then a profit will result. The interesting thing about this sort of arbitrage profit is that the portfolio must be managed dynamically. Trading must take place to lock in profits. It is difficult to believe, but even at the time of writing, there are many CBs that have

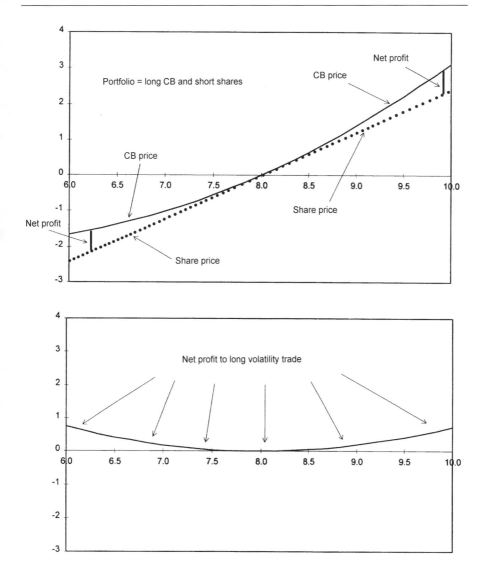

Figure 1.8   The long volatility trade

zero implied volatilities and many more with implied volatilities as low as 10%. These instruments continue to provide a large source of zero-risk or very low-risk income for the large hedge funds.

2
Using computer spreadsheets

Pricing even the simplest CB requires a computer solution. Throughout this book we demonstrate that even the most complex CBs can be valued using a spreadsheet. The purpose of this chapter is to review the more complex aspects of modern spreadsheets and can be skipped without loss of continuity.

Almost everyone knows how to use a basic spreadsheet. Most people will be able to use either Lotus or Excel to find the sum of a column or row of numbers. But spreadsheets have come a long way since their invention in the early 1980s. They can now do the most sophisticated calculations. The new statistical and random number generation features enable the user to model some very complex real-life processes — there is no longer the need to become a computer programmer. Spreadsheets lend themselves particularly well to the modelling of CBs. As will become apparent in later chapters, finding the fair value or price of a CB involves a technique known as 'backward induction' — a process perfectly suited to a spreadsheet solution.

Throughout this chapter we have assumed that the reader is familiar with the basic elements of a spreadsheet and in particular that of Microsoft Excel. Topics such as opening a worksheet, data entry, selecting data, moving data, copying data, deleting data, the formula bar and the construction of simple arithmetic formulae will not be discussed. Readers unfamiliar with these terms are referred to the many excellent texts available at most bookshops. Here we review some of the more advanced features of Microsoft Excel that will be used to model and simulate share and CB prices.

2.1 FEATURES OF EXCEL USED IN CB MODELLING

Naming cells It is often quite confusing transferring algebraic equations into spreadsheet formulae. Much of the confusion arises because what was the symbol a in an equation such as $y = ax + b$ becomes an absolute reference cell address such as B1. A much easier way to reference cells or a range of cells is to give them a name.

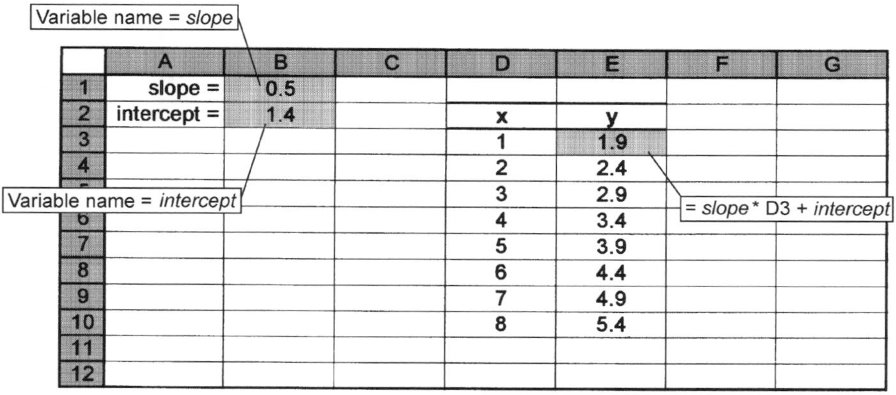

Variable name = *slope*

	A	B	C	D	E	F	G
1	slope =	0.5					
2	intercept =	1.4		x	y		
3				1	1.9		
4				2	2.4		
5				3	2.9		
6				4	3.4		
7				5	3.9		
8				6	4.4		
9				7	4.9		
10				8	5.4		
11							
12							

Variable name = *intercept*

= slope * D3 + intercept

Figure 2.1 Using named variables in formulae

The name of the cells can be used in the formulae instead of the awkward absolute cell reference. Say we wish to calculate and plot the values of y versus x in the linear relationship: $y = ax + b$, where $x = 1, 2, 3, \ldots 8$ with the parameters a and b general.

Input the list of x values in the cells D3 to D10 . Select the cell B1 and click the down arrow next to the cell reference box. Insert the name *slope* and press return. Select the cell B2, click the down arrow next to the cell reference box, type *intercept* and press return. You have now allocated names to these two cells

Input the values 0.5 and 1.4 into cells B1 and B2. We have thus set the slope parameter to 0.5 and the intercept parameter to 1.4.

In the cell E3 write the formula: = *slope* * D3 + *intercept* and copy into cells E4 to E10. The E and D columns now correspond to the y and x values represented by the equation:

$$y = slope \,.\, x + intercept$$

So each of the individual y values in the E cells are calculated from each of the individual x values in the D cells.

$$E3 = slope \,.\, D3 + intercept$$
$$E4 = slope \,.\, D4 + intercept$$
$$\vdots$$
$$E10 = slope \,.\, D10 + intercept$$

Naming cells in this way obviates the need for complex absolute cell references.

Statistical functions In this book we refer to the 'average', 'mean absolute deviation', 'variance', 'standard deviation' and the 'correlation coefficient'. Their

Array name = sample

	A	B	C	D	E	F
1						
2			Sample			
3			0			
4			28			
5			9			
6			35			
7			12			
8			23			
9			17			
10			41		= AVERAGE(C3:C10)	
11						
12		Average =	20.63		= AVEDEV(sample)	
13		Average deviation =	11.13			
14		Variance =	189.98		= VAR(C3:C10)	
15		Standard deviation =	13.78			
16						
17					= STDEV(sample)	

Figure 2.2   Statistical functions

definitions and meaning will be discussed in Chapter 3. These statistical functions operate on a list or array of numbers and return a single number. The array can be referenced using the standard notation of say C3:C10 or by naming the array. Figure 2.2 shows both methods. The list of data: 0, 28, 9, 35, 12, 23, 17, 41 sits in the range of cells C3 to C10. This array of data is named 'sample' by selecting the range, clicking the arrow next to the cell reference box and typing in *sample*.

The average of the list of numbers is calculated by using the in-built function = AVERAGE(C3:C10). An alternative method would be to refer to the array of numbers using its name as in = AVERAGE (*sample*).

The mean absolute deviation is calculated using the function = AVEDEV(*sample*) or AVEDEV(C3:C10). This returns the average of the deviations from the mean, ignoring the sign of the deviation.

The variance is calculated using either = VAR(*sample*) or = VAR(C3:C10).

The standard deviation is calculated using either = STDEV(*sample*) or = STDEV(C3:C10).

The correlation coefficient is a measure of the association between two variables or two lists of numbers. Correlation coefficients are calculated using the CORREL( ) function. Figure 2.3 illustrates an example of the calculation of the correlation coefficient between two lists of numbers in the arrays C3:C10 and D3:D10.

The correlation coefficient between the variables in columns C and D is 0.17. What does this mean? By definition the correlation coefficient is a number that must lie between -1 (perfect negative correlation) and $+1$ (perfect positive correlation). The value of 0.17 is not significantly different from zero. Although it is difficult to make any sort of statement with only eight pairs of numbers, there is no evidence that the variables are correlated in any way and this notion is reinforced by the scatter diagram.

The CORREL( ) function can also be used to see if there is any temporal dependence or temporal autocorrelation in a time series. Most models of share price behaviour assume that sequences of price changes are independent. If variables are independent then they must also be uncorrelated. When looking at a single sequence of numbers such as the list of x values in Figure 2.3 the autocorrelation coefficient of lag 1 is a measure of the correlation between each number and the previous one. This can be calculated using the CORREL( ) function by inputting the two variables as the arrays C3:C9 and C4:C10. Although the arrays contain

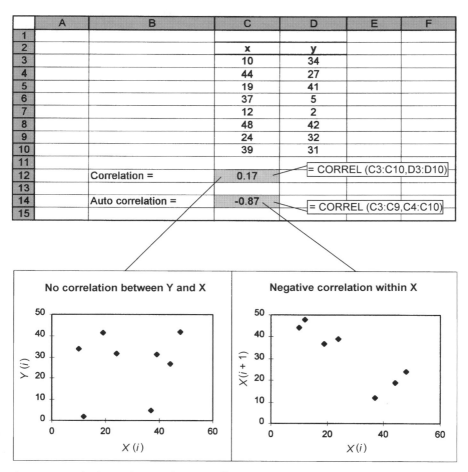

Figure 2.3 Calculating the correlation coefficient

mostly the same entries, the function considers them to be two separate lists of numbers. In the example given, the autocorrelation coefficient turns out to be -0.87. There is a strong degree of negative correlation between the two lists of numbers. This implies that large values in one list correspond to small values in the other list. Since the list is the one sequence of numbers we conclude that there is a high degree of reversalling — large numbers follow small and small follow large. Looking at the sequence of x values we see that this is indeed the case. So although there appears to be no link or correlation between x and y, there is a high degree of negative correlation within the x series. If x were a sequence of price changes this would have serious implications for the assessment of the other parameters of risk and return. More of this in Chapter 3.

The NORMDIST( ) function is very useful in evaluating the prices of options or warrants. It is known as the cumulative normal density function. This function returns the area to the left of the input value. The function gives the probability that a realisation from the standard normal distribution is at or less than the input value.

The maximum function   Excel has a function that is particularly useful in the CB modelling process — the MAX( ) function. The MAX (a, b) function returns the larger of the two arguments — a or b. On expiry the holder of a CB has to choose between two options. Should he convert and take up shares, or redeem and take cash? Obviously, he should take the maximum of the two values. As will be shown later the CB model starts on the last day by applying the MAX( ) function to these two values. The MAX( ) function can have up to 30 arguments and returns the largest.

Conditional statements — the IF function   Excel's IF( ) function is a very powerful tool. It is possible using this feature to construct quite sophisticated models. The IF( ) function can also be nested at many levels. In its simplest form, the IF( ) statement has three arguments: a *conditional statement*, a *true value* and a *false value*.

$$= \text{IF } (conditional\ statement,\ true\ value,\ false\ value)$$

When executed the conditional statement is tested. If the answer to the statement is true then the true value argument is returned to the cell. If the answer to the statement is false then the false value argument is returned. Figure 2.4 illustrates two examples. The cell B2 contains the number 26 and the cell B3 contains the number 12. Cell B5 has the expression: $= \text{IF}(B2 > B3, 1, 0)$. The value returned to cell B5 depends on the values in the cells B2 and B3. If B2 is greater than B3 then a 1 is returned, otherwise a 0 is returned. In this case 26 is greater than 12 and so the value 1 appears in cell B5. If the numbers were reversed a 0 would appear in cell B5.

	A	B	C	D	E	F
1						
2		26				
3		12		= IF (B2 <B3, 1,10)		
4						
5		1				
6						
7		100		= IF (B8 <=B7, "Yes', "No")		
8		120				
9						
10		No				

Figure 2.4 The IF ( ) function

Figure 2.4 also shows an example when words or strings are returned. The cells B7 and B8 contain the numbers 100 and 120 respectively. Cell B10 has the expression: = IF(B8 <= B7, "Yes", "No"). If the number in cell B8 is less than or equal to the number in cell B7 then the word 'Yes' is returned, otherwise the word 'No' is returned. In this case since 100 is not less than or equal to 120, cell B10 contains the word 'No'.

The random number generator Excel has a number of random number generator features but probably the simplest is the RAND( ) function. This function returns a random number between 0 and 1 and is very useful in simulating certain random events. Figure 2.5 is an illustration of how this works. Imagine the infinite set of different possible numbers that could be generated between the values of 0 and 1. The straight line connecting the points 0 to 1 thus represents the totality of all possible outcomes. Say we wish to simulate an event that only has a chance of 3 in 10 (30% or 0.3) of occurring. This could be represented by the sub-set or sub-interval of all those points between 0 and 0.3. Imagine throwing a dart at the straight line and that the distribution of throws along the straight line is uniform, i.e., there is just as much chance of landing on, say, the 0.95 point as landing on the 0.37 point. If we were to throw 1,000 darts we would expect the dart to land in our interval of 0 to 0.3 approximately 30% of the time. And this is how we simulate the event with a probability of 0.3. We generate a random number using the RAND( ) function and then use an IF( ) statement to see if it is less than 0.3 or not. If the number is less than 0.3 then we say that the event has occurred. If the number is greater than 0.3 then the event has not occurred. This simple function can be used as the basis of some very complex simulation experiments. Some examples are given in the next section.

Nested statements CBs are American-style instruments and as such can be converted or put back to the issuer usually at certain times prior to expiry. These

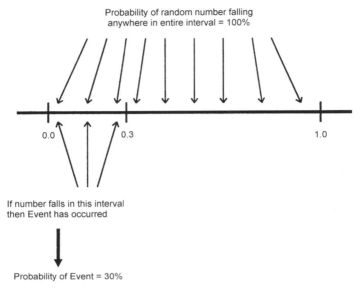

Probability of random number falling
anywhere in entire interval = 100%

If number falls in this interval
then Event has occurred

Probability of Event = 30%

Figure 2.5 Random numbers and event probability

complications, including the issuer's call option, can be incorporated in the CB modelling process using nested IF( ) and MAX( ) statements.

Consider an example in which the value of a CB unconstrained by the American-style option features is given by the named variable *CBunconstrained*. The variable *calltrigger* is the *parity* value above which the CB should trade at parity. *CBputprice* is the minimum price the CB can have. The CB price subject to these constraints is given by the expression:

$$= \text{MAX}(CBunconstrained, CBputprice, \text{IF}(parity{>}calltrigger, parity, CBunconstrained))$$

Now consider an example of nesting IF( ) statements to simulate one of three different events. Say the event A has a probability of 0.3, event B has a probability 0.2 and C a probability of 0.5. We generate a random number on the interval 0 to 1. If the number lies between 0 and 0.3 we say that A has occurred; if the number lies in the interval 0.3 to 0.5 (a probability 'distance' of 0.2) then B has occurred; otherwise C has occurred. This can be done using the expression:

$$= \text{IF}(A1 < 0.3, \text{``A''}, \text{IF}(A1 < 0.5, \text{``B''}, \text{``C''}))$$

with the random number function in cell A1. If the random number is less than 0.3 then "A" is returned. If not then the second nested IF( ) statement is invoked. If the random number is less than 0.5 (and by definition it must be greater than 0.3) then "B" is returned and if not "C" is returned.

2.2 SIMULATING RANDOM EVENTS

Tossing coins This example shows how RAND( ) and IF( ) can be used to simulate the outcome of tossing a coin ten times. Figure 2.6 is a schematic representation of the procedure and Figure 2.7 is the Excel spreadsheet.

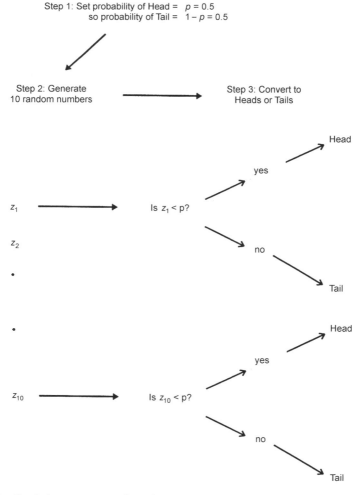

Figure 2.6   Simulating ten tosses of a coin

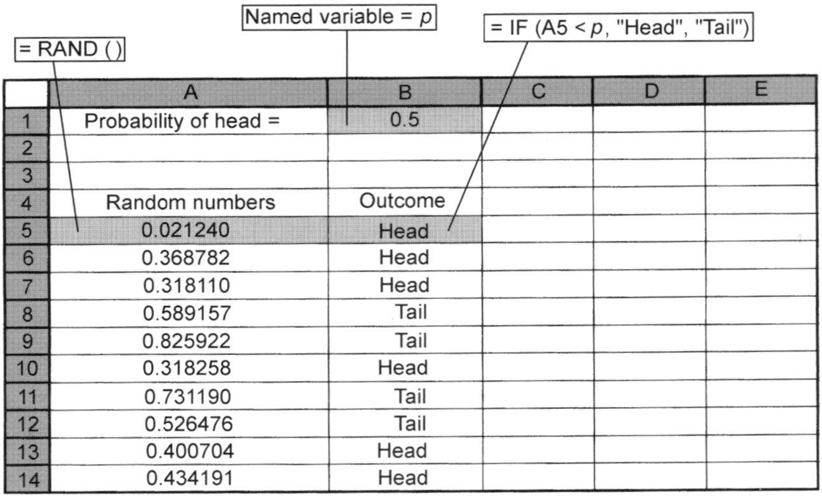

	A	B	C	D	E
1	Probability of head =	0.5			
2					
3					
4	Random numbers	Outcome			
5	0.021240	Head			
6	0.368782	Head			
7	0.318110	Head			
8	0.589157	Tail			
9	0.825922	Tail			
10	0.318258	Head			
11	0.731190	Tail			
12	0.526476	Tail			
13	0.400704	Head			
14	0.434191	Head			

Named variable = p

= RAND ()

= IF (A5 < p, "Head", "Tail")

Figure 2.7 Simulation of ten coin tosses

Step 1: Set the probability of a head The probability of a head is denoted by the named variable p and is set to 0.5 (though this could be set to any value).

Step 2: Generate 10 random numbers The cells A5:A14 contain the statement: = RAND( ). This generates 10 independent random numbers.

Step 3: Convert random numbers to 'Heads' or 'Tails' The cell B5 contains the statement: = IF(A5 < p, 'Head', 'Tail'). If the random number in B5 is less than 0.5 then this is equivalent to tossing a coin and getting a 'Head'. If the number is greater than 0.5 the result is a 'Tail'. The cells in the range B6:B14 contain similar expressions to represent ten coin tosses. In the example simulation there are six heads and four tails.

Step 4: Repeat simulations with F9 key The RAND( ) functions produce a new random number each time any cell anywhere in the worksheet is changed, or alternatively by pressing the recalculation key: F9. Each time the F9 key is pressed, a completely new set of simulations are generated.

Independent price series Central to Chapters 3 and 4 is the modelling of share price behaviour as a sequence of independent events. The simplest way of simulating a share price series is first to generate a series of price changes and then generate the prices. Figure 2.8 is a schematic representation of the procedure and Figure 2.9 is the Excel spreadsheet.

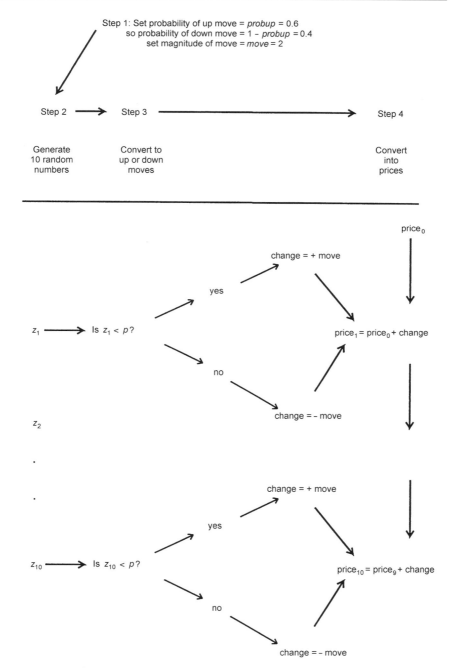

Figure 2.8 Simulating an independent price sequence

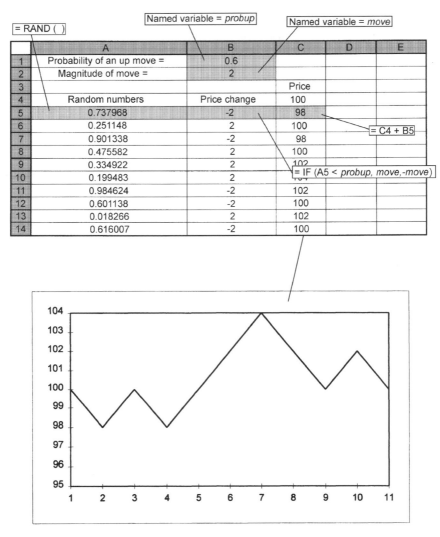

Figure 2.9 Simulating an independent price series

Step 1: Set the probability of up move, size of move and initial price The named variables *probup* and *move* represent the probability of an up move and the magnitude of the up or down move respectively. The given example is one in which there is a bias to the upside — the probability of an up move is 0.6 and so the probability of a down move is 0.4. The magnitude of each price move is 2.

Step 2: Generate 10 random numbers   The cell range A5:A14 contain the = RAND( ) statement.

Step 3: Convert random numbers to up or down moves   The cell B5 contains the statement = IF(A5 < *probup, move, −move*) and so return a value of +2 if the outcome is an up move and −2 if a down move. Cell B5 is repeated over the range B6:B14.

Step 4: Translate up and down moves into prices   The cell C4 has the starting price of 100. Cell C5 has the expression = C4 + B5 thus returning the original price plus the price move. This expression is copied all the way down to cell C14. This then is one realisation of a sequence of random prices.

Dependent price series   Figure 2.10 illustrates a simple example of simulating a price series with non-independent changes. The procedure is very similar to that used in generating an independent series but with one extra step — at each realisation the probability of an up move is (possibly) reset. The example given is specially concocted to generate a series with an excessive degree of reversalling. With independent series the probability of an up move is always the same at, say, 0.5. So even if the previous five moves were all up — the probability of the next move being up is still 0.5. Some market participants believe that price series exhibit some sort of memory in that after so many up moves there should always be a correcting down move. This example shows how one can incorporate this type of behaviour into a model. For the independent series the probability of an up move is fixed at a value of, say, 0.5. In this model the probability of an up move depends on whether the previous move is up or down. The named variable *probupup* is the probability of an up move if the previous move was up and in this example is set to 0.4 — after an up move there is a 40% chance of a further up move and a 60% chance of a down move. This obviously introduces a certain degree of reversalling — a down move is more likely to follow an up move. The named variable *probupdown* is the probability of an up move if the previous move was down and here is set to 0.7 — after a down move there is a 70% chance of an up move and a 30% chance of a down move.

To see how this works consider the seventh row. A random number is generated in cell A7. Which probability to use is determined from the direction of the previous move. The moves appear in the C column and so which probability to use for the move in C7 depends on the value in C6. The conditional statement: = IF(C6 > 0, *probupup, probupdown*) is in cell B7 and returns the 0.4 if the previous move was up or 0.7 if the previous move was down. In the example given the previous move was up and so the probability value to apply is 0.4 . The random number in cell A7 is 0.615926 and so a down move results.

Setting these probabilities in this way means that the probability of getting a long stream of moves in one direction is much less likely than with an ordinary sequence of independent moves. The autocorrelation coefficient of −0.8 calculated on the

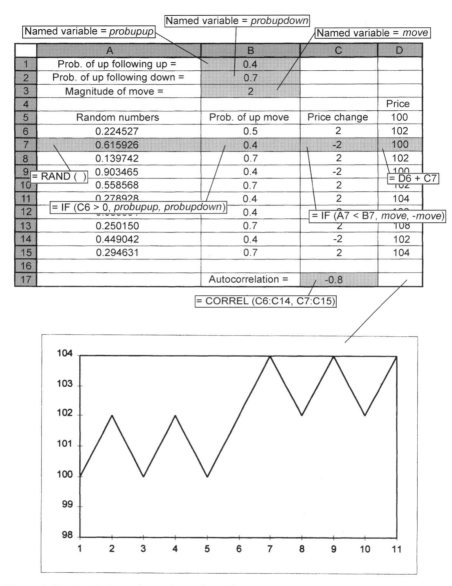

Figure 2.10   Simulating a dependent price series

sequence of moves reinforces the fact that the price series is highly negatively correlated.

By altering *probupup* and *probupdown* to, say, 0.6 and 0.3 respectively, the reverse happens. With these values there will be a much greater tendency for the price series to stick in one direction — the series of changes will be positively correlated. More complex examples of generating specially constructed non-independent time series are discussed in Chapter 4.

The birthday problem   (This section can also be skipped without loss of continuity). Although nothing to do with CBs or indeed any aspect of finance, the birthday problem is a classic conundrum that is complex to solve using probability theory but simple to illustrate using the RAND( ) and IF( ) statements. It is included here to illustrate how very complex problems involving random events in conjunction with convoluted conditional arguments can be solved. As we shall see later on, modelling CBs involves just such arguments. The solution to the birthday problem is so non-intuitive that even the most mathematically minded find the answer difficult to believe. The conundrum is as follows: A room has 23 randomly chosen people: what is the chance that two or more individuals have the same birthday? The most common guess at the answer to this question is $23/365 = 0.06$ or about 6%. The real answer is 50%. If you don't believe it try testing it out using the spreadsheet solution in Figure 2.11.

Step 1: Generate 23 random numbers   The cells A2:A24 contain the list of numbers 1 to 23 in order. The cells B2:B24 have the statement: = RAND( ) and so there are 23 independent random numbers on the interval 0 to 1.

Step 2: Convert random numbers to random birthdays   Cell C2 has the statement: = INT(364*B2 + 0.5) + 1. This has the effect of converting the random number generated in cell B2 into a random integer between 1 and 365. The cells C3 to C24 have similar expressions. We can think of the 23 different cells in the array C2:C24 as corresponding to the birthday of each of the 23 different people in the room. The birthdays here are, however, given in terms of the day of the year. So a value of 1 corresponds to a birthday on 1 January; a 2, 2 January and so on until 365 represents a birthday on 31 December. Leap years are ignored. The array C2:C24 is thus appropriately named as the variable *birthday*.

Step 3: Sort birthdays in ascending order   The cell D2 contains the expression: = SMALL(*birthday*, A2) and this works as follows. The function SMALL(*array*, k) returns the kth smallest value in *array*. Here $k = $ A2 $= 1$ and so the cell D2 will contain the smallest value in the birthday array. The cells D3 to D24 have identical expressions. Thus the range D2:D24 is all the different birthdays ranked from smallest to largest.

Step 4: Highlight those with the same birthday   If there are two individuals with the same birthday then they will appear in the D column one after the other. Note that in our example there are two people born on the 128th day of the year. This fact is drawn to our attention because the final column of numbers contains a "1"

= SMALL (*birthday*, A2)

= RAND ( )   Named variable = *birthday*   = IF (D2 = D3, 1, 0)

= INT (364*B2 + 0.5) + 1

	A	B	C	D	E
1		Random numbers	Birthday	Sorted	Match
2	1	0.2254	83	3	
3	2	0.983913	359	21	0
4	3	0.285895	105	31	0
5	4	0.854401	312	56	0
6	5	0.357768	131	83	0
7	6	0.937598	342	105	0
8	7	0.840314	307	128	0
9	8	0.641343	234	128	1
10	9	0.150741	56	131	0
11	10	0.378265	139	139	0
12	11	0.446407	163	142	0
13	12	0.928341	339	152	0
14	13	0.740527	271	163	0
15	14	0.414574	152	169	0
16	15	0.386438	142	234	0
17	16	0.055511	21	266	0
18	17	0.348218	128	271	0
19	18	0.082796	31	299	0
20	19	0.006300	3	307	0
21	20	0.818226	299	312	0
22	21	0.350230	128	339	0
23	22	0.727446	266	342	0
24	23	0.462900	169	359	0
25					1
26					Success

Same birthdays

= SUM (E3:E24)

= IF (E25 > 0, "Success", "Failure")

Figure 2.11   The birthday problem

opposite the second occurrence of 128, whereas most entries are "0". This is achieved by the clever use of the IF( ) function. In cell E3 the expression: = IF(D2 = D3, 1, 0) returns a "1" if the birthday in cell D3 is the same as that in D2 and "0" otherwise. So if one match occurs there will be one "1" and twenty-two "0"s. If two matches occur there will be two "1"s and twenty-one "0"s and so on. The sum of the number of matches is given in cell in E25.

Step 5: Do we have a success?   The original problem posed was: 'What is the probability of at least two people having the same birthday?' This can be translated into the question: 'How many times will the cell E25 have an entry that is greater than 0?' Cell E26 contains the expression: = IF(E25 > 0, "Success"," Failure"). If, as in the example given, there are at least two people with the same birthday then the cell E25 will be greater than 0 and we interpret this in cell E26 as a success — yes, we have found a room with 23 people containing at least two with the same birthday. The reader is invited to construct this spreadsheet example (or copy directly from the disk supplied) and make a note of the number of times a success occurs. Try pressing the F9 key 20 times. This is equivalent to carrying out the experiment 20 times — going into 20 different rooms, each with 23 people and seeing if there are any matches. Approximately half of the 20 rooms will result in a 'success'.

What is even more striking and even more counter-intuitive is the result if we carry out this simulation experiment with the number of people in each room changed to 50. With rooms of 50 people, the success rate increases to 97%. Put another way, in a room of 50 people, the probability that everyone has a different birthday is only 3%.

2.3   BACKWARD INDUCTION — A SIMPLE CB MODEL

The basic idea behind the pricing of CBs (or indeed most derivative products) is a process known as 'backward induction'. This involves getting the value of the instrument on expiry and working back through time to find the value today. The procedure works because the value of the expiring CB is fixed and is a function of the share price on the day of expiry. The share price on expiry is a function of the share price today. We illustrate the process with a simple additive one-period model:

Step 1: Start with a given share price today $= S$.

Step 2: Work forwards through time to get the possible values on expiry   Assume the share price can only increase or decrease by the amount: *move*. On expiry the share price can therefore be either $S + move$ or $S - move$.

Step 3: Compute the expiring CB values   Assume the conversion price is E and that there are no coupons. The expiring CB values will be the maximum of the share price or E. So if the share price is up at $S + move$ the CB value will be given by

$$CB_{up} = MAX(S + move, E)$$

and similarly if the share price is down the CB value will be given by

$$CB_{down} = MAX(S - move, E).$$

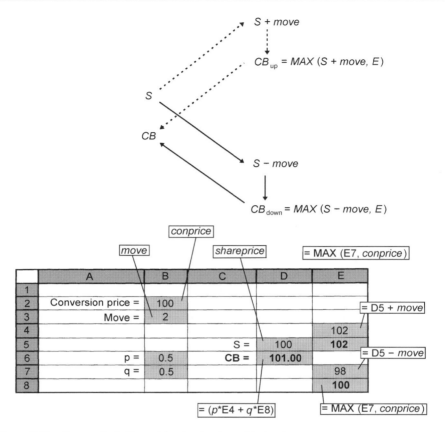

Figure 2.12   One-period CB model using backward induction

Step 4: Work back through time   The value of the CB today is given by the expression:

$$CB = p.CB_{\text{up}} + q.CB_{\text{down}}$$

where $p = q = 0.5$

With $S = E = 100$ and *move* = 2 Figure 2.12 shows that the CB value is = 101.00.

2.4   USING THE DATA TABLE FEATURE TO CREATE TABLES AND FIGURES

In the above example with the share price at $S = 100$ the CB price turns out to be 101.00. Throughout this book the CB price is plotted against the share price and so

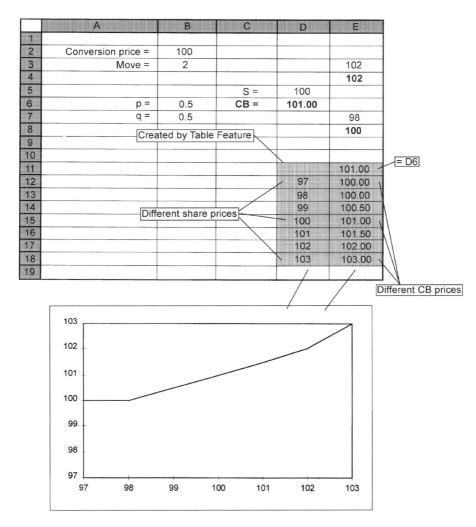

Figure 2.13   Using data table feature

it is necessary to be able to produce a list or table of one price against the other. In order to see how the CB price varies as S varies we can try substituting various S values or use Excel's data table feature. The data table is set up so that the range D12:D18 contains the various share prices: 97. 98. ..., 103. The E11 cell contains the formula: = D6 which corresponds to the cell containing the CB model price. In order to generate the table containing the CB price at each level of share price one first selects the rectangular range D11:E18. Then choose Table from the data menu.

The input parameter that is to be varied in this example is the share price and in the main body of the spreadsheet the share price is input into cell D5. Since the values of the variable input appear in a column, specify D5 as the Column Input Cell and choose OK. A column of values corresponding to the CB price appears in the range E12:E18. Charting the resultant output is straightforward.

2.5   FINDING THE IMPLIED VOLATILITY OF A CB USING THE GOAL SEEK COMMAND

The theoretical value of a CB depends usually on seven inputs: the share price, the conversion price, the interest rate, the time to expiry, the coupon level, the dividend rate and the volatility parameter. The first six are known and easy to measure. The volatility parameter is unknown and is often estimated using historic analysis. Alternatively, one can simply make a subjective guess at what the future volatility is likely to be. Substituting the seven inputs into the model will give the CB price. It is often useful to ask the reverse question, i.e., if the market price of the CB today is such and such what does this imply about the future volatility of the underlying share? In other words, what volatility input into the model will give a theoretical price that exactly matches the market price — what is the implied volatility of the CB?

One solution is to try different volatilities repeatedly in the appropriate cell in the spreadsheet until the theoretical model price exactly matches the market price. This will work but can be tedious. The real virtue of using Excel is that there is a special function that can solve this sort of problem quickly — the Goal Seek Command. In the context of the simple one-period additive CB model the *move* parameter can be thought of as defining the volatility of the share price. If this parameter is large (small) we can think of the underlying share price volatility as being large (small). In Figure 2.14 we have a spreadsheet with a formula in cell D6 giving the theoretical value of the CB in terms of the volatility or *move* parameter as an input. We now know the result of the formula (the CB market price) but we do not know the input value the formula needs to reach the result. The Goal Seek Command varies the value in the cell we specify until the formula that is dependent on that cell returns the result we want.

In the example in Figure 2.14 the formula for the CB is in cell D6 and the unknown *move* value is in cell B3. Say we wish to find the implied volatility if the CB price is not 101.00 but 103.00? Choose Goal Seek from the tools menu. In the Set Cell box put D6. In the To Value box put 103.00 (you are setting the formula given in cell D6 equal to 103.00). In the By Changing Value box put B3 and choose OK. The result appears quickly as 6.00. So if a volatility or *move* value of 6.00 is input into the model, the theoretical CB price is 103.00. The implied volatility or *move* parameter of this CB is 6.00. It is that simple. This is an extremely useful feature and saves the time and expense of writing programs that search through all

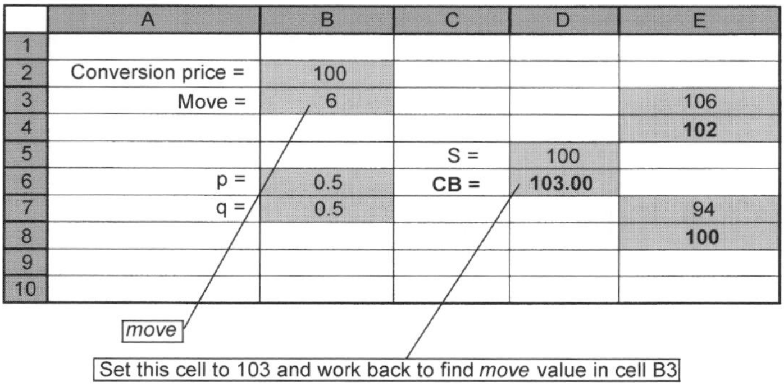

	A	B	C	D	E
1					
2	Conversion price =	100			
3	Move =	6			106
4					102
5			S =	100	
6	p =	0.5	CB =	103.00	
7	q =	0.5			94
8					100
9					
10					

move

Set this cell to 103 and work back to find *move* value in cell B3

Figure 2.14 Using the goal seek feature to find implied volatility

the different possible volatility values to get a match between the theoretical price and the market price. As will become obvious later on, the implied volatility is probably one of the most useful measures of relative value. Hedgers and other low-risk players only get involved in CBs with low implied volatilities.

3
Returns distributions and associated descriptive statistics

The terms 'risk' and 'return', as used in the investment world, have a specific meaning. In this chapter we show how to calculate various measures of the risk and return of an investment from the historical price series. The object of this chapter is to show how a distribution of profits and losses can be generated from a price sequence and how a few simple statistics can be used to describe such distributions.

To price any derivative product that runs on the back of an equity, one usually needs five basic inputs: (1) the underlying equity price, (2) the exercise (or conversion) price, (3) the time to maturity, (4) the relevant interest rate and (5) the volatility. In most situations the first four inputs are directly observable. The fifth input, the volatility, is an estimate of how much the future equity price is likely to vary. Estimating volatility is crucial to the pricing of CBs. In this chapter we define volatility and illustrate a number of methods of calculation.

3.1 MEASURES OF RETURN

It may seem a trivial exercise to talk about defining returns, but there are a number of different measures and it is important to know which one is being referred to. Throughout this book we refer to a profit or a loss as a return. If we invest £100 in some vehicle that turns into £110 in one year, then the return is obviously 10% per annum. There are, however, other ways of expressing this return and the one that is used in most risk and return calculations (the log relative return discussed below) is not so intuitive. Furthermore, some of these measures are used because of certain assumptions about the distributions of financial prices. Some of these assumptions are certainly not straightforward. Below we list five different ways of expressing return.

1. *Actual return*   If a £100 investment turns into a sum of £110 then the actual return is £10 or a profit of £10. If a £100 investment turns into a sum of £80 then

the actual return is $-£20$ or a loss of £20. In what follows we will eventually have to use algebraic notation when referring to returns and so we start by defining the actual return in terms of prices. If the price of something on day 1 is represented by p_1 and the price on another day, say day 2, is represented by p_2, then the actual return is simply the difference between p_2 and p_1 and is defined as

$$Actual\ return = p_2 - p_1$$

This is the simplest return measure. A profit is denoted by a positive value and a loss by a negative value. Theoretically there is no upper limit on the value of the actual return. So a £100 investment could turn into £1,000,000, producing an actual return of £999,900. If we restrict attention to those situations in which the maximum one can lose is the initial investment, then the lowest possible value for the actual return is $0 - p_1 = -p_1$. An investment of £100 turning into one worth £0 represents an actual return of $-£100$.

2. *Fractional return* The fractional return expresses the profit or loss as a fraction of the original investment. If an investment of £100 turns into a sum of £110 then the profit of £10 is expressed as a fraction of the £100 or $10/100 = 0.10$. Using the above notation of the prices of the investment on day 1 and day 2 , the general definition of the fractional return is

$$Fractional\ return = \frac{p_2 - p_1}{p_1}$$

This return measure is a more useful way of comparing profits and losses on differently priced entities. If one stock is bought at £100 and then sold at £110, the actual and fractional returns are £10 and 0.10 respectively. If another stock was bought at £1,000 and sold at £1,100, the actual and fractional returns are £100 and 0.10 respectively. The first measure gives the actual change in value and the second gives the change as a proportion of the initial investment. There is no theoretical upper limit on the fractional return and the lowest possible value is -1.

3. *Percentage return* The fractional return is usually multiplied by 100 and referred to as the Percentage Return. This is the most commonly reported measure of profit or loss and is defined as

$$Percentage\ return = 100 \times \frac{(p_2 - p_1)}{p_1}$$

A profit of £10 on £100 invested or a profit of £100 on £1,000 both represent 10% returns. There is no theoretical upper limit on the percentage return and the lowest possible value is -100%.

4. *Relative return* The relative return is defined as

$$Relative\ return = \frac{p_2}{p_1}$$

£100 turning into £110 gives a relative return measure of 110/100 = 1.10. Turning £1,000 into £700 gives a relative return measure of 700/1000 = 0.70. Most readers will be familiar with the fact that the relative return is simply the fractional return +1. The lowest possible value for this measure is 0 and of course there is no maximum. The relative return measure is often more convenient to use than the other measures. As an example, consider a sum of £3,250 invested in a scheme that produces a return (using the relative measure) of 1.06. The final value of the investment is simply £3,250 × 1.06 = £3,445. This is quicker than using the reported percentage return of 6% to calculate the actual profit as 6% of £3,250 = £195 and then adding to the original £3,250 to arrive at £3,445. The relative return measure enables one to carry out the two steps simultaneously. We quickly get to the new investment value of £3,445. And this is important since one usually needs then to reinvest the new sum into either the same or an alternative scheme.

The above methods of reporting profits or losses on investments are different ways of saying the same thing. The actual return is the actual monetary profit enjoyed or the real loss suffered. The relative return expresses this sum as a proportion of the original investment. The percentage return is just another way of representing the fractional return as a proportion of 100%. And the relative return is sometimes used as a more convenient way of calculating the future total value of investments.

5. *Log relative return*   Although the above standard return measures all have an intuitive meaning and are used to report profits and losses, they are rarely used in the valuation of derivative products. The measure that is used in the valuation of derivatives is the Log Relative Return defined as

$$Log\ relative\ return = \log\left(\frac{p_2}{p_1}\right)$$

The log term in the above expression refers to the natural log or log to the base *e*. Most calculators have functions that give the value of the log of a number. Most calculators should have a button with the symbol *loge* or *ln* (for natural log). We will leave the discussion of the meaning of this final return measure to later but give a simple example of the calculation. An investment of £100 turning into £110 has a log relative return of log (110/100) = log(1.1) = 0.0953. For simplicity the log relative return is often referred to simply as the log return.

At this stage it is useful to compare the values of all five measures for different profits and losses. Table 3.1 lists the values for various different outcomes obtained by investing £100.

The first four return measures are all intuitively obvious but the log relative return is not. Notice, however, the similarity between the fractional return values and the log relative values when the price changes are small. With an actual change

Table 3.1 Comparison of return measures

Amount invested on day 1	Value on day 2	Actual return	Fractional return	Percentage return	Relative return	Log relative return
	£0	−£100	−1.00	−100%	0.00	N/A
	£10	−£90	−0.90	−90%	0.10	−2.3024
	£50	−£50	−0.50	−50%	0.50	−1.6094
	£80	−£20	−0.20	−20%	0.80	−0.2231
	£85	−£15	−0.15	−15%	0.85	−0.1625
	£90	−£10	−0.10	−10%	0.90	−0.1054
	£95	−£5	−0.05	−5%	0.95	−0.0513
£100	£100	£0	0.00	0%	1.00	0.0000
	£105	+£5	+0.05	+5%	1.05	+0.0488
	£110	+£10	+0.10	+10%	1.10	+0.0953
	£115	+£15	+0.15	+15%	1.15	+0.1398
	£120	+£20	+0.20	+20%	1.20	+0.1823
	£150	+£50	+0.50	+50%	1.50	+0.4055
	£200	+£100	+1.00	+100%	2.00	+0.6931
	£250	+£150	+1.50	+150%	2.50	+0.9163

of +£5 the fractional and log relative returns are +0.0500 and +0.0488 respectively. With an actual change of −£5 the fractional and log relative returns are −0.0500 and −0.0513 respectively. It is possible to show that for very small price changes the two measures are almost identical.

Log relative return = fractional return (for small returns)

When the fractional returns are 0.01, the log relative returns are 0.00995, which is very nearly equal to 0.01. The smaller the actual return the better the approximation. This approximate identity is noted, since in this and many other books on the calculation of risk and return, only the log values are reported. Often the given returns are those calculated on a daily basis and so will invariably be very small indeed. Recalling this approximate identity will enable the reader to get a better feel for the real profits and losses experienced. If an investment produced the following stream of daily log returns: 0.002, −0.003, 0.001 and 0.000 one could interpret the daily fractional returns changes to be the same and thus the daily percentage price changes to be 100 times these numbers, or: +0.2%, −0.3%, +0.1% and 0%.

This approximation is valid only for small returns. The relationship between the log returns and the other measures becomes much more complex for non-trivial price changes. Also, it is not possible to calculate a value for the log return corresponding to losing everything; there is no such thing as the log of zero. We return to the discussion of the log returns later.

3.2   RETURN DISTRIBUTIONS

Investment returns are rarely certain. In the real world, when we invest in a certain stock, the future outcome is usually unknown. This chapter is concerned with trying to estimate the most likely return one will receive and also the degree of uncertainty of such returns. This process involves arriving at descriptive statistics associated with the distribution of returns. To introduce the idea of a distribution of returns it is useful to consider a hypothetical construct.

Consider the imaginary situation of playing a game that has an uncertain payback. The game, known as 'Game A', costs £100 to play and an individual is invited to play many times. Some of the time the game pays back £110, i.e., giving the player a 10% return and some of the time the game pays back £90 causing the player to lose 10%. It is also possible to make or lose 20%, 30% and 40%. The player is not allowed to reinvest his winnings and place a larger bet — the price for playing the game is always £100. Also, the game is devised so that there is no pattern in the sequence of profits or losses. So if a player loses ten times in a row, this does not make it more likely that he will win at the next play. The payback characteristics are given in Table 3.2 and Figure 3.1 which depict a typical result of playing this game 100 successive times. The table gives the frequency of each different outcome and we can use these to calculate probabilities. A loss of £40 occurred three times out of 100 tries and so our best estimate of the probability of losing £40 in the future is 3%. The frequencies given in the table and the resultant pictorial representation (a histogram) are two different ways of looking at what is known as the 'distribution of returns'. Note that the distribution is symmetric about some central value and that the likelihood of enjoying a large profit or suffering a large loss is small. Most of the returns are distributed around a value near zero. So is it worth playing such a game? We answer this in the next section.

Table 3.2   'Game A' return distribution

Initial stake	Payback	Actual return (a)	Frequency (b)	Total return = (a) × (b)
	£60	−£40	3	−£120
	£70	−£30	5	−£150
	£80	−£20	10	−£200
	£90	−£10	15	−£150
£100	£100	£0	25	£0
	£110	+£10	17	+£170
	£120	+£20	10	+£200
	£130	+£30	10	+£300
	£140	+£40	5	+£200
		Totals	100	£250
		Average		£2.50

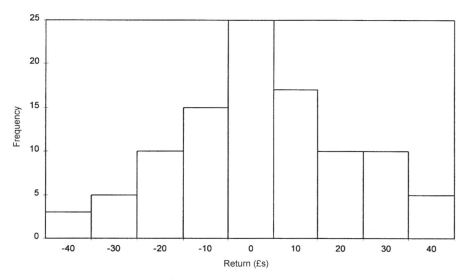

Figure 3.1 Game A return distribution

It should be noted that there is an important piece of information relating to the return distribution that is missing from both the table and the picture. Both representations omit information on the sequence of returns. If we were not told that no special pattern existed, we would not be able to discover this from either representation. And this fact is often forgotten in the literature. It is possible to imagine a specially concocted sequence of returns that have an identical distribution but in which the first five were profits of £40, followed by ten profits of $30, and so on until finally we experience three losses of £40. This sequence of returns would most definitely have a pattern and anyone observing the play would quickly realise that the paybacks were gradually diminishing. Statisticians call such predictable sequences of numbers, 'non-serially independent'. The problem with looking at return distributions using only pictures like those of Figure 3.1 is that all sense of the time is lost. We know that £40 was lost on three occasions but we don't know when and whether the series has any special pattern. When we come to discuss returns as sequences of price changes, it is important to remember that the resultant distributions and associated computations completely ignore the issue of time.

3.3 AVERAGES AND EXPECTED RETURNS

Closer inspection of Figure 3.1 will show that the distribution is not perfectly symmetric and that there is more of the distribution on the positive side than on the negative side. The 'centre' of the distribution appears to be above zero and so it looks as if this game might be worth playing. Table 3.2 gives the details of the realised profits and losses experienced by playing 100 times. On five occasions a profit of £40 was enjoyed producing a sum of 5 × £40 = £200, on ten occasions a profit of £30 was enjoyed producing 10 × £30 = £300 and so on. In total, a sum of £250 was accumulated and this was after 100 games. The average return is thus £250/100 = £2.50 per game. If these frequencies of paybacks are reproducible then this game is certainly worth playing. The only limit to accumulating infinite wealth would be the speed at which one could play. For every 100 games we would expect to accumulate £250. For every 10,000 games we would expect to accumulate £25,000. Whatever the number of games we play, our expected total profit would be £2.50 times the number of plays. This is why statisticians refer to the long run average of a distribution as the 'expected value'. The expected value of this distribution is £2.50 and is usually denoted symbolically as

$$E(\text{'Game A'}) = £2.50$$

or sometimes as

$$E(A) = £2.50$$

Note that playing any one particular game will produce only one of the returns in Table 3.2, but never £2.50. So in this and many other examples, the expected value can never be achieved in one attempt. It is the long-run average. Note also, that although in the long run the player wins £2.50 per game, it is not necessarily a risk-free exercise. If you were allowed only ten attempts, then you could be unlucky and lose everything. What if you were allowed only one? Would you risk losing £40 in the hope of wining £40?

Consider now being allowed to play a different game — 'Game B'. The cost of playing is the same as Game A (£100), but the payback characteristics are different. The distributions of returns are given in Table 3.3. The distributions of both games are shown in Figure 3.2.

The expected return to Game B is higher at £3.80. The distribution is still symmetric but centred around a higher average. So is B a better bet? The answer is yes if you are allowed a large number of attempts. In the long run you will win £3.80 − £2.50 = £1.30 more per game. So in 10,000 plays you would expect to be better off by £13,000. But what if you are allowed only ten plays, or maybe only one play? The returns to Game B are far more spread out than those of Game A. Although there is a higher chance of winning £40 (10% *versus* 5%) there is also a higher chance of losing £40 (7% *versus* 3%). Intuition tells us that B is riskier than A. And although the expected return is higher, is it worth taking the higher risk? Before we answer this question we need to come up with some method of quantifying risk or quantifying the clearly observable fact that distribution B is more spread out than A.

Table 3.3   'Game B' return distribution

Initial stake	Payback	Actual return (a)	Frequency (b)	Total return = (a) × (b)
	£60	−£40	7	−£280
	£70	−£30	8	−£240
	£80	−£20	9	−£180
	£90	−£10	11	−£110
£100	£100	£0	13	£0
	£110	+£10	17	+£170
	£120	+£20	13	+£260
	£130	+£30	12	+£360
	£140	+£40	10	+£400
		Totals	100	£380
		Average		£3.80

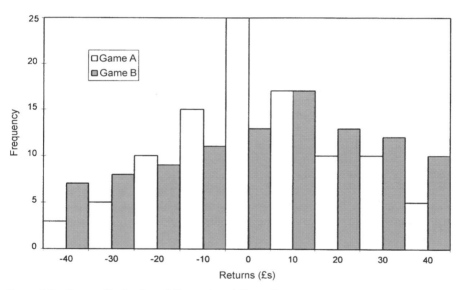

Figure 3.2   Return distribution of Game A and Game B

3.4   A MEASURE OF DISPERSION — MAD, VARIANCE AND STANDARD DEVIATION

An obvious method of measuring the spread of a distribution around some central point is to find how far each observation is from the centre and calculate the average. This is done for the Game A distribution in Table 3.4.

Note that a return of £40 is £37.50 above the mean and this occurs on five occasions; the return of £30 is £27.50 above the mean and occurs on ten occasions

Table 3.4 The MAD — average deviation from the mean — Game A

Actual return (a)	Mean return (b)	Deviation from mean (c) = (a)−(b)	Frequency (d)	Total deviation = (c) × (d)	Absolute deviation (e)	Total absolute deviation = (e) × (d)
−£40	+£2.50	−£42.50	3	−£127.50	£42.50	£127.50
−£30	+£2.50	−£32.50	5	−£162.5	£32.50	£162.5
−£20	+£2.50	−£22.50	10	−£225.00	£22.50	£225.00
−£10	+£2.50	−£12.50	15	−£187.50	£12.50	£187.50
£0	+£2.50	−£2.50	25	−£62.50	£2.50	£62.50
+£10	+£2.50	+£7.50	17	+£127.50	£7.50	£127.50
+£20	+£2.50	+£17.50	10	+£175.00	£17.50	£175.00
+£30	+£2.50	+£27.50	10	+£275.00	£27.50	£275.00
+£40	+£2.50	+£37.50	5	+£187.50	£37.50	£187.50
		Total	100	£0		£1,530
		Average		£0		£15.30

and so on. The measure of spread or dispersion we are looking for is an average of these deviations. These deviations sum to zero and so hence have an average of zero. This is, of course, no fluke. By the definition of an average, half of the total deviations will be negative and half will be positive. This measure will always come out as zero and so is not very useful.

However, all is not lost. The problem is the negative deviations. The negative signs tell us that that particular return is lower than the average. We are interested in looking for a simple measure of dispersion away from the mean and not particularly interested in whether a given return is above or below this value. The solution is to find the average of the deviations ignoring the negative signs. This is shown in column (e). The process of removing the sign from a number in mathematics is known as taking the 'absolute value'. The absolute function gives the magnitude of a number irrespective of its sign. The total absolute deviation is £1,530, giving an average of £15.30 per go and this is the measure of spread we are looking for — the mean absolute deviation (MAD). We read this value as meaning the following: when playing Game A, on average, an individual return is £15.30 away from the expected value of £2.50. The game is quite risky. We would much prefer a game whose expected value was £2.50 with a MAD of £5.30 per game. Better still would be a situation in which we were simply given £2.50 every time — a game with no variation in payback at all.

We now return to consider Game B. Carrying out the same calculations on the second distribution we find that the MAD is £19.85. As suspected, the returns to Game B are more spread out from the average than those of 'A'. Although Game B on average pays out more than Game A, the variation around the average is much higher. Game B is riskier. Which game is better depends on one's individual risk preferences. As in the real world of investments, higher returns are usually associated with higher risks.

As a measure of risk, the MAD has very appealing features, the most obvious one being that almost everyone has an understanding of an average. The MAD is the average of how far each outcome of an uncertain trial is from the expected value. If we had two investments that in the long run had the same expected value and one had a MAD of £10 and the other one of £20, we could say that the second is twice as risky as the first.

Intuitively appealing though it is, the MAD is not used as a common measure of risk. Two much more frequently used measures are the variance and the standard deviation. These measures use an alternative trick to get around the problem encountered above when totalling up the deviations from the mean — the fact that the positive ones are cancelled by the negative ones. If instead of simply ignoring the signs (i.e., using the absolute function) we square the deviations, we will always end up with a positive number and this then can be totalled; see Table 3.5 for the results.

The total of all 100 squared deviations is 36,875 and so the average squared deviation is 368.75. This measure of dispersion is known as the variance and is used in all future mathematical calculations and models involving risk or volatility. This is usually expressed mathematically as

$$Variance \text{ (Game A)} = 368.75$$

or algebraically as

$$\sigma_A^2 = 368.75$$

Table 3.5 The variance and standard deviation — Game A

Actual return (a)	Mean return (b)	Deviation from mean $(c) = (a) - (b)$	Squared deviation $(d) = (c) \times (c)$	Frequency $= (e)$	Total deviation $(f) = (e) \times (d)$
−£40	+ £2.50	−£42.50	1,806.25	3	5,418.75
−£30	+ £2.50	−£32.50	1,056.25	5	5,281.25
−£20	+ £2.50	−£22.50	506.25	10	5,062.50
−£10	+ £2.50	−£12.50	156.25	15	2,343.75
£0	+ £2.50	−£2.50	6.25	25	156.25
+ £10	+ £2.50	+ £7.50	56.25	17	956.25
+ £20	+ £2.50	+ £17.50	306.25	10	3,062.50
+ £30	+ £2.50	+ £27.50	756.25	10	7,562.50
+ £40	+ £2.50	+ £37.50	1,406.25	5	7,031.25
		Total		100	36,875.00
		Average	= Variance		368.75
		$\sqrt{}$(Average)	= St. dev.		£19.20

The problem with the variance is (1) it is in non-meaningful units and (2) it tends to exaggerate large deviations. Recall that the distribution is all about returns in £s. The average is measured and reported in £s and it would make sense to report the dispersion also in £s. The variance is a measure of the deviations squared and so the answer is 368.75 square £s — a meaningless concept. Also note that observations furthermost from the centre have a disproportionate contribution to the average. The −£40 returns contribute 1,806.25 squared units, whereas the −£10 returns contribute only 156.25 squared units. This is due to the nature of the squaring function. Squaring large numbers results in very large numbers.

Both of these difficulties are overcome by taking the square root of the variance. This gives us a value of £19.20 and is known as the standard deviation of the distribution.

$$\textit{Standard deviation} \text{ (Game A)} = \sqrt{\textit{Variance} \text{ (Game A)}}$$

or algebraically

$$\sigma_A = \sqrt{\sigma_A^2}$$
$$= \sqrt{368.75}$$
$$= £19.20$$

By definition the standard deviation is in the same units as the data and the square root process reverses (somewhat) the exaggerating effect of the squaring process. The standard deviation is another attempt at measuring how spread out the returns are. It is similar to the MAD but uses the squaring and square root process to arrive at a result. The two measures will be similar but not exactly the same. The standard deviation is the universally reported measure of dispersion but the variance is the one used in all further mathematical work. So what does the standard deviation tell us about Games A and B? Carrying out the same calculations for Game B we get a variance of 553.66 or a standard deviation value of £23.53. Game B is riskier than game A.

3.5   THE CONCEPT OF A POPULATION, SAMPLE AND SAMPLING VARIATION

When we considered playing Game A or B 100 times, the tables and histograms were said to represent the distributions of the payoffs. Strictly speaking this is not so. Table 3.2 shows only a sample of 100 outcomes of Game A. It is possible that another 100 plays will give a slightly different set of paybacks. So what does this say about the average and standard deviation of the returns? Maybe they are not really £2.50 and £19.20 respectively. Maybe in the long run the returns are negative and maybe the standard deviation is much higher. In this section we discuss the concept of a population and a sample. In the real world we have to use sample values to estimate what the real underlying population values are.

Until now we have assumed the games to be like those of tossing a coin or spinning a roulette wheel. We have assumed that one could play the game indefinitely. Imagine now a slightly different situation in which the outcomes to Game A are defined as the numbers written on balls that are drawn at random from a box. Assume the box contains 10,000 balls. Some of the balls are numbered −£40, some −£30 and so on. The player pays £100 and picks a ball at random. After noting his return, and either paying up if a loss occurs or pocketing the cash if a profit occurs, the ball is returned to the box. Table 3.2 could be the result of 100 such draws. Statisticians call the set of all 10,000 balls the 'population' and the subset of 100 drawn at random as a 'sample'. The average and standard deviations of the sample were £2.50 and £19.20 respectively. But is this really the average and standard deviation of the whole population? Can we be sure that the long-run average is really £2.50? Say another player (player number 2) came along and played another 100 times; what would his sample average and standard deviation be? Say they were £2.30 and £20.65 respectively. A third player (player number 3) also plays 100 times and reports values of £2.55 and £18.23. Figure 3.3 depicts the situation after 100 players each make 100 attempts. Each one would report an average and a standard deviation.

Let us concentrate initially on the sample averages. We can view each average as an attempt at estimating the unknown population average. The only way of truly discovering the population average is to empty the box and calculate the average of all 10,000 numbers. Say this population average is in fact £2.40; what would the distribution of the sample averages look like? The answer depends on the sample size. It is not intended here to go into the mathematics of sampling but note that if the sample size is large enough (and 100 is certainly large enough) then the resulting distribution is what is known as 'normal' or 'Gaussian' and this is depicted also in Figure 3.3. The normal distribution is a symmetric bell-shaped curve centred around the true population average. We say that the distribution of averages is a 'sampling distribution'.

In reality if we were attempting to estimate the long-run average returns to Game A, we would take just one sample of 100. However, Figure 3.3 shows that the resultant sample average could be quite some distance from the true value. Although the most likely value will be near the true value of £2.40 one could get values as high as £7.00 or as low as −£1.00. The fact that the sample estimate may be quite different from the true population value is known as 'sampling variation'. This point should be borne in mind later on when we discuss the estimation of true population mean returns on stocks and CBs. We are invariably in a situation of using sample values as estimates of underlying population values. There will always be sampling variation and so even though one has the right model one may still be using the wrong inputs.

Can one reduce sampling variation? Yes. The obvious way is to increase the sample size. Rather than sample 100, try 400 or better still 1,000. The degree of error in estimating the population mean is directly related to the sample size, but

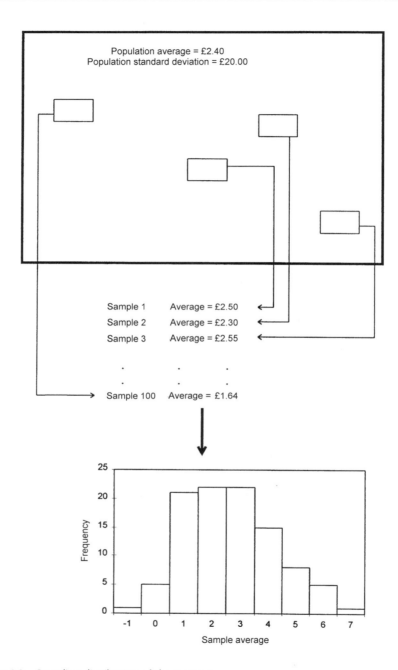

Figure 3.3 Sampling distribution of the average

not in a linear fashion. The relationship depends on the inverse of the square root of the sample size. Increasing the sample size by a factor of 4 to 400 would reduce the error by one half since $1/\sqrt{4} = 1/2$. If it makes sense and if it is possible, make the sample size as large as possible.

We now consider estimating the standard deviation. Figure 3.4 depicts the situation of the 100 different samples of size 100. Each sample will produce an estimate of the population value. Say the true population value is £20.00. We see that the estimates are also distributed around £20.00 but can be as high as £23.00 or as low as £17.00. Not surprisingly, the standard deviation is also subject to sampling error. As with the sample average, the cure is to increase the sample size. Later on we shall see that even if it were possible it often does not make sense to increase the sample size too much. When investigating return distributions on stocks, increasing sample size means looking further back into the past. Looking further back in time could actually increase errors from other considerations, but more of this later. The point of this section is to emphasise that the variables input into CB valuations are usually estimates and are subject to estimation error.

3.6 ADDING DISTRIBUTIONS

Eventually, we will be leading on to estimating and modelling stock risk. Many researchers use daily returns distributions to make inferences about annual risks. If there are 250 trading days in a year do we simply multiply the daily risk by 250 to arrive at an annual estimate? No.

Before we look at adding 250 different returns together let us consider the very much simpler example of adding just two. Say an individual were to play Games A and B simultaneously. Each go now would cost £200 and the profit or loss would be the sum of each separate game. With luck, £40 might be won on both A and B thus returning £80 or a profit of 40%. What would the long-run average or return and risk be? The answer to the first part is straightforward — we simply add the separate averages. This is expressed using expectation notation as

Expected return (A + B) = Expected return (A) + Expected return (B)

or

$$E(A + B) = E(A) + E(B)$$

The long-run average would be £2.50 + £3.80 = £6.30 per game and this is intuitively obvious. But what about the risk or the standard deviation? The answer depends on whether there is any way in which the two separate outcomes are linked. If the outcome to Game A is completely independent to that of Game B then the combined risk is obtained by summing the variances, not the standard deviations.

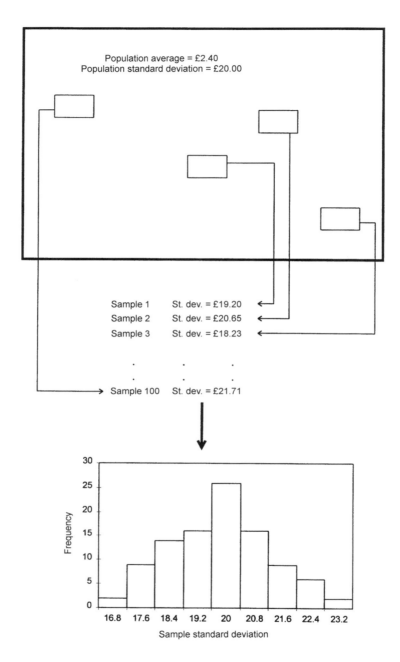

Figure 3.4   Sampling distribution of the standard deviation

$$\textit{Variance of } (A + B) = \textit{Variance of } (A) + \textit{Variance } (B)$$

or

$$\sigma^2_{(A+B)} = \sigma^2_A + \sigma^2_B$$
$$\sigma^2_{(A+B)} = 368.75 + 553.66 = 922.41$$

$\therefore$
$$\sigma_{(A+B)} = \sqrt{922.41} = £30.37$$

So the standard deviation is £30.37. Note that this is not the same as the sum of the individual standard deviations (£19.20 + £23.53 = £42.73). Provided the outcomes of Games A and B are independent, the above expression involving the sums of variances always holds and it is possible to show that the standard deviation of the sum is always less than the sum of the individual standard deviations. This result may seem strange at first, but experienced investors know the concept as 'diversification'. The risk of playing Games A and B together is less riskier than playing each one separately because of the lack of a connection between the outcomes. A particular outcome of A might be a loss of £40, but this may be offset by B resulting in a profit of £20.

The situation is completely different if there is some connection or correlation between A and B. It is possible to imagine a specially concocted situation in which the outcomes of A and B are positively correlated in some way. Such a situation would be if profits (losses) from A coincide with profits (losses) from B. In this case there would be little or no benefit from diversification — the joint standard deviation would be higher than £30.37. It is possible to show that if the outcomes are perfectly correlated in the sense that the returns were perfectly matched, then the standard deviation of the joint game would exactly equal the sum of the separate standard deviations. At the other extreme, if the outcomes are perfectly negatively correlated then it is possible to find a situation in which the joint standard deviation would be zero. In this case, the losses suffered from one game would be completely offset by the profits from the other — the long-run average of the joint game would still be £6.30 but it would be £6.30 each and every time.

We can extend this argument to include a third game, Game C.

$$E(A + B + C) = E(A) + E(B) + E(C)$$

and

$$\sigma^2_{(A+B+C)} = \sigma^2_A + \sigma^2_B + \sigma^2_C$$

The expression involving expectations is true for all situations but the one involving sums of variances is only true for A, B and C being mutually independent. If C has an expectation of £1.50 and a standard deviation of £20.00 then

$$E(A + B + C) = £2.50 + £3.80 + £1.50 = £7.80$$

$$\sigma^2_{(A+B+C)} = 368.75 + 553.66 + (20.00)^2 = 1,322.41$$

$$\therefore \qquad \sigma_{(A+B+C)} = \sqrt{1322.41} = £36.36$$

As before, the standard deviation is less than the sum of the individual standard deviations. This process can be extended to include as many games as we like. The expected value is always the sum of the individual expectations and, provided all games are mutually independent, then the variance is the sum of the individual variances.

3.7   ADDING THE SAME DISTRIBUTIONS

We return now to the simple situation of adding the results of two games, but with a difference. The player has one go at Game A and then another go at Game A. Here we treat one 'new game' result as being the sum of the two plays of Game A. Provided the two individual tries are independent, we can substitute A for B in the above expressions.

$$E(A + A) = E(A) + E(A)$$
$$E(2A) = 2 \times E(A)$$
$$= 2 \times £2.50 = £5.00$$

and

$$\sigma^2_{(A+A)} = \sigma^2_A + \sigma^2_A$$
$$\sigma^2_{2A} = 368.75 + 368.75 = 737.75$$
$$\sigma_{2A} = \sqrt{737.75} = £27.15$$

This new game then has twice the expected return, but less than twice the standard deviation. The new standard deviation is, in fact, exactly the old one multiplied by $\sqrt{2}$ or 1.414. This is easy to see if we recompute as follows.

$$\sigma^2_{(A+A)} = \sigma^2_A + \sigma^2_A$$
$$\sigma^2_{(2A)} = 2\sigma^2_A$$
$$\sigma_{(2A)} = \sqrt{2}\sigma_A$$

Playing A twice is not twice as risky as playing it once. Extending the argument to playing A three times we have.

$$E(A + A + A) = E(A) + E(A) + E(A)$$

or

$$E(3A) = 3E(A)$$

and

$$\sigma^2_{(A+A+A)} = \sigma^2_A + \sigma^2_A + \sigma^2_A$$
$$\sigma^2_{(3A)} = 3\sigma^2_A$$
$$\sigma_{(3A)} = \sqrt{3}\sigma_A$$

The expected value and standard deviation of three tries at Game A is £7.50 and £33.26 respectively. If we extend this to any number of games, say n, then:

$$E(nA) = nE(A) \tag{3.1}$$

and

$$\sigma_{(nA)} = \sqrt{n}\sigma_A \tag{3.2}$$

So if we have 100 tries at A and count this as one game (costing £10,000 to play!) then the expected value and standard deviation are $100 \times £2.50 = £250$ and $\sqrt{100} \times £19.20 = £192$. As the value of n increases, so does the standard deviation, but only at the rate of $\sqrt{n}$ and this is illustrated in Figure 3.5

With $n = 100$ the expected value has increased 100 times but the standard deviation only 10 times. And this is why we intuitively know that it makes sense, if allowed, to play as many times as possible. In the long run, although the risk is

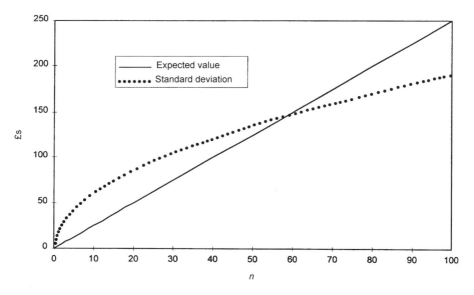

Figure 3.5   Characteristics of game $n \times A$

increasing, the expected return is increasing faster. As an extreme example say we altered n to 10,000. A single outcome of this final game will now be the sum of 10,000 tries at A and will cost £1,000,000 to play. The expected value and standard deviation of returns are $1,000,000 \times £2.50 = £2,500,000$ and $\sqrt{1,000,000} \times £19.20 = £19,200$ respectively. The probability of losing is extremely small.

This special feature of the non-linear increase in standard deviation is all due to expressions of the type (3.1) and (3.2) and we use this fact later on to estimate annual stock volatility from daily numbers. But the expression is valid only if each try at A is independent from the other goes. If there is any dependence such as losses or profits tending to 'stick together' then the expression is invalid and the total standard deviation may be more or less than $\sqrt{n}\sigma_A$.

3.8 FROM STOCK PRICES TO RETURNS

We now address the issue of calculating risk and return statistics for sequences of stock prices. Consider the set of daily stock prices given in Table 3.6 and the top panel in Figure 3.6. On day 1 the price is 100 units (the currency is not important). On day 2 the price has increased to 102 and we say that the actual return or price change is $102 - 100 = +2$ units. On day 3 the price has fallen back to 101 and so the new return is $101 - 102 = -1$ unit. The sequence of price changes can be thought of in much the same way as the outcomes to Game A above, with one important difference. To enter Game A we had to pay £100 every time, but in the case of buying stock you only pay once — on day 1. Nevertheless, we can still consider the sequence of price changes to be returns if we think of the situation slightly differently. With Game A, the player was not allowed to reinvest his profits in future games — it always cost £100. When buying stock it is as if the

Table 3.6 Stock prices to returns

Day (t)	Price p_t	Return $= p_t - p_{t-1}$
1	100	
2	102	$+2$
3	101	-1
4	104	$+3$
.	.	.
.	.	.
.	.	.
28	111	$+1$
29	110	-1
30	106	-4
31	110	$+4$

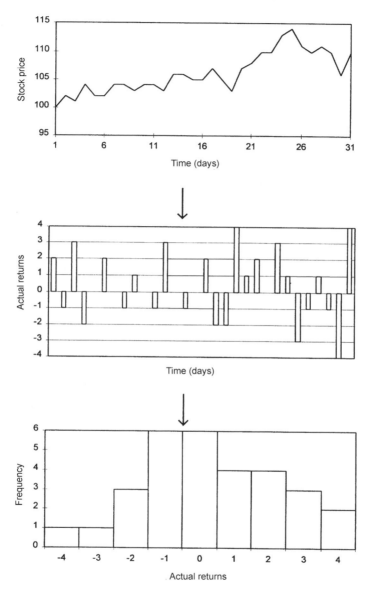

Figure 3.6 From prices to returns to distributions

returns are always reinvested. On day 2 when the return is +2 we add this to the original investment of 100 and obtain 102. On day 3 the loss of 1 is subtracted from 102 to get 101 and so on. The series of price changes are still returns, but the returns are continually reinvested. The chart of the price changes as they evolve is given in the middle panel of Figure 3.6. Positive returns correspond to days when the price in the price chart increases, and negative returns correspond to days when the price falls. Note that there are two occasions when the price increased 4 units, three occasions when the price increased 3 units and so on. The distribution of returns is given in the lower panel. This shows that the most frequent returns are −1 and 0 and that the distribution is symmetric and clustered around the zero mark. The average and standard deviation of this distribution is 0.33 and 2.02 respectively.

The average of 0.33 has a direct interpretation for the price chart. On day 1 the price is 100 and 30 days later it is 110. This represents an average price change of $10/30 = 0.33$ per day. This figure is exactly the same as that calculated from the frequency distribution because the sum of the price changes must be equal to the total price change of 10 units. The average could be referred to as the trend. One would end up with the same final stock price if the price simply increased 0.33 units each and every day.

To interpret the standard deviation we start with the lower panel of Figure 3.6, go on to consider the middle and then the top panel. The standard deviation is a measure of the spread of the distribution in the lower panel. It can also be thought of as a measure of the average width of the channel within which the price changes fluctuate in the middle panel. And this in turn can be thought of as a measure of the volatility of the original price series in the top panel. On its own, a standard deviation of 2.02 doesn't mean much. Figure 3.7 shows another price

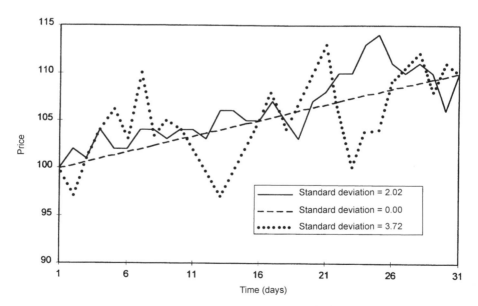

Figure 3.7 Price series with different standard deviations (volatilities)

series with the same average but with a higher standard deviation of 3.71. A higher standard deviation corresponds to a more volatile price series. A lower value corresponds to a less volatile series. The lowest possible value for a standard deviation is zero and this corresponds to a series that moves exactly the same amount every day. The straight line representing the trend has a zero standard deviation or zero volatility.

The values of 0.33 and 2.02 are estimates for daily returns but it is usual practice to quote these statistics in annual terms. If we assume that one year has 250 trading days and that price changes are independent, then we can use the expressions (3.1) and (3.2) to calculate the annual expected value and standard deviation for the series in Table 3.6 as: $250 \times 0.33 = 83.33$ and $\sqrt{250} \times 2.02 = 31.84$ respectively.

3.9 FROM STOCK PRICES TO MORE APPROPRIATE RETURNS

When considering the outcomes to Games A, B and C or the stock price sequence above we have exclusively talked about the actual returns. This is because it is very easy to look at simple price changes or absolute profits or losses. In reality, however, one invariably uses one of the other return measures. Say two stocks both produced an actual return of £10 with one priced at £100 and the other at £50. The percentage returns are 10% and 20% respectively. In the investment world it is percentage returns that really count. There is a problem, however, associated with averaging percentage returns. To illustrate this consider the price of a certain stock on four consecutive days: £100, £110, £132 and £165. The three individual daily percentage returns are 10%, 20% and 25% respectively. The average of these returns is $(10 + 20 + 25)/3 = 18.33\%$. However the average daily return is not 18.33. Starting with £100 and increasing at 18.33% each day would produce prices of £118.33, £140.03 and £165.70. The discrepancy is due to the complication of the way in which returns are compounded. The real average daily percentage return is 18.17%. Starting with £100 and increasing at 18.17% each day would produce prices of £118.17, £139.63 and £165.00. To find the true average percentage returns one has to multiply all the individual relative returns and then find the cube root.

$$\text{Average relative return} = \sqrt[3]{(110/100) \times (132/110) \times (165/132)}$$
$$= 1.1817$$
$$\therefore \text{ Average percentage return} = 18.17\%$$

Similarly, if there were 30 daily returns as in Table 3.6 we would have to multiply all 30 relative returns and then find the 30th root. There is, however, an alternative method and that is to find the ordinary average of the logged returns and then take the anti-log or in this case find the exponential of the answer.

$$\text{Average of logged returns} = (\log(110/100) + \log(132/110) + \log(165/132))/3$$
$$= (0.09531 + 0.18232 + 0.22314)/3$$
$$= 0.16693$$

$\therefore$ $\qquad\qquad$ Average relative return $= \text{Exp}(0.16693) = 1.1817$

$\therefore$ $\qquad\qquad$ Average percentage return $= 18.17\%$

The equivalence of the two approaches is due to the special property of logarithms. Multiplying relative returns is the same as adding logged returns. Finding the cube root of a number is the same as dividing the log by 3. So by converting the prices to price relatives and then to log relatives one can arrive at the long-run average and standard deviation of the percentage returns. This is done for the same price sequence in Table 3.7.

The average and the standard deviation of the logged series are 0.00318 and 0.01898 respectively. Converting these back to percentage returns we get 0.32% and 1.92%. Annualising the figures we get $250 \times 0.32 = 80.00\%$ and $\sqrt{250} \times 1.92 = 30.36\%$. Compare these to the actual return figures of 83.33 and 31.84. When expressed as a percentage of the initial value of 100 the results are not that dissimilar and this is often the case.

This is how the annualised estimates of volatility or standard deviations are calculated and reported. Using the log relative returns gets around the complication caused by compounding.

Table 3.7 Stock prices to logged returns

Day (t)	Price p_t	Logged return $= \log(p_t/p_{t-1})$
1	100	
2	102	$+0.01980$
3	101	-0.00985
4	104	$+0.02927$
.	.	.
.	.	.
.	.	.
28	111	$+0.00905$
29	110	-0.00905
30	106	-0.03704
31	110	$+0.03774$

4
Modelling the share price process

There have been many studies of the empirical (i.e., actual) distribution of stock prices. Most studies actually examine the distribution of stock price returns defined as percentage changes or relative changes. The results are varied but the consensus is that in the long run, the distribution of returns is not that different from lognormal with a non-constant volatility. In this book we do not intend to go into a detailed description of the lognormal distribution but outline a much more intuitively appealing and straightforward binomial model. The virtue of this approach is that as we increase the number of binomial steps, the model becomes much more believable as a description of a random stock price process. The real advantage is that as we increase the number of steps without limit, the model approaches the lognormal distribution.

Many practitioners still use the binomial model without really understanding the implications for the evaluation of derivatives in general. In this chapter we derive expressions for the expected return and the volatility of returns. We show why, under certain circumstances, the volatility is independent of certain probability aspects. We also give examples of stock prices that are not temporally independent and highlight the implications for CB modelling.

4.1 THE EXPECTED VALUE AND STANDARD DEVIATION OF A BERNOULLI TRIAL

We begin by considering one of the simplest models of price behaviour — the Bernoulli trial. In this model the price of something at the end of a given period can be either up or down a fixed amount. We start by assuming the stock price today is £100. If we assume that the price tomorrow can be either £102 or £98, then we say that the price change follows a Bernoulli process. What is the expected value and standard deviation of this price change? Recall that the expected value is the long run average and that the standard deviation is a measure of the spread of all the possible outcomes around this long-run average. In the very simple situation of a Bernoulli trial, there are only two outcomes and in this case these are +£2 and −£2.

It should be obvious that the long-run average price change will be somewhere between these two numbers. The answer will depend on the number of times the price increases or decreases. Although we do not intend to go into the mathematics here, the expected value and standard deviation of a Bernoulli trial is a function of the probability of the up and down movements and is given by:

$$E(\text{price change}) = u(2p - 1)$$
$$\sigma(\text{price change}) = 2u\sqrt{p(1 - p)}$$

where u = magnitude of up move
       p = probability of an up move
       $1 - p$ = probability of a down move

In this particular example, if we assume that the probability of an up move is equal to that of a down move, then $p = 0.5$. Substituting this into the above expression we get

$$E(\text{price change}) = u(2(0.5) - 1) = 0$$
$$\sigma(\text{price change}) = 2u\sqrt{0.5(1 - 0.5)} = u$$

And since $u = £2$ we have an expected value of £0 and a standard deviation of £2. These results are intuitively obvious. Imagine investing in 100 stocks all priced at £100. If each price could only rise or fall by £2 and a rise or fall were equally likely then the average price change would be zero.

4.2   THE SIMPLE ADDITIVE MODEL OF STOCK PRICE CHANGES

In the very simple Bernoulli model above, the stock price can be only one of two values at the end of a period. We now develop a slightly more realistic model in which the final price can be a number of different values. We do this by building on the idea of a Bernoulli process. We start by assuming that the stock price at the beginning of the period in question is £100. We then consider breaking the period into a number of sub-periods. We then assume that the stock price over each of these sub-periods follows a Bernoulli process.

4.2.1   The 12-Period-a-Year Additive Stock Price Binomial Model

For simplicity, assume that we wish to model the stock price at the end of one year. Break the year up into 12 equal sub-periods of time, say one month each, and assume that the stock price change over each month is given by the above Bernoulli process. We could simulate the outcomes of this process with the tossing of a coin. If the outcome is a head (H), the stock price increases by £2; if it is a tail (T), the

Table 4.1   Simulation no.1 of additive stock price model

Month	Outcome of coin toss	Price change	Price
			Initial Price = £100
1	H	+ £2	100 + 2 = £102
2	H	+ £2	102 + 2 = £104
3	T	− £2	104 − 2 = £102
4	H	+ £2	102 + 2 = £104
5	T	− £2	104 − 2 = £102
6	T	− £2	102 − 2 = £100
7	H	+ £2	100 + 2 = £102
8	H	+ £2	102 + 2 = £104
9	H	+ £2	104 + 2 = £106
10	H	+ £2	106 + 2 = £108
11	T	− £2	108 − 2 = £106
12	H	+ £2	106 + 2 = £108
	Total Price Change	+ £8	

stock price decreases by £2. To simulate the path taken by the stock in a given year let us toss the coin 12 times. Say the outcomes are:

H   H   T   H   T   T   H   H   H   H   T   H

Table 4.1 shows how the price series evolves.

The upper panel in Figure 4.1 gives a pictorial display of the simulated stock price chart. The final stock price at the end of the 12 months can also be deduced simply using the expression

$$\text{Final stock price} = \text{initial stock price} + \text{number of up moves} \times 2$$
$$- \text{number of down moves} \times 2$$
$$= 100 + 8 \times 2 - 4 \times 2$$
$$= £108$$

Consider another simulation of the stock path. Starting again at £100 we toss a coin another 12 times.

H   T   T   T   H   H   H   T   H   H   T   T

The resulting stock path is shown in the middle panel of Figure 4.1. The final stock price is

$$\textit{Final stock price} = 100 + 6 \times 2 - 6 \times 2 = £100$$

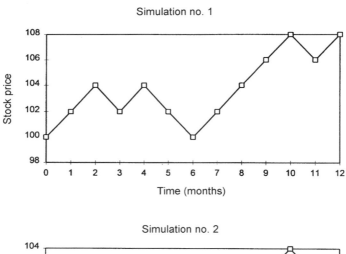

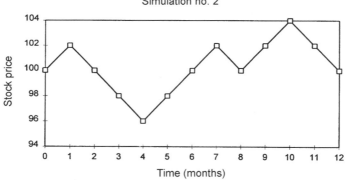

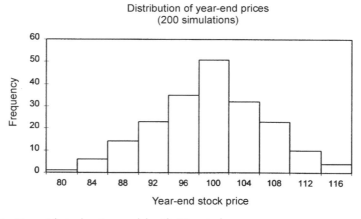

Figure 4.1   Binomial stock price model with 12 periods per year

These two outcomes are just two possible stock price paths. Each one is sometimes referred to as a 'realisation' of the model. We are interested in modelling the final stock price or stock price change at the end of a year and so continue to simulate the above process 200 times. The results appear in the lower panel of Figure 4.1.

The average and standard deviation of the 200 year-end stock prices are £99.54 and £7.36 respectively. Since we are interested in returns we translate this to −£0.46 and £7.36 respectively and this makes sense. The stock price change at the end of 12 months is simply the sum of the 12 individual price changes. Provided these price changes are serially independent, we can use expressions (3.1) and (3.2) derived in Chapter 3 to calculate the annual average and annual standard deviation from the one-month values.

$$E(\text{year price change}) = 12 \times E(\text{monthly price change})$$
$$= 12 \times 0 = £0$$

and

$$\sigma(\text{year price change}) = \sqrt{12} \times \sigma(\text{monthly price change})$$
$$= \sqrt{12} \times \text{magnitude of monthly price change}$$
$$= \sqrt{12} \times 2 = £6.93$$

The sample values of −£0.46 and £7.36 are very near the true population values of £0 and £6.93. Note also that there are now 13 different possible year-end stock prices and these are £76, £80, £124 rather than the simple Bernoulli model of just two. Even though this is an improvement, the stock price charts do not look that realistic. We have to improve the model and this is done in the next section.

4.2.2 The 48-Period-a-Year Stock Price Model

We now consider the situation of simulating the stock price over one year but reducing the time interval for each period and at the same time increasing the number of periods per year. Instead of 12 equal periods, say we use 48 periods. In this way there will be 49 different possible final stock prices — each one being made up of 48 different possibilities of up and down movements. In order to keep the annual standard deviation the same as when using only 12 periods per year we must reduce the extent of the up and down movements. If the magnitude of each up and down movement is now £X then this is also the standard deviation for each period and since

$$\sigma(\text{year price change}) = \sqrt{48} \times X = £6.93$$

then

$$£X = 6.93/\sqrt{48} = £1.00$$

At first sight this may seem strange in that the extent of the up and down move has only halved from £2 to £1 whereas the number of periods per year has been multiplied by four. But this is all due to the nature of summing uncertain outcomes and the addition of variances noted in Chapter 3. Increasing the number of periods by n will only increase the standard deviation by $\sqrt{n}$. Increasing the number of periods by n can thus be compensated for by reducing the magnitude of the movement by only $\sqrt{n}$.

Starting at a price of £100 we could toss a coin 48 times. Each head would represent a price rise of £1 and each tail a price fall of £1. Figure 4.2 shows the results of two different realisations of such a process. Also given is the distribution of the year-end prices for 200 such simulations. The sample average and standard deviations of the 200 simulations are £100.00 and £6.94 respectively. The year-end final stock prices can now range from a low of £52 (corresponding to a sequence of 48 tails) to a high of £148 (corresponding to a sequence of 48 heads). With this model there are 49 different possible year-end prices and this is certainly better than 13. The price charts, however, still do not look that realistic. We need to increase the number of periods per year again.

4.2.3   The 300-Period-a-Year Stock Price Model

We now increase the number of periods a year to 300. To keep the volatility of the year-end prices fixed at £6.93, we again reduce the magnitude of the up and down movements. From 48 to 300 represents an increase of 300/48 = 6.25 fold. Accordingly we reduce the up and down movement by $\sqrt{6.25}$ = 2.5. The new movement is thus = 1/2.5 = £0.40. Figure 4.3 shows two realisations and the distribution of year-end prices.

The mean and standard deviations of the 200 simulations are 100.30 and £6.98 respectively. There are now 301 different possible final stock prices. It is clear that as one increases the number of periods per year, the stock price charts become more realistic. It is fascinating that such a simple model can produce such life-like charts.

There is a body of quite well-paid 'experts' who believe that it is possible to predict the future path of a stock by looking at the past. These experts (known as Chartists or Technicians) believe that stock prices have certain 'support' and 'resistance' levels. A support level is where buyers appear and a resistance level is where sellers appear. If the price gets down to a support level then buyers come out of the woodwork and begin buying — thus supporting the price. If the price moves up to a resistance level then sellers sell, pushing the price down. Chartists spend a lot of time looking for trend lines and turning points. Their language is full of statements such as 'let the trend be your friend' that are supposed to help an investor make decisions. To date there is absolutely no evidence that Chartism works. For every Chartist that finds evidence of a pending bull market there will be one who sees a portent of a bear market.

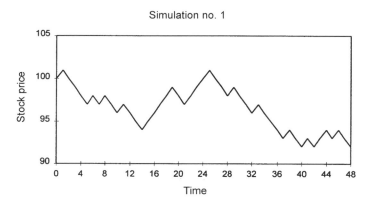

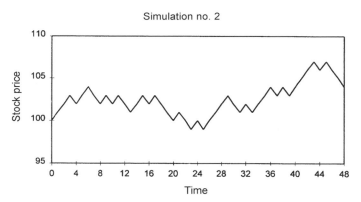

Figure 4.2   Binomial stock price model with 48 periods per year

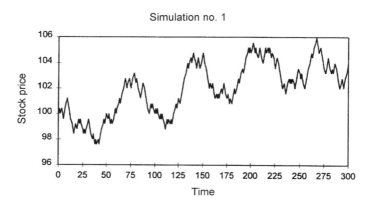

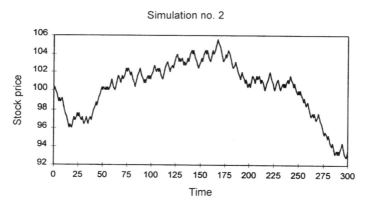

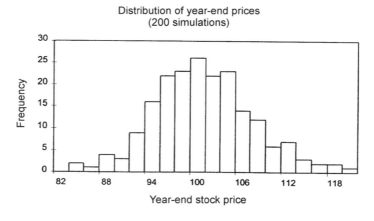

Figure 4.3 Binomial stock price model with 300 periods per year

However to be fair, it is easy to see why these people believe that stock charts have some special predictable properties. Look at the top panel in Figure 4.3. The sequence of prices certainly seems to follow a repeatable pattern, but they do not. The sequence was generated from a purely random process. Look at the second panel in Figure 4.3. There seems to be a definite up trend followed by a down trend, but there is not. And it is all due to a well-known classic human flaw — the eye will see order when there is not. There are many instances of this very human characteristic in other fields. The point of this section is that the very simple model of stock price movements produces results that look very much like real stock prices. The resultant charts even illustrate what appear to be non-random characteristics.

If we continue to increase the number of periods per year and at the same time reduce the magnitude of the up and down moves, it can be shown that the year-end prices or price changes approach a limiting distribution. In the limit, the distribution converges to the well-known 'normal distribution'. The normal distribution is characterised by a symmetric bell-shaped curve centred at the long-run average and extending infinitely in both directions.

4.2.4   Drawbacks of the Additive Model

Realistic though they appear, there are two serious drawbacks of the above model as a description of the stock price generating process.

1. *The proportional rate of return varies with price levels*   Consider the last example in which the moves are £0.40 each and say that in a given simulation the first 100 moves were all down. $100 \times -0.40 = -£40$ so the stock price would now be £60. With the current model the next two possible stock price values are £60.40 or £59.60, i.e., a move up or down of 0.67%. Originally, with the stock at £100, the possible moves of £0.40 represented a change of 0.40%. If the stock price were ever to get to £140, the fixed moves of £0.40 would represent changes of only 0.29%. This model with fixed moves then implies that as stock prices fall, the relative stock price changes increase and that as stock prices increase, the relative changes decrease. This may not be exactly consistent with experience. Surely it would be better if the proportional changes in prices were the same at all price levels?

2. *The model allows for the possibility of negative stock prices*   In the last example with 300 periods per year it is possible, though unlikely, that all 300 tosses of the coin are tails. In such a situation the net stock price change would be $= -300 \times 0.40 = -£120$ resulting in a final year stock price of $-£20$. This is clearly a silly result. We cannot have a model that allows for the possibility of negative stock prices.

4.3   THE MULTIPLICATIVE BINOMIAL MODEL

Fortunately, with one small change to the original model, both of the complications associated with the additive model vanish. Instead of modelling the process additively we model it multiplicatively. We go back to the first situation of simulating 12 periods per year. Instead of assuming that the stock price at the end of each period is equal to the previous price plus or minus £2, we assume the stock price is either increased by 2% or decreased by 2%. This is equivalent to multiplying the previous stock price by 1.02 or 0.98. As before, we assign a probability of p to an up move and $(1 - p)$ to a down move and we let $p = 0.5$. So using the same set of coin-tossing outcomes as in the first example, i.e., H H T H T T H H H H T H, we generate the stock price sequence in Table 4.2.

The final stock price is £108.07, compared to £108.00 with the additive model — not much difference. As with the additive model we can increase the number of periods per year and decrease the magnitude of the relative price change and we get more and more realistic price charts. To emphasise the advantage of this model over the additive model we compare the situation each one would be in after 300 successive down moves. With the additive model change set to 0.40 the stock price would be $100 - 300 \times 0.4 = -£20$. If the multiplicative down move is set to 0.996 the stock price would be $100 \times 0.996 \times 0.996 \times \ldots$, (300 times) = £30.05. With the multiplicative model the stock price gets smaller and smaller with each successive down move but it can never go negative.

Table 4.2 Simulation no.1 of multiplicative stock price model

Month	Outcome of coin toss	Multiplier	Price
			Initial Price = £100.000
1	H	1.02	100.000 × 1.02 = £102.000
2	H	1.02	102.000 × 1.02 = £104.040
3	T	0.98	104.040 × 0.98 = £101.959
4	H	1.02	101.959 × 1.02 = £103.998
5	T	0.98	103.998 × 0.98 = £101.918
6	T	0.98	101.918 × 0.98 = £99.880
7	H	1.02	99.880 × 1.02 = £101.878
8	H	1.02	101.878 × 1.02 = £103.915
9	H	1.02	103.915 × 1.02 = £105.994
10	H	1.02	105.994 × 1.02 = £108.113
11	T	0.98	108.113 × 0.98 = £105.951
12	H	1.02	105.951 × 1.02 = £108.070

4.3.1 The Role of the Probability Parameter *p*

Up until this stage we have, for simplicity, always let the probability of an up move equal to the probability of a down move, i.e., $p = 0.5$. This is intuitively pleasing and easy to simulate using a coin. However if p is not 0.5 then this has implications for the long-run average of the price process. If we let $p = 0.53$ then the probability of a head or an up move is greater than 50% and we would expect, in the long run, the price to increase over time. Similarly if we let $p = 0.47$ then the probability of an up move is lower than 50% and we would expect, in the long run, the price to decrease over time. Figure 4.4 shows the realisations of three such multiplicative models. The multiplier is set to 1.004 (i.e., an increase of 0.4%) and the down multiplier set to 0.996 (i.e., a decrease of 0.4%). The three realisations correspond to models with $p = 0.50$, $p = 0.53$ and $p = 0.47$.

As suspected, a high p value results in a positive drift in the price and a low p value results in a negative price drift. So the choice of p directly affects the direction, and hence expected return on the stock in the long run.

How is the volatility affected? We can get an idea of this by simulating 200 realisations with each different p value. The results are in Figure 4.5. With $p = 0.47$ we see that on average the stock price ends up at £92.22. Biasing the coin in favour of tails and increasing the likelihood of a down move has the effect of producing a stock price that is lower than the starting stock price. The standard deviation of year-end stock prices is £6.70. With p set to 0.5 the average and standard deviations are £100.35 and £6.74 respectively. With p set to 0.53 the average and standard deviations are £107.74 and £6.82. The important point to note about these statistics

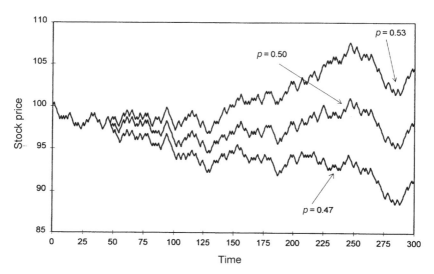

Figure 4.4 Multiplicative model with different p values ($u = 1.004$ and $d = 0.996$)

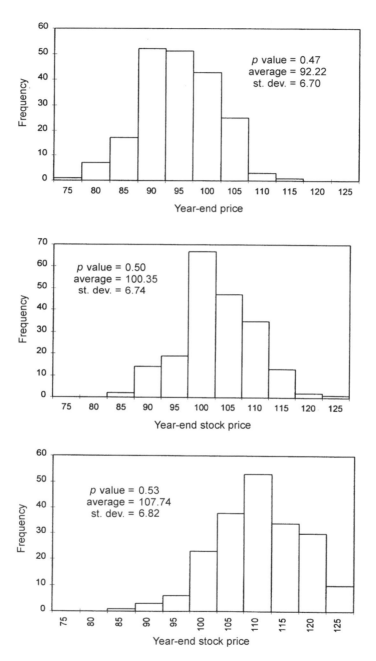

Figure 4.5   Simulations of multiplicative model ($u = 1.004$ and $d = 0.996$)

and the three histograms is that although different p values give different long-run stock price changes, *the spread of prices around the long-run average seems to be the same*. This is no fluke.

4.3.2   A Special Multiplicative Model

There is a specially contrived multiplicative model in which one can set the long-run average and volatility separately. By fixing the magnitude of the individual movements, but varying the probability of an up move, one can produce a model that has fixed volatility but a variable average. It will become obvious later on that this has special implications for the valuation of CBs.

Until now we have always considered simulating the stock process over one year. We now consider a more general situation in which the time span is t years. We also let the number of sub-periods be n, so each sub-period spans a time of t/n years. If we wish the annual volatility to be σ and the annual average return to μ then we set

$$u = \exp(\sigma\sqrt{t/n}) = \text{up multiplier} \tag{4.1}$$

$$d = 1/u = \text{down multiplier} \tag{4.2}$$

and

$$p = \frac{\exp(\mu t/n) - d}{u - d} \tag{4.3}$$

As an example, say the period concerned was $t = 4$ years and we want a 50-step model ($n = 50$) that will generate a stock price with an annual volatility of 30% ($\sigma = 0.30$) and an average annual return of 10% ($\mu = 0.10$). Substituting these values in the above expressions gives $u = 1.0886$, $d = 0.9186$ and $p = 0.5261$. If we were to simulate a model in which the up and down multipliers were set to these values and the probability of an up move was always 0.5261, then in the long run, the stock price would rise by 10% per year and exhibit a volatility of 30%.

Consider now another model in which we keep all parameters the same except μ, which we alter to $\mu = 0.05$. Substituting the values into the above expressions gives $u = 1.0886$, $d = 0.9186$ and $p = 0.5024$. The only difference between this model and the previous one is that the probability of an up move is lower. This model will produce a price series with a long-run stock price rise of 5% per year and exhibit a volatility of 30%. It should be clear that if σ remains constant at 0.30 then the magnitude of the up and down movements is fixed and, whatever the value of p, the volatility of the price series will always be 30%. The only characteristic altered by varying μ will be the probability of an up move. High values of μ will produce high values of p and low values of μ produce low values of p. We could rearrange equation (4.3) above and express μ in terms of p as follows

$$\mu = \frac{n \log[p(u - d) + d]}{t} \qquad (4.4)$$

and think of the problem slightly differently. By fixing σ and hence u and d we are considering a fixed price lattice as shown in Figure 4.6.

With $n = 50$ there will be 51 different final nodes. The lowest final node is arrived at if a tail occurs 50 times. Accordingly, we multiply £100 by 0.9186, 50 times producing a stock price of £1.44. The second lowest node is arrived at if a tail occurs 49 times and a head once. Accordingly, we multiply £100 multiplied by 0.9186, 49 times and 1.0886 once, producing a stock price of £1.70 and so on. The clever thing about this construct is that no matter what value we set for the probability parameter p, the volatility of the resultant price series will always be σ. Different p values will produce different long-run averages but will always produce a series with the same volatility.

One can think of this stock price model in a slightly different way by considering the lattice (also known as a binomial tree diagram) given in Figure 4.6. We start at £100 and walk through the lattice. At each node we have two choices — to step up or to step down. We make the decision by tossing a coin. If a head occurs then we step up and if a tail occurs we step down. At the next node we repeat the procedure. With this model the final stock price can only be one of the 51 different end nodes

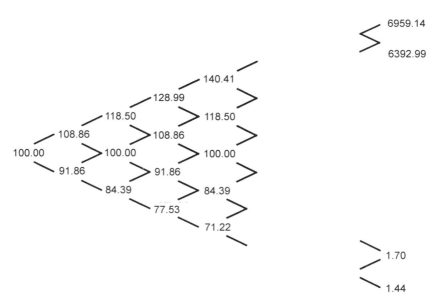

Figure 4.6   Price lattice with $\sigma = 0.3$, $n = 50$, $t = 4$, $u = 1$ and $d = 0.9186$

Table 4.3 $\sigma = 0.3$, $n = 50$, $t = 4$, $u = 1.0886$ and $d = 0.9186$

p	0.35	0.40	0.45	0.50	0.55	0.60	0.65
μ	−0.2766	−0.1685	−0.0613	+0.0449	+0.1503	+0.2548	+0.3584
σ	0.3	0.3	0.3	0.3	0.3	0.3	0.3

and whatever happens we will eventually arrive at one of them. The magnitude of the 51 different individual prices is determined only by the u parameter and has nothing to do with the probability of a head or tail. So with this model the final distribution of stock prices is always fixed at the 51 different values. Now imagine repeating the exercise a large number of times. Each time we start at the first node and walk through the lattice tossing a coin at each node. Sometimes we will end up at a price of £1.44, sometimes we will end up at a price of £1.70 and so on. If the p value is high we tend to end up with prices higher than £100. If the p value is low we will tend to end up with prices lower than £100. But whatever the value of p, the volatility of the final stock price distribution will always be the same. This point is emphasised in Table 4.3. Substituting different values of p into equation (4.3) will produce different values of μ. Table 4.3 shows a range of values of p and the resultant μ for this model.

Setting p to the very low value of 0.35 will produce a stock price that in the long run will always drift down at an average rate of 27.66% per annum. Setting p to the very high value of 0.65 will produce a stock price that in the long run will always drift up at an average rate of 35.84% per annum. But whatever the value of p in this model the volatility will always be 30%.

4.3.3   The Limiting Distribution of the Special Multiplicative Model

The characteristics displayed by the special multiplicative model above are really valid only if the number of sub-periods is large. If we increase the value of n above from 50 to 100, the time span of each sub-period reduces from 0.02 years to 0.04 years and the number of final nodes increases from 51 to 101. Increasing n to 1,000 produces a model with sub-periods of length 0.004 years and with 1,001 different final stock prices. As n increases without bound the length of sub-period decreases and the number of different final stock prices increases. It is possible to show that as n tends to an infinitely large number, the resulting stock price distribution approaches the well-known lognormal distribution. As noted at the beginning of this chapter, much empirical research shows that the lognormal model is a reasonable description of the stock-price distribution. The virtue of considering the stock-price-generating process as a series of discrete up and down movements is that it lends itself to a very simple model for the valuation of derivative products — particularly CBs. And the clever thing about this formulation of the stock-price process is that we can separate considerations of volatility and price drift.

4.4   A MODEL WITH TIME DEPENDENCE

Up until this stage in all models, additive or multiplicative, we have assumed that each of the up and down moves is independent of the previous move. If the probability of an up move is 50%, then this is still the case even if the previous 100 moves were up. Statisticians describe such sequences as 'serially independent'. We now consider situations when this may not be true.

The stock price charts shown in Figures 4.1 to 4.3 were actually generated using the Microsoft Excel random number generator, not by tossing a coin. This software allows the user to produce stock price sequences with any predefined set of probabilities. The random number generator produces a number that is uniformly distributed on the interval 0 to 1. To simulate the tossing of a coin with the probability of a head set to $p = 0.5$, we generate a random number on the interval 0 to 1. If the random number is between 0 and 0.5 then we take this as representing the realisation of a head or in terms of the model, an up move. If the random number is between 0.5 and 1 then we take this as representing the realisation of a tail or a down move. The random number function generates serially independent random numbers, so in this case the probability of an up move will always be 0.5 irrespective of the previous sequence of up moves. However, it is just as easy to generate stock prices that have a built-in non-serial independence. The problem, however, is that there are an infinite number of ways in which a price series can have serial dependence. Here we look at one type of dependence in which the probability of an up move becomes a function of what has happened in the recent past.

There are some individuals who believe that if a stock price increases, say, five days in a row, then the probability of a down move must increase. The rationale behind this sort of thinking is that the stock price must eventually 'correct itself'. One often hears that a certain stock price or stock market or even currency is due for a 'correction'. If this were the case then modelling the stock price as a series of independent up and down movements is not appropriate. One way of modelling this type of correcting serial dependence now follows.

Start as with the standard model, i.e., at an initial price of £100 and fix the probability of an up move as p and a down move as $(1 - p)$. For simplicity in our example we initially set $p = 0.5$. Proceed as in the standard model, but keep a track of the preceding five moves, in particular the sum of the number of up moves (W_t). If the sum of the number of preceding up moves is either large or small then we reset the value of p to make the probability of the price series correcting more likely. As an extreme example we could set the time dependent p values as

If $W_t = 0$ then set $p = 0.7$
If $W_t = 1$ then set $p = 0.6$
If $W_t = 2$ then set $p = 0.5$
If $W_t = 3$ then set $p = 0.5$

If $W_t = 4$ then set $p = 0.3$
If $W_t = 5$ then set $p = 0.2$

In this way, if the five preceding moves were all down, i.e., there were no up moves or $W_t = 0$, then the probability of the next move being up would be set to 0.7 or 70%. So after five successive down moves, the chance of the next move also being down would be much lower at 30%. Similarly, if the five preceding moves had four down and one up ($W_t = 1$), then the probability of the next move being up would be set to 0.6 or 60%. By constantly updating the p values in this special way we will end up with a price series that will most definitely not be serially independent. There will be fewer long sequences of up or down moves than would normally occur in a purely random series. Figure 4.7 shows one simulation of such a series with n set to 300, $t = 1$ year, $\sigma = 0.3$, $u = \exp(\sigma\sqrt{t/n}) = 1.0175$ and $d = 1/u = 0.9828$. For comparison, the serially independent series with p set to a constant value of 0.5 is also shown. As expected we see that the serially dependent 'correction type' series has very few periods in which the price moves significantly in one direction. It is easy to see that the net effect of the serial dependence is that the year-end final stock price distribution will be less spread out than that generated by a serially independent model. This type of serial dependence will cause the year-end prices to be more clustered around the long-term price drift.

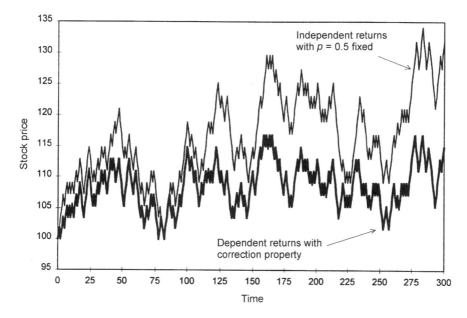

Figure 4.7   'Correction' type dependent returns vs. independent returns

A second type of serial dependence would be one which exhibits the opposite property. This type of dependence would be characterised by price moves tending to stay in the same direction rather than reverse. Once a sequence of up (down) moves is established, the probability of further up (down) moves is more likely rather than less likely. There are some individuals who believe that prices behave in this way. The rationale behind their thinking is that once a price begins to move in one direction other players will notice the trend and start to pile in. If this were the case, once a trend is established other participants would act in such a way as to cause the trend to continue. If prices did move in this way we could say that they build up a 'momentum'. We can model this type of process as follows. Begin with an initial stock price of £100 and set the probability of an up move, p, to 0.5. As before, keep track of the number of up moves in the five preceding moves, W_t. In order to make the sequences of up or down moves more likely than that caused by a purely random process we could simply invert the p values in the previous model as follows

If $W_t = 0$ then set $p = 0.2$
If $W_t = 1$ then set $p = 0.3$
If $W_t = 2$ then set $p = 0.5$
If $W_t = 3$ then set $p = 0.5$
If $W_t = 4$ then set $p = 0.6$
If $W_t = 5$ then set $p = 0.7$

So if the five preceding moves were all down ($W_t = 0$) then the probability of an up

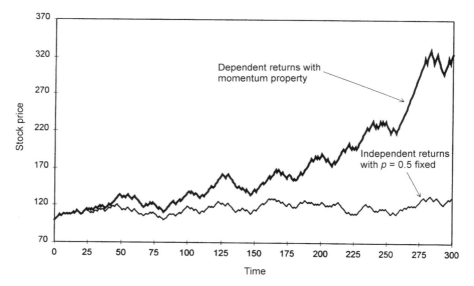

Figure 4.8   'Momentum' type dependent returns vs. independent returns

move is reduced to 0.2 or 20%. After five successive down moves the chance of further down moves would be 80%. Similarly, if the five preceding moves were all up ($W_t = 5$) then the probability of the next move being up is 70%. Figure 4.8 shows one simulation of such a series with identical parameters and an identical sequence of random numbers to those used to generate Figure 4.7. Since the same sequence of random numbers is used in both simulations, the serially independent series with p set to a constant value of 0.5 is also the same in both figures. As expected we see that the serially dependent 'momentum type' series has long periods in which the price moves significantly in one direction.

In Section 4.3 we showed that by setting the magnitude of the up and down parameters u and d, as defined by expressions (4.1) and (4.2), we uniquely fix the volatility of the series at σ. We now see that if the sequence of up and down movements is not independent then this is no longer the case. If the up and down movements follow the serially dependent 'correction' type pattern as given in the first example, then the year-end prices will tend to be much less varied than a purely random process — the annual volatility will be much lower than σ. If the up and down movements follow the serially dependent 'momentum' type pattern as given in the second example, then the year-end prices will tend to be much more varied than a purely random process; the annual volatility will be much greater than σ. This has serious implications for the valuation of CBs.

5
The basic convertible bond model

CBs can sometimes behave like equity, sometimes like bonds and sometimes a mixture of the two. CB price behaviour can be very complex. Under certain circumstances, the instrument is highly sensitive to the price of the underlying equity and completely insensitive to fluctuations in interest rates. Under other circumstances the reverse is the case. Until recently most participants in the CB market used quite naïve models such as adding bits and pieces of other well-known instruments together. One such technique was to consider a CB as an equity warrant plus straight bond. We show below and in Chapter 8 that most of these techniques are flawed.

A CB is a very complex instrument in that it has embedded options. Both the holder and the issuer have an option. If either should exercise their right then the other option is extinguished. This is why one cannot model a CB as a bit of this and a bit of that. However, complex though they are, this does not mean that they are intractable. Like all complex problems, it is often easier to start with something very simple. In this chapter we begin with the concept of pricing a two-way bet. This then leads on to a simple one-period model for a CB. Extending the model to two periods, then three periods and eventually to a model with 50 or 100 periods, we end up with a pricing algorithm that is remarkably good at describing how CB prices vary in the real world.

5.1 A SIMPLE TWO-WAY BET — THE ZERO ARBITRAGE APPROACH

There are a number of ways of approaching the modelling of CB prices but by far the most intuitively appealing is that of the zero arbitrage approach. The basic idea behind the zero arbitrage approach is that one should not be able to have a 'free lunch'. It should not be possible to construct a portfolio that always makes a profit. One should not be able to make a profit without having to take on some risk. If such a situation did exist then individual participants would come into the market and act in such a way as to destroy the free lunch. This action may manifest itself in the form of individuals rapidly buying up some very cheap investment and simultaneously selling short some other related vehicle. The zero arbitrage approach argues that most investments or combinations of investments should be priced in such a way as not to allow a risk-free profit.

Before looking at the basic CB model consider the following hypothetical gambling situation involving two highly correlated investment instruments A and B. One can think of A and B as being investments in a regular market or as payoffs to a specially concocted game.

Instrument A   This is priced today at £100 and in one year's time will be either at £130 or £90. So if you invest £100 in A you will, for sure, either make 30% or lose 10% with no other possibilities. It is important to point out here that one is not given any indication of the probability of making a profit or loss. It could be that there is a 95% chance of losing or that there is an 80% chance of winning. The fascinating aspect of the following argument is that it turns out not to matter.

Instrument B   This is priced today at £50 and in one year's time will be either £60 or £40. Once again we have no idea of the probabilities. However, what we do know is that the two investments are perfectly correlated in that in one year's time, if A is up at £130, then we know for sure that B will be up at £60. Similarly, if A falls to £90, then B will fall to £40. The situation is depicted graphically in the top panel of Figure 5.1.

You are allowed to buy or sell short instrument A or B, separately or any combination of A and B together. You are given an initial sum of £1,000 cash. There are no transaction costs, no bid to offer spreads and no taxes. In this game, margin rules dictate that selling short requires 100% up-front investment and the short proceeds are not enjoyed by the seller. Consider the following two strategies with the relevant possible outcomes.

Strategy 1   Buy 10 units of A at £100 — the £1000 is fully invested. If A is up in one year you make $10 \times (130 - 100) = £300$ or 30% profit. If A is down you lose $10 \times (100 - 90) = £100$ or 10%.

Strategy 2   Sell short 20 units of B at £50 — the £1000 is fully invested. If B is up at £60 you lose $20 \times (60 - 50) = £200$ or 20%. If B is down at £40 you make $(50 - 40) = £200$ or 20%.

With either strategy you could win or lose. You might get lucky or you might not. Now consider a third strategy.

Strategy 3   Buy five units of A at £100 and simultaneously sell short ten units of B at £50 — the £1,000 is fully invested. Consider the two possible scenarios.

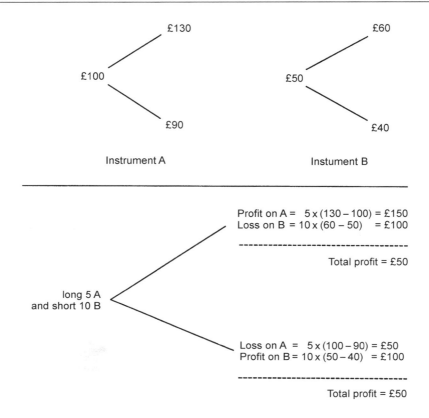

Portfolio of A and B

Figure 5.1   Two-way bet — the concept of fair value

(a) At the end of the year if A is up at £130 then B is up at £60. You are long of
    five units A and make a profit of 5 × (130 − 100) = £150. However, you are
    short of ten units of B and so make a loss of 10 × (60 − 50) = £100. The net
    result with both instruments up is a total profit of £50 or 5% on the original
    investment.
(b) At the end of the year if A is down at £90 then B will be down at £40. You are
    long of five units A and make a loss of 5 × (100 − 90) = £50. However, you
    are short of ten units of B and so make a profit of 10 × (50 − 40) = £100. The
    net result with both instruments down is a total profit of £50 or 5% on the
    original investment.

So, which strategy would you choose? Betting on the outcome of A or B being
up or down (strategies 1 or 2) can give a much higher return than strategy 3, but in
either case there is always the chance of experiencing a loss. Strategy 3 always

makes a return of 5%, whatever happens. There is no risk in strategy 3; the return is always the same.

If such a situation existed in reality, it of course would be possible to borrow on the strength of the risk-free investment idea. Say one borrowed four times the original stake of £1,000 and invested the total £5,000 into strategy 3. The resulting return would be $5 \times 50 = £250$. Say the borrower charged £50 for the use of his funds, the net profit would always be £200 or 20% of the original stake — completely risk free. If there were no limit on the amount one could borrow then the gearing could potentially make the risk-free return limitless.

Surely something must be wrong here?

It is. Clearly, by buying A and selling B short, we end up with a risk-free return because either A is priced too low or B is priced too high. In reality, other individuals would spot this anomaly and all would get involved in borrowing large sums of money to buy A and sell B. Eventually the continual buying of A and selling of B would force prices back into line or back to some value that would remove the possibility for further risk-free gains.

What is the right price of A and/or B to wipe out these risk-free profits? It is easier to solve this problem if we keep the price of A fixed and solve for different, i.e., lower, values of B. This is not an unreasonable approach as we shall see later when this simple technique eventually becomes the CB model. Then we shall assume that A is the underlying stock price and that B is the CB price. One invariably thinks of the derivative product as being priced 'off' the underlying stock and not the other way round. So in this very naïve situation we will think of B as being priced off A and assume A is the right price, whatever that means.

These risk-free profits are there because B is too expensive. Let us try a lower value of, say, £30. We apply strategy 3 again: buy five units of A and sell ten units of B. What happens in each scenario?

(a) At the end of the year if A is up at £130 then B is up at £60. You are long of five units A and make a profit of $5 \times (130 - 100) = £150$. You are short of ten units of B and so make a loss of $10 \times (60 - 30) = £300$. The net result with both instruments up, is a total loss of £150.

(b) At the end of the year if A is down at £90 then B will be down at £40. You are long of five units A and make a loss of $5 \times (100 - 90) = £50$. You are short of ten units of B and so make a loss of $10 \times (50 - 40) = £100$. The net result with both instruments down, is a total loss of £150.

So whatever happens we always suffer a loss of £150. Obviously if we had instigated the strategy in the reverse sense, we would always end up with a profit of £150. It is left as an exercise for the reader to prove that by selling short five units of A and buying ten units of B will always produce a profit. Once again then, it is possible to produce a risk-free return.

Surely something is wrong again?

It is. This time it is because B at £30 is far too cheap relative to A. If this situation existed in reality, other individuals would spot this anomaly and all get involved in borrowing large sums of money to sell A and buy B. Eventually the continual selling of A and buying of B would force prices back into line or back to some value that would remove the possibility for further risk-free gains. So £50 is too expensive and £30 is too cheap. What is the 'right' price for B? What is the right price in the sense that whatever strategy we employ we cannot make a risk-free return. The reader is invited to try different values for B between £50 and £30 and see what value gives a return of zero.

The answer is £45.

Buying (selling) five units of A at £100 and selling (buying) ten units of B at £45 will always result in a net profit of zero. This then is what we would call the 'fair' price or 'arbitrage-free' price or the 'theoretical' price of B. Any other price will result in risk-free arbitrage possibilities.

5.1.1   Calculating the Hedge Ratio

In all of the above we always considered a fixed ratio of A to B of 5 to 10, or 50%. What is interesting is that if we try any other ratio it is not possible to get a return that is entirely risk free. And this is the case even if the price of B is the so-called arbitrage-free value of £45. As an example, consider buying seven units of A at £100 and selling ten units of B at £45 (a ratio of 70%). If the prices of A and B increase to £130 and £60 respectively, a profit of £60 results. However, if the prices of A and B fall to £90 and £40 respectively, a loss of £20 results. The profit occurs on the upside because the portfolio has too many units of A. The loss occurs on the downside also, because the portfolio has too many units of A. The portfolio is actually net long of A whereas if a ratio of 50% had been used, the portfolio would have been perfectly neutral with respect to A. In the jargon of the market-place we would say that the portfolio with a ratio of 50% of A to B would be perfectly hedged. This crucial ratio is known as the 'hedge ratio'. Later on we will also learn that an alternative term for the hedge ratio is 'delta'.

But how does one arrive at the magic hedge ratio of 50%? One way of course would be to try many different values such as 10%, 20%, 30%, etc. However, there is a method that will always give the correct answer and involves finding the extent of the up and down movements of A and B. In our example B can end up at £60 or down at £40, a range of £20; A can end up at £130 or down at £90, a range of £40. The ratio of £20 to £40 is 50%. And that's it. The hedge ratio is 50%.

It is instructive to see why this simple ratio of ranges always gives the right answer. To do this we need to express the situation algebraically. Assume that the price of instrument B is £Y and that the hedge ratio, h, this time is expressed as a fraction. The portfolio is thus short of one unit of B and long h units of A. With the prices up at the end of the year, the profit on A will be $h \times (130 - 100) = £30h$ and the loss on B will be $£(60 - Y)$. So the net profit or loss will be

$$\text{Net profit if prices are up} = 30h - (60 - Y)$$
$$= 30h + Y - 60 \qquad (5.1)$$

With the prices down at the end of the year, the loss on A will be $h \times (100 - 90) = £10h$ and the profit on B will be $£(Y - 40)$. So the net profit or loss will be

$$\text{Net profit if prices are down} = (Y - 40) - 10h$$
$$= -10h + Y - 40 \qquad (5.2)$$

The idea behind the risk-free arbitrage approach is that the net profit to the portfolio should not only be zero but it should be zero in both cases. So whatever the value of the price of B (i.e., £Y) the results of equations (5.1) and (5.2) should be identical. Equating both sides of these two equations we get

$$30h + Y - 60 = -10h + Y - 40$$

Rearranging, we see that the Y term drops out and that

$$40h = 20$$

or

$$h = 20/40 = 0.5$$

The hedge ratio actually turns out to be 0.5 or 50%. The magnitude of the ratio tells us the relative position size. So a portfolio short of 10 units of B should be hedged with a long position of 50% of 10 or 5 units of A. A portfolio long of 200 units of B should be hedged with a short position of 100 units of A. And this is the case whatever the price of B, even if it is not at the fair value. Equating expressions (5.1) and (5.2) ensures that whatever the net profit or loss, using the exact hedge ratio will ensure identical results. This is why in the first example, with B priced too expensively at £50, a profit of £50 results with A up or down. Similarly, with B priced too cheaply at £30, a loss of £150 results with A up or down. The hedge ratio is what it is, whether B is fairly priced or not.

5.1.2 Calculating the Fair Value

Now that we have the hedge ratio, how do we find the fair value without trial and error? The solution is simple. We know that the hedge ratio is 50% so we can look at one of the two possible outcomes — say A and B moving up together. If A moves up from £100 to £130, this represents a gain of £30. The risk-free portfolio will only have 50% of A and so the profit due to A will be 50% of £30 or £15. To be risk free and profit free, the total portfolio return must be zero. If the portion in A produces a profit of £15, then the portion in B must produce a loss of £15. But B ends up at £60 and so it must have started off at £45. This is fair price for B. It is easy to show, following the same argument with a down move that the fair price for B is also £45.

The algebraic solution would be to consider equation (5.1). For a risk-free return the left-hand side must be equated to zero.

$$\text{Net profit if prices are up} = 30h + Y - 60 = 0$$

Rearranging we get

$$Y = 60 - 30h$$

Substituting $h = 0.5$ gives

$$Y = 60 - 30 \times -0.5 = £45$$

5.1.3   The Probability of Profit or Loss; What Relevance?

In most gambling examples, simple or otherwise, there is usually the question of the probability of a profit or loss. Note that in all of the examples considered in this chapter so far, probability has not been mentioned. There is a special reason for this — it is completely irrelevant when considering the risk-free arbitrage. To illustrate this point assume that the probability of the price of A rising to £130 is 80% and that the probability of A falling to £90 is 20%. If we bet solely on the outcome of A, the long-run expected payoff would be $= 0.8 \times 130 + 0.2 \times 90 = £122$, or a profit of £22. So it clearly would be worth having a bet on A. And certainly, if we were allowed a large number of tries, then in the long run we would make a large profit. However, if we were allowed only one try, there is always the chance (a 20% chance) that we could lose.

If, as in the first example, B were mispriced at £50 rather than the correct fair price of £45, we could instigate the risk-free strategy of buying five units of A and selling ten units of B and make £50 *always*, i.e., with a probability of 100%. As previously pointed out, on the strength of the risk-free profit, we would be able to borrow large sums of money and invest in considerably larger amounts than our original stake. Depending on the borrowing ratio (or gearing) allowed, it is easy to see that receiving a small profit with a 100% probability is always preferable to receiving a large profit with an 80% probability. Why take a risk when it is not necessary?

The above argument applies even if we increase the probability of winning with A to 99%. This point should not be forgotten later on when we begin to look in more detail at CB pricing. The probability of A increasing has no bearing on the fair value of B. The portfolio is long one instrument and short the other. If there is a mispricing then the portfolio will always return a profit, whatever the outcome of A or B. And the real reason that probability is irrelevant is that the prices of A and B are perfectly correlated — there is no uncertainty as to their joint outcome.

5.1.4   A General Algebraic Expression for the Hedge Ratio and Fair Value

In the above two-way bet examples we used real numbers to illustrate the process of calculating a fair value. We will shortly see that this process can be extended to produce a very realistic model for how CB prices behave in reality. However, it will be necessary to make the mathematics more general. Rather than, say, considering the value of A increasing to £130 or falling to £90 we must now resort to a more general argument.

Let us assume that the prices of A and B today are $£X$ and $£Y$ respectively. Furthermore, let us assume that in one year's time A will either increase to a value of $£X_{up}$ or fall to a value of $£X_{down}$. The corresponding values for B will be $£Y_{up}$ and $£Y_{down}$. As before, we have no idea what the probabilities are of A or B increasing or decreasing, but we do know that whatever happens, they will both be up or both be down. Now consider a portfolio short one unit of B and long h units of A. The net portfolio profit if both prices are up is given by:

$$\text{Net profit if prices are up} = \text{profit on A} - \text{loss on B}$$
$$= h(X_{up} - X) - (Y_{up} - Y) \qquad (5.3)$$

The net profit if both prices are down is:

$$\text{Net profit if prices are down} = \text{profit on B} - \text{loss on A}$$
$$= (Y - Y_{down}) - h(X - X_{down}) \qquad (5.4)$$

Although these expressions look complex, in any given example, (5.3) and (5.4) contain only two unknowns; the value of the hedge ratio, h and the price of B, $£Y$. All other terms are known. The solution involves solving the two simultaneous equations with the two unknowns and can be arrived at by considering the two following binding conditions:

1. The net profit of the portfolio must be the same if A is up or down. We thus equate (5.3) and (5.4):

$$h(X_{up} - X) - (Y_{up} - Y) = (Y - Y_{down}) - h(X - X_{down})$$

Expanding and rearranging we note that X and Y drop out leaving

$$h = \frac{Y_{up} - Y_{down}}{X_{up} - X_{down}} \qquad (5.5)$$

2. The net profit of the portfolio in either case must be zero. Taking either (5.3) or
    (5.4) and equating to zero we get

$$Y = \frac{Y_{\text{up}}(X - X_{\text{down}}) + Y_{\text{down}}(X_{\text{up}} - X)}{(X_{\text{up}} - X_{\text{down}})} \tag{5.6}$$

So expressions (5.5) and (5.6) are simply the general algebraic equivalent of the
arguments followed with real numbers in Section 5.1.2. The reader is invited to
substitute the relevant values of $X = 100$, $X_{\text{up}} = 130$, $X_{\text{down}} = 90$, $Y_{\text{up}} = 60$ and Y_{down}
$= 40$ into the above equations to show that $h = 0.5$ and $Y = 45$.

Using these general expressions it is possible to concoct an infinite number of
examples. We will always be able to get a solution involving two numbers; the
hedge ratio and the fair value. The reader is invited to find the hedge ratios and fair
values of the instrument B in the examples given in Figure 5.2.

5.2 THE ONE-PERIOD CB MODEL

We now begin to build a simple binomial model that will explain how CB prices
vary. We use the binomial model for stock prices and the idea outlined above that
prices one asset (instrument B) in terms of another (instrument A). We begin by
imposing some very unrealistic assumptions, get a mathematical expression that
gives the CB price in terms of the stock price and then gradually amend the model
by relaxing the assumptions and introducing reality.

Consider an imaginary zero coupon CB issued by ABC Bank. The terms are as
follows:

ABC Bank convertible bond
Nominal value: £5,000
Conversion price: £8.00
Conversion ratio: 625
Coupon: zero
Present price of the underlying share: £7.84
Dividend yield of underlying share: zero
Maturity: 1 year

In the market-place CBs are invariably priced as a percentage of par and when
converted give the holder a certain number of shares (the conversion ratio). It is far
easier however, to understand what is going on, if we convert everything into a per
share basis (as in Chapter 1) and consider instead a new type of CB. This new CB
can be converted into one share or on maturity redeemed at the conversion price.
For the purposes of this simple model we assume that the underlying shares pay no
dividend and that interest rates are zero. Also for simplicity we assume that in one
year's time (on expiry) the share price will be either £9.00 or £7.20.

Use the arguments of Section 5.1.2 or the algebra of Section 5.1.4 to find the hedge ratio and the fair value of B in the following

(1)

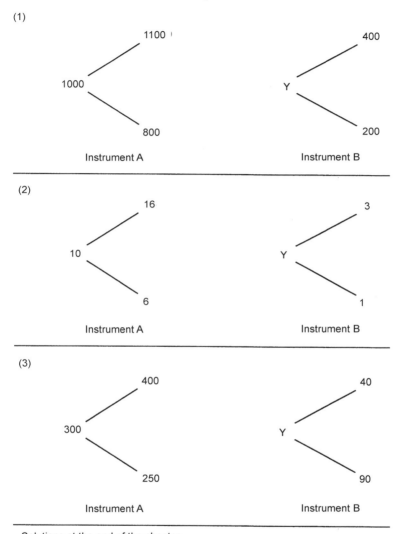

Figure 5.2   More examples

What will the holder of the CB do on expiry? He can convert and take one share valued at whatever the then current share price, or redeem and take the cash sum of £8.00. What should he do? Clearly if the share price is up at £9.00, he will take the shares and if the share price is down at £7.20 he will take the cash sum of £8.00. So

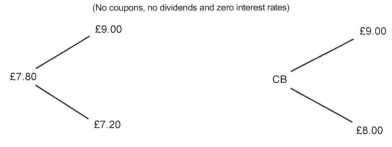
(No coupons, no dividends and zero interest rates)

£9.00   £9.00

£7.80   CB

£7.20

£8.00

Instrument A = ABC Bank stock   Instrument B = ABC Bank CB

Figure 5.3   The one-period binomial CB model

we can illustrate the situation in the same way as we did when considering the two-way bet and this is shown in Figure 5.3.

Using the simple logic of Section 5.1.1 or the mathematical expressions (5.5) we calculate the hedge ratio as

$$h = \frac{9.00 - 8.00}{9.00 - 7.20} = 5/9 = 55.5\%$$

and use expression (5.6) to calculate the CB fair value, CB_f, as

$$CB_f = \frac{9.00(7.80 - 7.20) + 8.00(9.00 - 7.80)}{(9.00 - 7.20)} = £8.33$$

So in this very unrealistic situation, if the CB were priced significantly below £8.33 per share then one could go long the CB and short the underlying in the ratio of 55.5% and make a risk-free return. Similarly, if the CB were priced significantly higher than £8.33 per share one could short the CB and go long the underlying in the same ratio and still make a risk-free return. We say that £8.33 per share is the fair value.

Most CB markets do not price these instruments on a per-share basis, so we have to convert £8.33 back into an understandable quoted market price, i.e., as a percentage of the original £5,000 nominal value. First we find the value of one bond and then we express this as a percentage of the nominal value of £5,000.

Value of one CB = price per share × number of shares = 8.33 × 625 = £5,206.25

$$\text{As a percentage of £5,000} = \frac{5,206.25}{5,000} \times 100 = 104.13\%$$

Throughout this book we will always calculate model CB prices on a per share basis but the market quotes them as a percentage of the nominal value. A quick way of getting from the per share price to the market price is to multiply by the factor 12.5 (i.e., 625 × 100 / 5000 = 12.5). In general the multiplication factor is given by:

$$multiplication\ factor = \frac{conversion\ ratio}{nominal\ value} \times 100$$

The market price of this bond is 104.13. Note that as before, we have arrived at this fair value without any reference to the probability of the underlying share price rising or falling.

5.2.1 The General One-period CB Model with Different Stock Prices

The argument above shows that the fair value of the CB is £8.33 per share if the current share price is £7.80. But what if the current share price were £7.85 or £7.90 or in fact any other value? We could go through the above arithmetic for each share price and calculate the corresponding fair CB price. However, it is easier if we construct a general formula giving the CB price in terms of the current share price. In the original formulation the share price could rise by a factor of 9.00 / 7.80 = 1.1538 or fall by a factor of 7.20 / 7.80 = 0.9231. If we let the share price today be S, and the up and down multipliers be u and d, then the general form of the problem is shown in Figure 5.4.

CB_u and CB_d are the values of the CB corresponding to the share price being up at $S.u$ or down at $S.d$. As in this particular case we can use (5.5) to calculate the hedge ratio as

$$h = \frac{CB_u - CB_d}{S.u - S.d}$$

and use (5.6) to calculate the CB fair value

$$CB_f = \frac{CB_u(S - S.d) + CB_d(S.u - S)}{(S.u - S.d)} \tag{5.7}$$

It is important to remember that although (5.7) looks complex it is just a generalised version of that used to calculate the CB fair value with numbers. All the

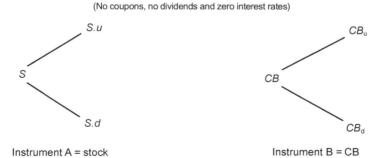

(No coupons, no dividends and zero interest rates)

Instrument A = stock   Instrument B = CB

Figure 5.4   The one-period binomial CB model

terms on the right hand side are known. We just substitute for S, u, d, CB_u and CB_d and out falls the CB value. Equation (5.7) is the initial building block for the CB model and as we shall see later will be extended to much more complicated situations. This basic equation however, is invariably presented in a different form as follows:

$$CB_f = \frac{CB_u(S - S.d) + CB_d(S.u - S)}{(S.u - S.d)}$$

$$= \frac{CB_u(S - S.d)}{(S.u - S.d)} + \frac{CB_d(S.u - S)}{(S.u - S.d)}$$

$$= \frac{CB_u S(1 - d)}{S(u - d)} + \frac{CB_d S(u - 1)}{S(u - d)}$$

$$= \frac{CB_u(1 - d)}{(u - d)} + \frac{CB_d(u - 1)}{(u - d)}$$

or

$$CB_f = pCB_u + qCB_d \tag{5.8}$$

where $p = \dfrac{(1 - d)}{(u - d)}$, and

$$q = \frac{(u - 1)}{(u - d)} = 1 - p$$

Expression (5.8) looks much neater than (5.7) and shows us that the CB value is a simple weighted average of the upper expiring value, CB_u, and the lower expiring value, CB_d; with the weights given by the parameters p and q. Here $u = 1.1538$ and $d = 0.9231$ and so the weights p and q are

$$p = \frac{(1 - d)}{(u - d)} = \frac{1 - 0.9231}{1.1538 - 0.9231} = 0.333$$

$$q = 1 - 0.333 = 0.667$$

and therefore

$$CB_f = 0.33CB_u + 0.67CB_d \tag{5.9}$$

So whatever the initial share price, the CB value is always a mixture of one-third of the upper value and two-thirds the lower value. In Figure 5.3 the upper value is £9, the lower value is £8 and so the answer $= 0.33 \times 9 + 0.67 \times 8 = $ £8.33.

At this point it is worth noting the common confusion relating to inferences about the meaning of the weighting parameters, p *and* q *(0.33 and 0.67 respectively in our example). Because* p *and* q *sum to one they are often referred to as probabilities. Because* p *is associated with* CB$_u$ *and* q *is associated with* CB$_d$, *the common inferential error is to read these as being the probability of an up and down move respectively. This is not necessarily so. In this specific example the probability of an up move could be 0.10 or 0.75 or indeed 0.99, but the* p *and* q *values would still be 0.33 and 0.67 respectively and the fair value would still be £8.33. This fair value model is completely free of probability considerations.*

We are looking for a general expression that will give the CB value in terms of the initial share price, S. Equation (5.9) gives the answer in terms of the final upper and lower CB values and so we must express these in terms of the initial share price. Recall that on expiry, the CB holder will have the option to take up the shares at whatever price or take the redemption value which will always be the redemption price or conversion price. The CB holder will always choose the greater of these two values and we can express this mathematically as

CB value on expiry = Max {share price on expiry, conversion price}

In this case the conversion price = £8, so

CB value on expiry = Max {share price on expiry, 8}

With the general initial share price of S, the CB value if the price increases is therefore

$$CB_u = \text{Max } \{S.u, 8\}$$

and similarly the CB value, if the price decreases is

$$CB_d = \text{Max } \{S.d, 8\}$$

So (5.9) can now be written as

$$CB_f = 0.333 \text{ Max } \{S.u, 8\} + 0.667 \text{ Max } \{S.d, 8\}$$

or

$$CB_f = 0.333 \text{ Max}\{1.1538\, S, 8\} + 0.667 \text{ Max}\{0.9231\, S, 8\} \qquad (5.10)$$

There is a problem, however, with this formulation in that we do not really have an explicit equation giving CB_f in terms of S. The Max { } functions are awkward in the sense that for any given share price, S, we have to calculate the values of 1.1538

S and 0.9231 S and ask the question: is either term greater than 8? There is a simple way around this problem and it involves breaking down the equation to one considering three different regions for S. The Max { } functions can be converted into individual linear equations using straightforward logic. Consider the term corresponding to the upper value first.

Is 1.1538 S > 8?

$\qquad$ Yes   Then: Max {1.1538 S, 8} = 1.1538 S

$\qquad$ No   Then: Max 1.1538 S, 8} = 8

The question: 'Is 1.1538 S > 8?' is identical to S > (8/1.1538) or S > 6.93 and so we have

Is S > 6.93?

$\qquad$ Yes   Then: Max {1.1538 S, 8} = 1.1538 S

$\qquad$ No   Then: Max {1.1538 S, 8} = 8

Therefore in (5.10), if the S is greater than £6.93 we can insert the linear expression 1.1538 S and if not, then insert 8. Following the same argument with the lower term in (5.10) we have

Is 0.9231 S > 8?

$\qquad$ Yes   Then: Max {0.9231 S, 8} = 0.9231 S

$\qquad$ No   Then: Max {0.9231 S, 8} = 8

which translates to

Is S > 8.67 ?

$\qquad$ Yes   Then: Max {0.9231 S, 8} = 0.9231 S

$\qquad$ No   Then: Max {0.9231 S, 8} = 8

Therefore in (5.10), if the S is greater than £8.67 we can insert the linear expression 0.9231 S and if not, then insert 8.

We can, therefore, rewrite (5.10) as three separate equations corresponding to the three regions defined by (a) S > 8.67, (b) 6.93 < S < 8.67 and (c) S < 6.93.

(a) $CB_f = 0.333\ (1.1538\ S) + 0.667\ (0.9231\ S)$, i.e., $CB_f = S$ if $S > 8.67$.

(b) $CB_f = 0.333\ (1.1538\ S) + 0.667\ (8)$, i.e., $CB_f = 0.38\ S + 5.33$ if $6.93 < S < 8.67$.

(c) $CB_f = 0.333\ (8) + 0.667\ (8)$, i.e., $CB_f = 8$ if $S < 6.93$.

The general CB value is thus given by one of the three equations. If the initial share price is high (above £8.67), then on expiry, even if it falls by a factor of 0.9231, it will still be higher than the conversion price and the holder will always opt to take the shares. So whether the shares rise or fall, the final CB price is always going to be identical to the final share price and the CB fair value must be identical to the initial share price, i.e., equation (a) holds. If the initial share price is low (below £6.93), then on expiry, even if it rises by a factor of 1.1538, it will still be lower than the conversion price and the holder will always opt for redemption at £8. This is the situation described by equation (c). In between the two extremes, the outcome for the CB holder is uncertain and so the fair value turns out to be a linear function of the underlying share price, i.e., equation (b). The top panel in Figure 5.5 illustrates this relationship between the CB price and the underlying share price as three straight lines.

Although simple, this picture does illustrate some of the basic properties of a CB. At the low end, the CB price is independent of the share price and just represents the value of a lump sum of £8. At the high end, the CB price mimics perfectly the share price. In the middle, the CB price depends on the share price, but not perfectly.

Before leaving this section it is worth while looking at another way in which the single CB model given by (5.10) involving Max { } functions reduces to the three equations or straight lines: (a), (b) and (c). Whether each Max { } function returns a direct multiple of the share price or the constant conversion price, £8, depends on the original value of S. If S is low, the £8 is returned. If S is high both functions of S are returned. If S is in between the two extremes, one Max function returns a multiple of S and the other £8. Figure 5.6 illustrates the three situations. So, in this simple one-period model, the CB price is one of three equations. The reason there are three equations is that on expiry, the stock price has one of two values and these two values split up the range of initial share prices into three separate zones.

5.2.2   The Hedge Ratio as a Function of Share Price

We see from the above argument that the one-period general CB model reduces to three equations. But what about the hedge ratio? It is left as an exercise for the reader to show that the hedge ratio given by expressions of the type (5.5) also reduce to three equations as follows

(a) $h = 1$, if $S > 8.67$

(b) $h = 5 - 34.67\ /\ S$, if $6.93 < S < 8.67$

(c) $h = 0$, if $S < 6.93$

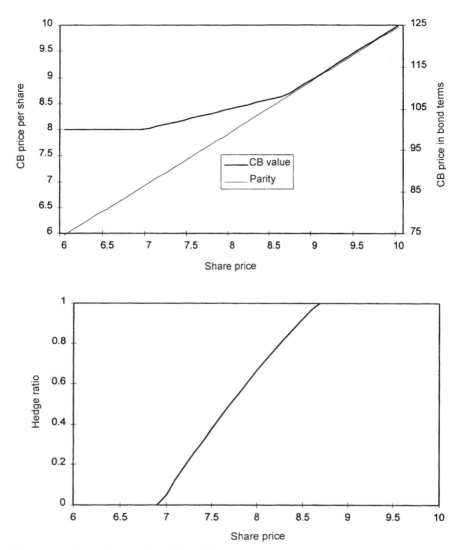

Figure 5.5   General one-period CB model

Constructing the riskless arbitrage portfolio is sometimes very simple. With high share prices (above £8.67) the hedge ratio is 1 or 100%. With low (below £6.93) share prices the hedge ratio is 0, i.e., no hedge required. With medium share prices (between £6.93 and £8.67) the ratio is somewhere in between the two. The lower panel in Figure 5.5 illustrates this relationship between the hedge ratio and the underlying share price.

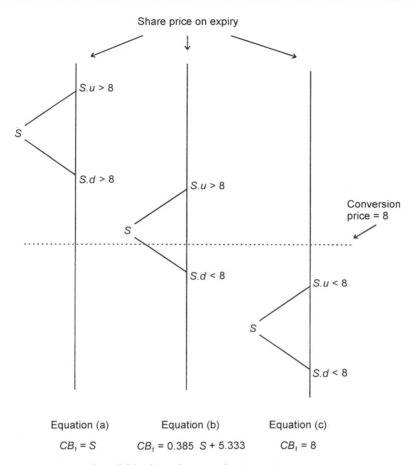

Figure 5.6 One-period model leads to three stock price regions

5.3 INTRODUCING INTEREST RATE CONSIDERATIONS

In reality we live in a world were there is always a cost of carry. If an arbitrage possibility were to present itself, we would have to take into account the cost of money. In the above examples involving CB price modelling it is therefore necessary to include interest rate considerations into the calculations. We return to the simple ABC Bank example given in Section 5.2. With zero interest rates, the CB fair price turned out to be £8.33 per share and the hedge ratio 0.55. The cost of carry of the hedged portfolio, assuming a long position in the CB and a short position in the shares, is calculated as follows. We buy one unit of CB at £8.33 and short 0.55 shares at £7.80. Usually, shorting shares results in a positive cash flow. Shorting 0.55 shares at £7.80 results in an inflow of $0.55 \times 7.80 = £4.29$ and this can be used to offset the £8.33 outlay. The initial cost of the portfolio is therefore $8.33 - 4.29 = £4.04$. For simplicity let us assume that interest rates for the one-year period are 5%. The borrowing costs for the portfolio would be 5% of £4.04 = £0.202. On expiry the portfolio breaks even with no interest charges and so with charges, a loss of £0.202 is locked in whatever happens to the share price. Clearly the CB price of £8.33 is now too high.

Including interest rate considerations into the CB model requires going back to the general formulation of the two-way bet given in Section 5.1.4. Recall that the special zero profit arbitrage price and hedge ratio was derived by solving two simultaneous equations. It is a simple matter to include in these profit calculations the interest costs. The portfolio is long one unit of CB at CB_f and short h shares at S. Therefore the net cost of the portfolio is $= CB_f - h.S$. Let r represent the interest rate expressed in fractional form (so $r = 0.05$ represents rates of 5%). The interest costs for the one year are therefore $= r.(CB_f - h.S)$ and this must be subtracted from the profit if the share price rises or falls.

The net profit to the hedged portfolio if both prices are up at expiry is now:

$$\text{Net profit if prices are up} = \text{profit on CB} - \text{loss on shares} - \text{interest costs}$$
$$= (CB_u - CB_f) - h(S_u - S) - r(CB_f - h.S)$$

Similarly, the net profit if both prices are down at expiry is:

$$\text{Net profit if prices are down} = \text{profit on shares} - \text{loss on CB} - \text{interest costs}$$
$$= h(S - S_d) - (CB_f - CB_d) - r(CB_f - h.S)$$

Solving these two equations subject to the two constraints given above we get

$$h = \frac{CB_u - CB_d}{S.u - S.d}$$

$$CB_f = \frac{pCB_u + qCB_d}{1 + r} \tag{5.11}$$

where $p = \dfrac{1 + r - d}{u - d}$, and

$q = 1 - p$

The fair value expression with interest rate costs is very similar to those without. The difference is in the specification of the p and q parameters and the dividing term, $(1 + r)$. Substituting $u = 1.1538$, $d = 0.9231$ and $r = 0.05$ gives $p = 0.550$ and $q = 0.450$, so the fair value is now

$$CB_f = \frac{0.550CB_u + 0.450CB_d}{1.05}$$

Using the same logic of Section 5.2.1 the CB price can be expressed as three linear equations.

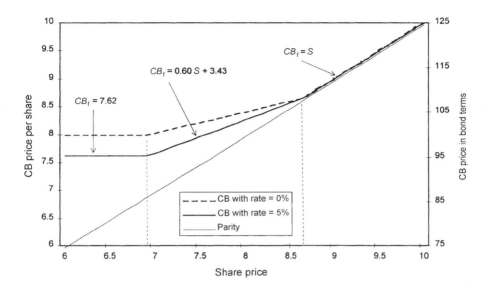

Figure 5.7 General one-period CB model ABC Bank with interest rate effects

(a) $CB_f = S$, if $S > 8.67$
(b) $CB_f = 0.60 \, S + 3.43$, if $6.93 < S < 8.67$
(c) $CB_f = 7.62$, if $S < 6.93$

This relationship between the CB price and the share price is shown in Figure 5.7 along with that when interest rates are zero.

Note that introducing interest rates reduces the value of the CB at low share prices, and this makes sense. At low share prices, the CB will always be redeemed on expiry. The expiring value is £8 and so the present price must represent this value discounted, i.e., 8/1.05 = £7.62. If interest rates were higher at, say, 20%, the present value would be even lower. So at low share prices the CB is very dependent on interest rates — just like a straight bond. At high share prices, the CB is completely independent of interest rates — the price is the same if rates are 0% or 5% or indeed 20%. At high share prices the instrument is essentially equity. In between these two extremes the dependency on interest rates is partial. This is exactly what we witness in the real market-place.

5.4 THE TWO-PERIOD CB MODEL

In the previous section we started by assuming that the underlying share price could only be one of two values on the expiration date. The motivation behind this approach is entirely due to the fact that a riskless portfolio can be constructed. If the final share price and the final CB price have only two values, then the two-way bet mathematics dictates that there is a unique CB price and a unique hedge ratio and that these values are completely independent of probability considerations. If we tried to model the instruments by using three or more final share prices, this would not be possible.

Clearly, the model is limited. It is nonsense to assume that a share price can only move to one of two values at some point in the future. In reality the share price might be one of 10,000 different values. Fortunately, there is a clever way around the problem. We begin by developing a model in which we can have three final share prices, but still keep the logic of the one-period model and hence the two-way bet mathematics. We illustrate by returning to the example of the ABC Bank CB.

First, we split the one-year period to expiry into two sub-periods, each of half a year. For consistency we redefine the up and down multiplicative parameters so that the extreme values are as before. This is done by taking the square root of the original values. So now $u = \sqrt{(9.0/7.8)} = 1.0742$ and $d = \sqrt{(7.2/7.8)} = 0.9608$. At each node in the share price tree, an up move results in the price being increased by a factor of 1.0742 and a down move results in the price being reduced by the factor 0.9608. In this way, the extreme share prices on expiry are still £9.00 and £7.80. If the interest rate is 5% over the two periods, it must be $100 \times \sqrt{(1.05 - 1)} = 2.47\%$ per half year. To calculate the new fair value we break up the share and CB trees into three sub-sets. Figure 5.8 depicts the new situation.

Consider the situation at the half-year mark with the share price up at £8.38. At this point the share price can now only rise or fall by the new u and d factors and correspondingly the CB can have only one of two values on expiry. We can thus consider this sub-set of the two-period model as a mini one-period model and this is shown separately also in Figure 5.8. So we have generated a completely new one-period problem that is easily solvable. With the share price up at £9.00, the expiring CB value will be £9.00. With the share price down at £8.05 the CB value will also be £8.05. Here $p = 0.5637$, $q = 0.4363$ and $r = 0.0247$. Using (5.11) we get the CB value to be:

$$\text{CB value at half-year mark} \atop \text{with share price at £8.38} = \frac{0.5637(9.00) + 0.4363(8.05)}{1.0247} = £8.38$$

(5.11) also gives the hedge ratio corresponding to a share price of £8.38 and substituting the above values we get:

$$\text{Hedge ratio at half-year mark} \atop \text{with share price at £8.38} = \frac{9.00 - 8.05}{9.00 - 8.05} = 1.00$$

In a similar fashion it is possible to consider the lower sub-set of share and CB prices starting at the half-year mark as another one-period model. Here the upper and lower CB values are £8.05 and £8.00 respectively. The u, d and r parameters are the same so using (5.11) again we have

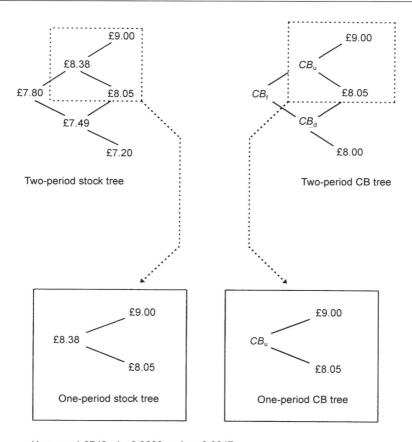

Here u = 1.0742, d = 0.9608 and r = 0.0247

This gives p = 0.5737 and q = 0.4363 and using (5.11)

$$\therefore\ CB_u = \frac{0.5737\ (9.00) + 0.4363\ (8.05)}{1.0247} = £8.38$$

Figure 5.8 Two-period CB model for ABC Bank

$$\frac{\text{CB value at half-year mark}}{\text{with share price at £7.49}} = \frac{0.5637(8.05) + 0.4363(8.00)}{1.0247} = £7.83$$

The hedge ratio here is 0.06.

We now have the two CB values at the half-year mark. These two values correspond to the share price rising or falling from the initial value of £7.80. So once again we have another one-period problem. We can consider the first half-year to be a new one-period model. Here the upper share and CB prices are both £8.38

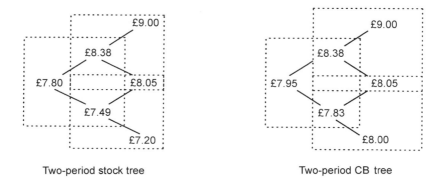

Two-period stock tree   Two-period CB tree

Final CB fair value = £7.95

Figure 5.9 Solution to two-period CB model for ABC Bank

and the lower share and CB prices are £7.49 and £7.83 respectively. Applying
(5.11) again we have

$$\frac{\text{Initial CB value}}{\text{with share price at £7.80}} = \frac{0.5637(8.38) + 0.4363(7.83)}{1.0247} = £7.95$$

The initial hedge ratio turns out to be 0.62. The completed solution is shown in
Figure 5.9.

In this example, the initial risk-free portfolio would be long one CB and short 0.62
shares. If, half-way through the year, the share price increases to £8.38, the portfolio
would be adjusted so that the hedge ratio is increased to 1.00. This would be done by
selling 0.38 more shares. If, however, half-way through the year the share price fell
to £7.49, the portfolio would be adjusted so that the hedge ratio is reduced to 0.06.
This would be done by buying 0.56 shares. So in this way we have again arrived at
an arbitrage-free price for the CB. If the price in the market were significantly
different from £7.95 per share, the above strategy could be implemented producing a
riskless profit. Note that the difference between the one- and two-period models is
that the portfolio has to be altered, or rehedged, half-way through the year. In the
jargon of the market-place we say that the hedging is 'dynamic'.

5.4.1 The General Two-period CB Model

The argument above shows us that the two-period CB model with the share price at
£7.80 is £7.95. We now need to develop a model in terms of a general share price,
S. With the up and down multipliers set at, u and d, the share price half way through
the year will be either $S.u$ or $S.d$. If the first share price move is up at $S.u$, then the

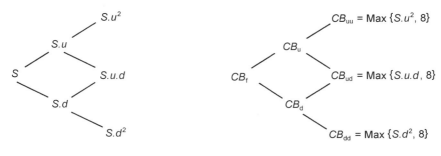

Two-period stock tree   Two-period CB tree

Figure 5.10   The general two-period CB model for ABC Bank

final two possible share prices are $S.u.u$ $(= S.u^2)$ or $S.u.d$. If the first share price move is down at $S.d$, then the final two possible share prices are $S.d.u$ $(= S.u.d)$ or $S.d.d$ $(= S.d^2)$. We let the expiring CB prices be denoted by: CB_{uu}, CB_{ud} or CB_{dd} corresponding to two up moves, an up and a down move and two down moves. We let the intermediate CB prices be CB_u, CB_d corresponding to the first move being up or down. The general model is depicted in Figure 5.10.

As in the particular case, we treat the final upper sub-set as a one-period model in which the two end CB prices are CB_{uu} and CB_{ud}. The fair value for the end of the first period with the stock price at $S.u$ is calculated by substituting these into (5.11) as follows.

$$CB_u = \frac{pCB_{uu} + qCB_{ud}}{1 + r}$$

For the lower sub-set we substitute CB_{ud} and CB_{dd} and get the fair value of CB_d with the share price at $S.d$ as

$$CB_d = \frac{pCB_{ud} + qCB_{dd}}{1 + r}$$

Finally, substituting these expressions for CB_u and CB_d into (5.11) we get

$$CB_f = \frac{pCB_u + qCB_d}{1 + r}$$

$$= \frac{\dfrac{p(pCB_{uu} + qCB_{ud})}{1 + r} + \dfrac{q(pCB_{ud} + qCB_{dd})}{1 + r}}{1 + r}$$

which after simplification becomes

$$CB_f = \frac{p^2.CB_{uu} + 2p.q.CB_{ud} + q^2.CB_{dd}}{(1 + r)^2} \tag{5.12}$$

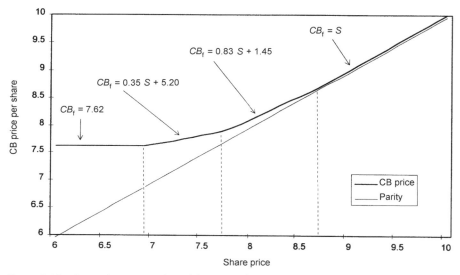

Figure 5.11   General two-period model ABC Bank

To convert this into an expression involving the share price, we must express the final CB values in the usual way, i.e. $CB_{uu} = \text{Max} \{S.u^2, 8\}$, $CB_{ud} = \text{Max} \{S.u.d, 8\}$ and $CB_{dd} = \text{Max} \{S.d^2, 8\}$. Substituting $u = 1.0742$ and $d = 0.9608$ and applying the logic of the Max $\{\ \}$ function, (5.12) becomes:

(a) $CB_f = S$, if $8.67 < S$
(b) $CB_f = 0.83 \ S + 1.45$, if $7.75 < S < 8.67$
(c) $CB_f = 0.35 \ S + 5.20$, if $6.93 < S < 7.75$
(d) $CB_f = 7.62$, if $S < 6.93$

This relationship is shown in Figure 5.11. Note that we now have four straight lines, each given by the equations (a), (b), (c) and (d) above, and that the gradient or slope of the lines decreases with decreasing share prices.

In the one-period model, the CB price is one of three equations. The reason there are three equations is that on expiry, the stock price has one of two values and these two values split up the range of initial share prices into three separate zones. With the two-period model, the CB price is one of four equations. The reason there are four equations is that on expiry, the stock price has one of three values and these three values split up the range of initial share prices into four separate zones.

5.5   THE THREE-PERIOD CB MODEL

We can extend the two-period model idea to allow the possibility of four final stock and CB prices by having a three-period model as shown in Figure 5.12. The solution is obtained, as before, by breaking the problem up into smaller one-period models, starting from expiry and working back to the present time. The general solution becomes:

$$CB_f = \frac{p^3.CB_{uuu} + 3p^2.q.CB_{uud} + 3pq^2.CB_{udd} + q^3.CB_{ddd}}{(1+r)^3}$$

The u, d and r values all have to be changed to reflect the fact that one year is now split up into three equal periods of a third of a year, so $u = (9.0/7.8)^{1/3} = 1.0489$, $d = (7.2/7.8)^{1/3} = 0.9737$ and $r = (1.05)^{1/3} - 1 = 0.0164$. These values give p and q as 0.5683 and 0.4317 respectively. Substituting these into the above equation and following the logic of the Max{} functions as before we get five equations:

(a) $CB_f = S$, if $8.67 < S$
(b) $CB_f = 0.93\,S + 0.61$, if $8.05 < S < 8.67$
(c) $CB_f = 0.63\,S + 3.03$, if $7.47 < S < 8.05$
(d) $CB_f = 0.20\,S + 6.22$, if $6.93 < S < 7.47$
(e) $CB_f = 7.62$, if $S < 6.93$

The CB price behaviour of the three-period model is shown in Figure 5.13

With the three-period model there are two intermediate steps between today and expiry. As with the two-period model it would be necessary to calculate the hedge ratio at each branch or node of the CB and stock price trees. The three-period model thus would require two rehedging trades.

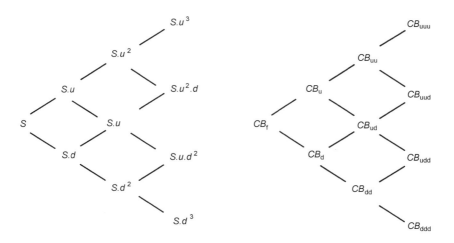

Three-period stock tree   Three-period CB tree

Figure 5.12   The general three-period CB model for ABC Bank

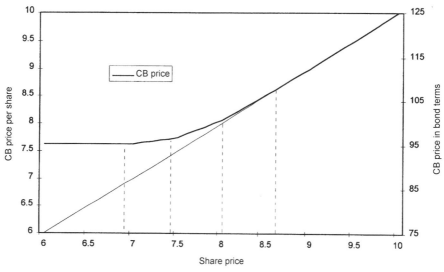

Figure 5.13   General three-period model ABC Bank

5.6   THE GENERAL *n*-PERIOD CB MODEL

We can clearly extend the above technique to a four-period or a five-period or
indeed a fifty-period model. As we consider models with increasing numbers of
periods, the fixed time to expiry is broken up into smaller and smaller sub-periods.
As the number of sub-periods increases, so does the number of possible final share
prices and so does the number of equations and straight lines that correspond to a
solution. Table 5.1 illustrates the relationship between the number of periods, the
number of final share prices, the number of equations that correspond to a solution
and the number of rehedging trades that the model requires. Also given are the
expressions for the general *n*-period model.

So, how many periods should one use and what difference does it make to the final
CB price? The more periods we use the more realistic the model. A 50-period model
with 51 different possible final share prices is more realistic than a two-period model
with only three. But should one use a 10,000-period model? In practical terms, 50 to
200 periods is often good enough. Remember that share and CB prices can in
practice be quite coarse and so one does not really need to have the possibility of
10,000 different share prices on expiry — 51 may be sufficient. But even so, what
about the tedium of estimating 52 different equations? In practice, the user never
really goes to the bother of finding all the separate equations. In practice, the CB
price is calculated using a spreadsheet or program that does the calculations using a
particular share price. The user is often not interested in the 52 different equations;
he just wants the CB price at a given share price.

Table 5.1 Increasing the number of periods in the CB model

No. of periods	No. of possible final share prices	No. of equations that form solution	No. of rehedging trades
1	2	3	0
2	3	4	1
3	4	5	2
.	.	.	.
.	.	.	.
50	51	52	49
.	.	.	.
n	$n + 1$	$n + 2$	$n - 1$

In the simple model for ABC Bank we started off with the one-period model by assuming that on expiry the upper and lower share prices were £9.00 and £7.20 respectively. Extending the model to two and then three and so on, we kept these two figures as the possible extreme values. This enabled us to arrive at the values for the u and d multipliers for each model. However, it is unrealistic to ask a CB user to come up with such estimates. The values of u and d set the possible range of future share prices. If u is large and/or d is small, the possible future share price range is large. For 'share price range' we could think of 'share price volatility'. If we think the share price is going to be very volatile then we would set u to be a large value and d to be a small value and vice versa. Recall that Section 4.3.2 showed that if we let

$$u = \exp(\sigma\sqrt{(t/n)})$$

and

$$d = 1/u$$

where t = time to expiry and
n = number of periods,

a share price that then moves up and down by factors u and d, would in the long run exhibit an annual volatility of σ, irrespective of the long-run average return. This is how the u and d values are arrived at in practice. The CB user makes an estimate (subjective or otherwise) of the likely future volatility of the underlying share price and this is used to get the u and d values.

In the case of the ABC Bank, 50-period CB model, if we think that the volatility is going to be 20% then $\sigma = 0.20$ and $u = \exp(\sigma\sqrt{(t/n)}) = \exp(0.2\sqrt{(1/50)}) = 1.0287$ and $d = 1/u = 0.9721$. The CB model values using 50 periods are shown in Figure 5.14.

To the naked eye, the 52 different equations represented by the 52 small segments of different straight lines look very much like a continuous curve. And this is how CB prices vary in reality. CB prices vary with respect to the underlying

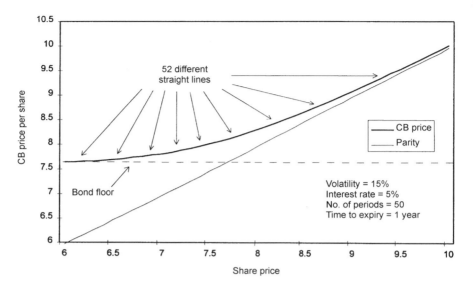

Figure 5.14 General 50-period model ABC Bank CB

share price in a smooth continuous fashion. At low share prices, the slope of the curve is low. At very low share prices, the CB price bottoms out and becomes completely independent of the share price. At very low share prices, the CB is a simple lump cash value of £7.62 — the discounted £8 conversion price. In the jargon of the market-place we say that the instrument has a floor — the bond floor value of £7.62 per share or 95.25 bond points. At high share price levels, the CB price mimics the share price perfectly. The transition between these two extreme types of dependence is smooth.

The 50-period model has the appearance of a very smooth curve but still only allows the possibility of 51 different share prices on expiry. Would more periods be better? It is interesting to note that if price is the only consideration, using more periods doesn't really make much difference. For example, with the current share price at £7.80, interest rates at 5% and a volatility of 15%, the 50-period and 100-period CB values differ by only 0.18p per share, or in bond terms, only 0.02 points. With this CB, 50 periods is more than adequate. We return to the issue of the choice of the number of periods in Chapter 6, when discussing CB sensitivities.

5.7   THE EFFECTS OF VOLATILITY

Now that we have a working model that gives realistic CB prices, it is interesting to examine the effects of varying some of the inputs. In particular, what effect does

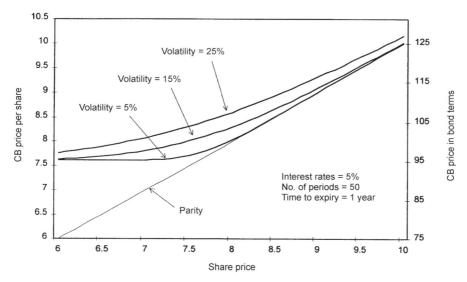

Figure 5.15   Effect of volatility on ABC Bank CB price

varying the volatility parameter, σ, have? Share prices can have volatilities as low as 0% and as high as 90%. In practice most stock markets have shares that exhibit volatility in the range of 5% to 30%. Figure 5.15 charts the ABC Bank CB with the volatility set to 5%, 15% and 25% (i.e., $\sigma = 0.05$, 0.15 and 0.25).

Note that at all share prices, increasing the volatility increases the CB price. This makes sense in that a share with a high volatility has a greater chance than one of a lower volatility, of being above the conversion price on expiry. This effect is most marked near the conversion price. With the share price at £7.80 the difference between the 5% value and the 25% value translates into 7.54 bond points. At very high and very low share prices, volatility effects the CB prices to a lesser extent. Note also that the degree of curvature is highest near the conversion price and is most marked on the low volatility curve. This last effect is particularly useful to hedge players looking to trade volatility. We return to the influence of volatility on CB pricing in Chapter 6.

5.8   THE EFFECTS OF INTEREST RATES

Keeping the volatility parameter fixed at 15% we investigate the effects of using different interest rates. Figure 5.16 shows the ABC Bank CB price using interest rates of 0%, 5% and 10% (i.e., $r = 0.00$, 0.05 and 0.10).

As suspected, interest rates affect CB prices most at low share prices and least at high share prices. At low share prices, the instrument behaves like a bond and at

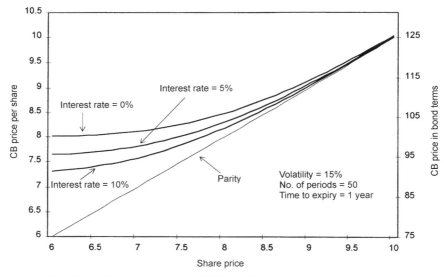

Figure 5.16 Effect of interest rates on ABC Bank CB price

high prices, it behaves like equity. This is exactly what happens in reality. When the share price is very much lower than the conversion price, a CB holder is only exposed to interest rate risk. When the share price is very much higher than the conversion price, a CB holder is only exposed to share price risk. In between the two extremes, the instrument is exposed to both types of risk, the degree depending on many factors.

Figure 5.16 gives a very good approximation of the sensitivity of CBs to interest rate changes. However, the issue of which interest rate to use in pricing CBs is more complex than presented here. In practice, the rate used is a combination of the short rate, the long rate and the spread associated with the probability of default risk. These and other complications will be dealt with in Chapter 6.

5.9 INTRODUCING COUPONS

Most CBs pay a coupon either annually or semi-annually and for some participants this is one of the main reasons for being involved. Often, though not always, the coupon expressed as a yield will be higher than the dividend yield on the underlying shares. Some of the early quantitative techniques used to compare CBs with the underlying, would use measures such as 'yield advantage' and 'break-even time'. These were crude attempts at pricing the premium over parity in terms of yield pick up. A CB invariably trades at a premium to parity but it also invariably rewards the holder with a higher yield. These early measures were attempts at asking the question: is the premium worth it?

Introducing the coupon payments into our CB model is quite straightforward. As before, we break the n-period model down into many one-period models. In each sub-period we apply the standard two-way bet mathematics to arrive at a hedge ratio and a CB price. The difference now is that at some of these sub-periods there will be an additional term to take into account on the CB side of the equations. The additional term will be the coupon. The first thing to do is to express the coupon as a payment on a per share basis. To illustrate we now redefine the ABC Bank CB as one that has a coupon of 2% paid semi-annually; 2% of £5,000 is £100, so each half-year one CB pays £50. Each CB is convertible into 625 shares and so the coupon is 50/625 = £0.08 per share per half year. The next step is to find in which of the n sub-periods a coupon is paid. As an example, if we were using a four-period model, the one year to expiry would be split up into four equal periods of three months. The coupon is paid every six months or every other sub-period. The situation is shown in Figure 5.17.

The first step is to calculate the value of the CB at each of the expiring stock price nodes. As before, the CB holder has the choice of converting and taking the shares or redeeming and taking the redemption price plus the final coupon. With the share price up at $S.u^4$, the choice is between this value and 8 + 0.08 = £8.08. So the CB value corresponding to the topmost expiring value is given by

$$CB_{uuuu} = \text{Max } \{S.u^4,\ 8.08\}$$

or more generally, if E = conversion price, then

$$CB_{uuuu} = \text{Max } \{S.u^4,\ E + \text{coupon}\}$$

The other expiring CB values are calculated in an identical fashion. Working back from period 4 to period 3 we apply the one-period model to each node. The CB value corresponding to the upper stock price $S.u^3$, is given by

$$CB_{uuu} = \frac{pCB_{uuuu} + qCB_{uuud}}{1 + r}$$

The values corresponding to the other nodes at period 3 are calculated in a similar fashion.

Working back to period 2 we now encounter another coupon payment of £0.08 per share. We can still apply the two-way bet mathematics but remember that the coupon is paid to the CB side of the portfolio if the stock price increases or decreases. It is left as an algebraic exercise for the reader to show that one simply adds the coupon value to the usual expression. The CB value corresponding to the upper stock price $S.u^2$ is therefore given by

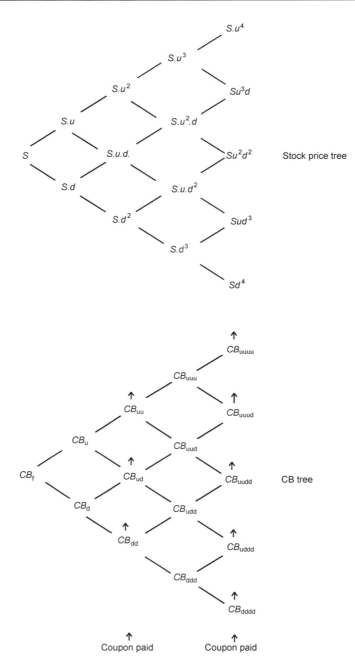

Figure 5.17 The four-period CB model for ABC Bank with coupons

$$CB_{uu} = \frac{pCB_{uuu} + qCB_{uud}}{1 + r} + 0.08$$

or more generally

$$CB_{uu} = \frac{pCB_{uuu} + qCB_{uud}}{1 + r} + \text{coupon}$$

This is repeated for all the nodes at the second period and we proceed to work back through the binomial lattice as before. The final equations will be a complex combination of Max { } functions and the coupon payments. As in all CB modelling, in practice, these equations are never explicitly evaluated. The solution is arrived at using iterative-type programs or the spreadsheets. With volatility set at 15%, interest rates set at 5%, the four-period model values for the ABC Bank CB with and without the 2% coupon are £8.30 and £8.18 per share respectively. These values translate into bond-quoted terms of 103.72 and 102.20, i.e., a difference of 1.52 bond points. The coupons do make a difference to the price and the longer the time to expiry the greater the difference. If this CB had ten years to expiry and a 50-period model were used, the difference in prices would increase to 15 bond points. Over ten years all the little 2% coupon payments make quite a considerable difference.

But what about the coupon effect at different share prices? Figure 5.18 shows how the one year ABC Bank CB price varies with respect to the underlying share price with the coupons set at 0%, 3% and 6%. The coupons have more effect at low share prices and less effect at high share prices. It is possible to show that, in this

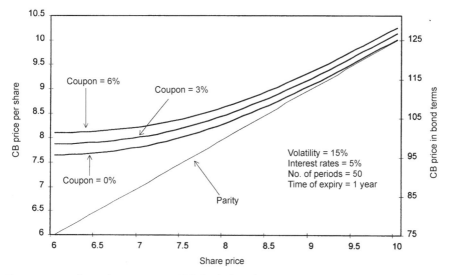

Figure 5.18   Effect of coupons on ABC Bank CB price

example, at very low share prices the difference between the 0% and 3% coupon CB tends, in the limit, to a fixed value of 5.77 bond points and at very high share prices, a fixed value of 2.91 bond points.

So, introducing coupons to the CB model requires only one additional term at certain specific points in the CB tree. The additional term is simply the coupon payment.

5.10   A FINAL NOTE ON THE VALUE AND MEANING OF THE p AND q PARAMETERS

In all of the above, the p and q parameters are given by

$$p = \frac{1 + r - d}{u - d}, \text{ and } q = 1 - p$$

where $u = \exp(\sigma\sqrt{(t/n)})$
$d = 1/u$ and
$r = (1 + \text{interest rate})^{t/n} - 1$

The p and q parameters are functions of u, d and r and hence functions of σ, t, n and the interest rate. With any given CB the value of t, the time to expiry, is known for sure and in modelling the instrument we choose a suitable value for n, the number of periods. The only other inputs required are the interest rate and σ, an estimate of the future share price volatility. So we can think of the final model p and q values as being dependent on two fixed and known entities (t and n) and two variable entities (σ and r). Once we choose suitable values for σ and r, the values of p and q are determined and at no time does the question of probability come into the model. As an example, say we have a CB that expires in four years' time and we let $n = 50$, $\sigma = 0.30$ (30% volatility) and interest rate $= 0.10$ (10%). Substituting these values into the above formulae gives

$$p = 0.53 \quad \text{and} \quad q = 0.47$$

These fixed p and q values would then be used in all 50 recurring iterative steps, starting with expiry and working back towards the present time to arrive at the final model CB value of, say 102.19. As mentioned before, this final CB value is completely independent of probability considerations.

The underlying share price process evolves by 50 different up and down movements. With the given parameters, the magnitude of each up or down movement is $u = \exp(\sigma\sqrt{(t/n)}) = 1.0886$ and $d = 1/u = 0.9186$ respectively. If the probability of an up move is 0.60 and that of a down move is 0.40 the CB fair value is 102.19. If the probability of an up move is 0.10 and that of a down move is 0.90, the CB fair value is still 102.19. The CB fair value will always be 102.19 because it is dependent on the *magnitude* of the up and down movements and not the *probability* of the up and down movements. So this means that if we set the probability of an up move to 0.53 and a down move to 0.47 (coincidentally the p and q values given above) then the CB value will still be 102.19.

Although the CB value is independent of probability considerations, the ultimate direction of the underlying share price is not. Recall from Section 4.3.2 that fixing the up and down multipliers to u and d as above, fixes the volatility of the share price to σ. Recall also however, that the long run average share return depends on the probability of the up and down moves. If the probability of an up move is large then the average share return will be positive. If the probability of an up move is small then the average share return will be negative. In fact, if the probability of an up move is set as follows

$$\text{Probability of an up move} = \frac{\exp(\mu t/n) - d}{u - d}$$

then the long-run average share return comes out to be μ. In the example above the annual interest rate is 10% so substituting $\mu = 0.10$, $u = 1.0886$ and $d = 0.9186$ we get

$$\text{Probability of an up move} = \frac{\exp(0.10 \times 4/50) - 0.9186}{1.0886 - 0.9186}$$
$$= 0.53$$

and so the probability of a down move $= 0.47$

Is this a coincidence? These probability values for the share price process are identical to the p and q values that are used in the CB modelling process. In the share price process they are probabilities, but in the CB model they are just two numbers that eventually give the fair value irrespective of probability. It is no coincidence that the p and q values are identical and there is a reason which we now explore.

It is possible to model CBs using a different approach to that of zero arbitrage. Instead of constructing a zero risk portfolio of long one thing and short another we now approach the problem probabilistically and this is illustrated in Figure 5.19. For simplicity assume that the CB pays no coupons, expires in one year's time and is convertible into one share that pays no dividends. Assume that the underlying share price can rise from S to $S.u$ or fall from S to $S.d$ with the corresponding final CB values being CB_u and CB_d respectively. In this model we approach the situation in much the same way we treated the gambling situations dealt with in Chapter 3. We are offered the chance to bet or buy the share price at S and/or the CB at CB_f. Let us assume that the probability of the share price rising is P and that the probability of the share price falling is Q (obviously $Q = 1 - P$). So the probability of the final CB value being CB_u or CB_d is P or Q respectively. Imagine being given the opportunity to play the CB game repeatedly. Some of the time the final outcome will be CB_u and some of the time it will be CB_d. What will the long-run average or

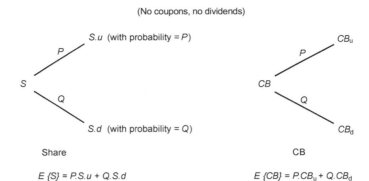

Figure 5.19 The probablistic one-period binomial CB model

expected value of the CB game be? The standard solution to this type of problem is given by

$$E\{CB\} = P.CB_\text{u} + Q.CB_\text{d}$$

So what should one pay today for something that in the long run will be worth $E\{CB\}$ in one year's time? We simply discount the expected value by the interest rate factor

$$CB_\text{f} = \frac{E\{CB\}}{1+r}$$

or

$$CB_\text{f} = \frac{P.CB_\text{u} + Q.CB_\text{d}}{1+r} \tag{5.13}$$

This new alternative fair value is thus the discounted expected future value of the CB price. The expected value is calculated using the probabilities associated with the underlying share price and the discounting is done using the appropriate interest rate. CB_u will always be greater than CB_d and so the higher the P value, the higher CB_f. In this model the fair value of the CB most definitely depends on the probability of the underlying share price rising or falling.

Note the striking similarity of CB fair value expressions (5.13) and (5.11). One equation is derived using a probability argument and the other using a zero arbitrage non-probability argument. The only difference is that in one we have probabilities P and Q and in the other we have numbers p and q that are not necessarily probabilities. What if we let the two sets of numbers be the same, i.e., $P = p$ and $Q = q$? If the probability of the share price rising is set to p, where

$$p = \frac{\exp(\mu t/n) - d}{u - d}$$

then this says something about the long-run average share price change. In fact with p set to this very special value, the long-run average share price change will be μ. So the probabilistic fair value and the zero arbitrage fair value are identical if the share price is assumed to have the same long-run average as the interest rate. And this is the principle behind what is known as the 'risk neutral argument'. Valuing a CB using the zero arbitrage approach is equivalent to valuing a CB assuming that the underlying share price moves in such a way as to have the same long-run average return as someone investing in risk-free cash deposits. The resulting fair value will be valid for share distributions that have any expected return but will also be valid for share distributions that have the expected return equal to the interest rate. This argument is valid for all derivative products and it means that when it is not possible to construct simple zero arbitrage portfolios, one can revert to the probabilistic approach, provided one uses a share distribution that has the appropriate long-run average return.

5.11   SUMMARY

In this chapter we have developed the basic n-period binomial CB pricing model. Starting with a very simple gambling situation in which there were only two correlated outcomes, we showed that is possible to arrive at a unique fair value of one instrument in terms of another. An important aspect of this approach is that the fair value is independent of probability considerations. The two-way bet approach was then applied to a one-period model with no coupons, no interest rates and only two possible expiring share prices. The idea was then extended to a two-period, then a three-period and eventually a general n-period model. Different volatilities, interest rates and coupon payments were then incorporated into the model. In this way, what started as a naïve and simplistic approach became a model that very nearly explains how CB prices vary in reality. We say very nearly because there are still some aspects of CBs and the underlying shares that have not been included. In the next chapter we deal with these final complications.

5.12   SOLUTIONS TO EXERCISES IN FIGURE 5.2

1. $h = 2/3$, $Y = 333$.
2. $h = 1/5$, $Y = 1.8$
3. $h = -1/3$, $Y = 73.3$. In this example, the hedge ratio is negative because B behaves like a put type option, i.e., increasing in value when A decreases in value. The perfectly hedged portfolio in this case would be long three units of B and long one unit of A.

6
Introducing the complications

The CB model derived in Chapter 5 incorporated share price volatility, interest rates, and coupon payments. For some CBs this model gives adequate results. There are, however, additional factors that have to be taken into account and these factors are usually associated with the fact that the options embedded in CBs are American style rather than European style. A European option can only be exercised or invoked on the final day of the instrument's life, whereas an American option can be exercised at any time. Having an American-style embedded option means that what was assumed to be an instrument with, say, ten years of life left can suddenly be extinguished. The American-style nature of many of the embedded options means that the valuation process becomes more complex. These complications are dealt with in this chapter and are as follows:

- dividend-paying shares;
- the issuer's call provision;
- the CB holder's put;
- incorporating different interest rates;
- CBs redeemable in one currency but convertible into shares denominated in another.

We deal with each of these complications in sequence.

6.1 INTRODUCING DIVIDENDS

In the real world most shares pay a dividend and we now have to introduce this complication into our model. Fortunately, the solution is quite simple. All we do is apply the two-way bet mathematics around the day that the share goes ex-dividend. To illustrate, we return to a one-period model with no coupons. Let us assume that the shares go ex-dividend just prior to expiry and that the dividend amount is £D.

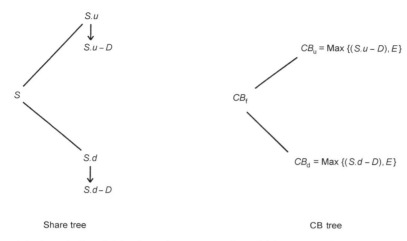

Share tree   CB tree

Figure 6.1   Introducing dividends to the one-period model (no coupons)

Recall that the risk-free arbitrage portfolio is long one CB and short h shares. With the up and down multipliers set at u and d, the final share price would be either Su or Sd. However, we must now assume that over the dividend date the shares would fall by the dividend amount and so the final share prices will be either $(Su - D)$ or $(Sd - D)$. A portfolio that is short shares over an ex-dividend date will of course have to pay out the dividend amount, D. The situation is depicted in Figure 6.1.

It is left as an exercise for the reader to show that by applying the two-way bet mathematics, the fair value for the CB with a dividend payment is almost identical to that without. The only difference is that one must use the amended share prices $(Su - D)$ and $(Sd - D)$ in the calculations. The reason for this simplicity is that the loss to the portfolio due to paying out D is completely offset by the lower final share prices. So introducing dividends just means amending the share price tree at all the nodes where one is paid.

However, an extra problem arises when using this type of share price amendment technique, especially when the number of periods is large. Without dividends, the real virtue of the binomial approach is that the share price tree *recombines*. In the four-period example given in Figure 5.17 there are six different ways the share price can finally end up at the value Su^2d^2. There are six different combinations of up and down moves, starting at S and ending at Su^2d^2. Because multiplication is commutative, i.e., it does not matter in which order multiplication occurs, the final value of Su^2d^2 is the same — the tree recombines. Introducing a dividend by subtraction spoils this very convenient recombining property. Introducing a single dividend payment of D at the second period would result in the share price tree shown in Figure 6.2.

There are now nine different final share prices instead of the original five. This is because introducing the dividend as a quantity that is subtracted, ruins the

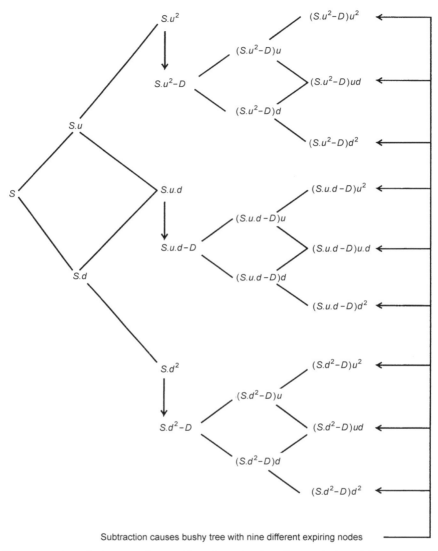

Subtraction causes bushy tree with nine different expiring nodes

Figure 6.2 Introducing one-dividend by subtraction into four-period model

recombining property offered by the commutative multiplicative operations. This effect increases exponentially with more dividends and more periods. A model with no dividend payments and 50 periods would have only 51 different final share prices: Sd^{50}, Sud^{49}, ... Su^{50}. Introducing ten dividend payments by subtraction would increase this number to 60,466,176. The share price tree would be very

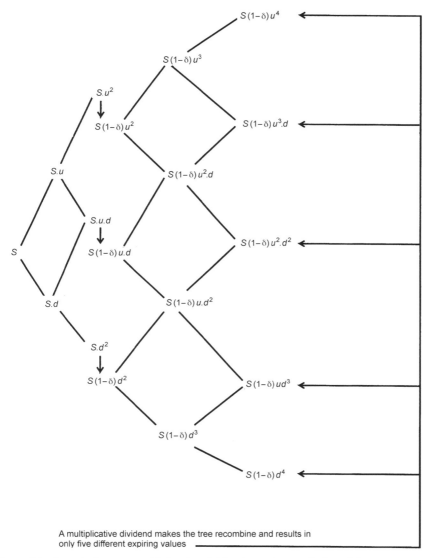

A multiplicative dividend makes the tree recombine and results in only five different expiring values

Figure 6.3 Introducing one-multiplicative dividend to a four-period model

bushy indeed. Even with modern fast computers, carrying out backward induction starting with 60,466,176 different end nodes is not feasible. The process would be absurdly time consuming.

There is, fortunately, a clever way around this problem and it involves expressing the dividend payments multiplicatively rather than by an absolute amount. If we express the dividend payment in terms of a yield given by δ (where, for example, $\delta = 0.01$ represents a yield of 1%), then the dividend amount is simply δ times the current stock price. Also, the stock price after a dividend payment is given by $S(1 - \delta)$. In this way the dividend payment effects are incorporated into the model in a multiplicative way and this has the virtue of keeping the recombining property intact. The new multiplicative approach for the four-period model is shown in Figure 6.3.

There is a difference in the two approaches to incorporating dividends. In one approach the dividend amount stays fixed at D and in the other the amount varies according to the level of the share price. In the multiplicative approach, as the share price falls (rises), so does the absolute dividend amount. This of course may not be an unreasonable assumption. If a particular share price fell by 50% it is unlikely that the dividend amount would stay fixed — it would probably also fall. A similar argument can be applied to share price rises. Most market participants use the multiplicative dividend adjustment technique.

Dividends are therefore very easily incorporated into our general CB model. All that is required is that the share price tree be amended by the $(1 - \delta)$ multiplicative factor at each of the appropriate nodes. As before, backward induction on the new amended share tree will give the CB fair value. We finish this section by calculating the effect dividends have on the ABC Bank CB. Assuming a volatility of 15%, interest rates at 5%, zero coupons, $n = 50$ and a dividend yield of 1%, a one-year CB would be priced at 101.72 in bond terms. This is compared to 102.22 if there were no dividends. The introduction of dividends has dropped the CB value by half a point. This price reduction effect is obviously due to the lowering of the final share prices and is more marked for longer-dated bonds. If this CB had ten years to expiry then the difference in price would be 3.11 points.

There is one final point to make when incorporating dividends and that is associated with the American-style feature of CBs. Although usually dividends are small, (especially in comparison to the coupons paid by CBs) there are some situations when an exceptionally large dividend payment will suppress the CB price so much that it may be worth exercising or converting early. This obviously has implications for the valuation process. As an illustration, consider the two-period ABC example used in Figure 5.9. This is replicated in the top panel of Figure 6.4. Let us assume there is a large dividend payment of 8% of the share price. The new situation is shown in the lower panel of Figure 6.4.

Without the dividend payment the CB would be worth £7.95 per share. With the dividend payment the CB price is reduced to £7.70 per share. But this cannot be right since the current share price is £7.80 and the CB is American style. If this situation existed in reality we could buy the CB at £7.70 per share, convert immediately into shares and sell at £7.80 per share, enjoying a risk-free profit. The CB cannot trade at a discount to the share price because there is always the possibility of conversion. So in this case the correct fair price for the CB must be £7.80 — the parity or intrinsic value. Incorporating this type of logic into the CB

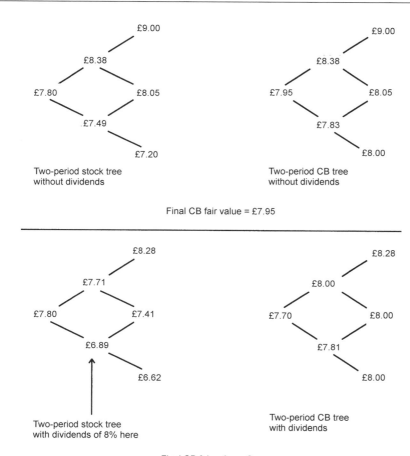

Final CB fair value = £7.95

Final CB fair value = ?

Figure 6.4 Two-period model for ABC Bank

modelling process is quite straightforward. We proceed as before calculating the fair values of the CB at each node but include one final extra step; that of checking that the CB price is at least at parity. If it is lower than parity then replace with the parity value.

6.2 INTRODUCING THE ISSUER'S CALL OPTION

Most CBs are issued with what is known as a call provision. A call provision gives the issuer the right to call back the bond at a predetermined price. The predetermined price is usually at or near the nominal bond value. CBs are called normally to invoke conversion. To illustrate let us look at a variation of the ABC Bank CB. We assume that today's share price is £7.80, the conversion price is £8.00, interest rates are 5% and volatility is 25%. The CB pays a semi-annual coupon of 5% and has two and a half years to expiry. The underlying share pays no dividends. The upper panel of Figure 6.5 illustrates the share price and CB price tree for a five-period model but shown in a slightly different format. In this new format the two trees are interwoven. The share price values appear in bold and the corresponding CB values appear in italics. The standard backward induction process gives the fair value at £9.61 per share which translates into 120.13 bond points. (This price is high because the coupon is large.)

We now consider an identical CB that has a call provision giving the issuer the right to call back the instrument in exchange for £8 per share (or 100 bond points). Like most call provisions this one is subject to two constraints.

1. The CB cannot be called under any circumstances for one year — in the jargon of the market, the *hard non-call period* is one year. Most CBs are issued with hard non-call periods. This ensures the investor that whatever happens to the underlying share price, the instrument will exist as a CB for at least this period. Hard non-call periods are typically two to four years from the issue date.
2. The CB cannot be called unless the share price is trading at a 30% premium to the conversion price. This is also typical of most CBs. This type of constraint means that the embedded share option component is always worth something. Without this constraint it would be possible for the issuer to invoke the call provision the moment the CB price increased slightly and thus make the instrument less attractive. In the context of our ABC Bank example, the constraint of 30% above the conversion price translates into a share price of £10.40. So to be called, the underlying share price has to be at or above £10.40.

What are the implications of the existence of a call provision on the CB price? The answer is given in the lower panel of Figure 6.5. Consider in detail the node corresponding to the underlying share price being £11.11. Without the call provision, the upper panel shows that at this node the CB price would be £11.68 per share — a slight premium to the parity. However, this node corresponds to the end of the first year and so the CB has passed out of the hard non-call period. Also, with the underlying share above the minimum required price (£10.40), there is the real risk that the CB holder will receive a call notice.

What will the situation be if the holder does receive a call notice? The call notice gives the issuer the right to call back the CB in exchange for £8.00 per share. If the holder does nothing his CB position is eradicated by the issuer and he receives a lump sum of cash equivalent to £8.00 per share. In this case, since each bond is convertible into 625 shares, doing nothing will result in the holder receiving £5,000 per CB. And this would be a shame since prior to the call notice with the underlying

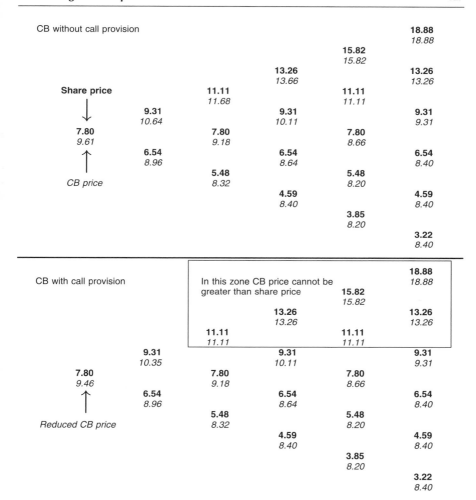

Figure 6.5   The effect of a call provision on CBs

share price at £11.11, each CB was worth at least 11.11 × 625 = £6,944. Doing nothing would result in £3.11 per share or £1,944 per CB being wasted.

If the CB holder receives a call notice what he must do immediately is to convert into shares and sell at the market price of £11.11. In this way he gets the embedded intrinsic value prior to the call notice. In fact this is often the very reason the corporation issues a call notice. The corporation knows that the CB holders will not want to receive the call price of £8.00 per share when the shares are trading at £11.11. By issuing the call notice they are essentially forcing the holders to invoke their conversion option. What this means then is that if a CB is in a situation where it can be called, then it should never trade at a premium to the underlying intrinsic value. In the upper panel of Figure 6.5, with the share price at £11.11, the CB is priced at £11.68 — a £0.57 premium to the shares. With the CB in danger of being called this cannot be so. It would not make sense to pay £11.68 for something that in the next instant may be worth only £11.11. So the call provision overhang will force the CB price down to parity at £11.11 and this is shown in the lower panel. The lower CB price at this node will have a knock-on effect throughout the remaining part of the tree. The final result is that the CB with the call provision is worth £9.46 per share compared to £9.61 per share. In bond points these values translate into £118.25 and £120.13 respectively.

As suspected, the call provision has the effect of reducing the price one should pay for a CB. And this makes sense. The call provision is, subject to constraints, American in style and thus has the possibility of reducing the life of the instrument. A trader involved in the above instrument may be buying into what he thinks is a two and a half year volatility play. This is why he pays a premium over parity. It is possible that in one year's time the share price could be above £10.40. If this were to happen he may then be in a situation in which the CB is called and hence extinguished. What was thought to be a two-year play may turn out to be only a one-year play. The instrument should be priced accordingly — lower than one without a call provision.

The effects of the call provision on the CB price vary with the underlying share price. Figure 6.6 illustrates that the effect is minimal when the share price is very

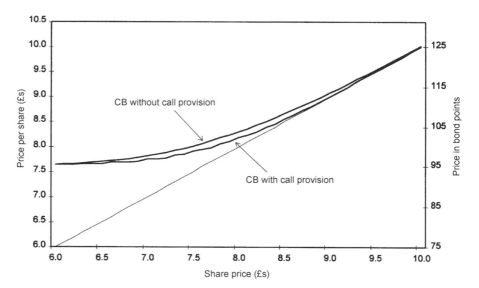

Figure 6.6 The effects of a call provision on ABC Bank convertible bond

low or very high and this is intuitively reasonable. At very low share prices the CB will be sitting at or very near the bond floor level. At these levels the probability of the share price reaching the call trigger point of 30% above the conversion price is so low as to have no effect on the CB price. At very high share price levels (provided the coupon is not too high) the CB would be trading at parity anyway and so the presence of the call provision has no effect.

6.3 INTRODUCING A BOND PUT

Some CBs are issued with a put. These puts give the investor the option to force the issuer to buy back the CB at some predetermined price. The predetermined price is usually, but not always, the nominal value. This forced buy-back is known as putting the bond to the issuer. The put option is the investor's to exercise (should he choose) and so must add some value. Accordingly CBs with puts usually trade at a higher price, although the degree depends on many factors.

To illustrate we again consider yet another version of the ABC Bank CB in Figure 6.7. Here we assume that the CB has two and a half years to expiry and pays a semi-annual coupon of 1%. Assume volatility is 25%, interest rates are 10% and that the shares pay no dividends. The upper panel of Figure 6.7 shows that the regular CB would be priced at £7.31 per share, or 91.38 bond points. The lower panel shows what effect the presence of a put option in one year's time will have. CB puts are usually only exercisable on one day and in this example this corresponds to the second period. With the share price down at £4.21 the unconstrained CB would be priced at £7.08 per share. The put option gives the holder the right to put the instrument back to the issuer at the conversion price — £8.00. If the CB were trading at £7.08 in the market it would be possible to buy at this price, immediately exercise the put and receive £8.00. This would represent a risk-free profit of £0.92 per share or £575 per CB. Clearly this will not happen. The presence of the put will ensure that the minimum price the CB can have will be £8.00 and so in the modelling process we must override the backward induction value. Note that in the lower panel of Figure 6.7 in the second period with the share price at £6.00, the put option would also force the CB value to £8.00. These increases in CB prices eventually have a knock-on effect to the initial CB price. In this example the price increases from £7.31 to £7.68 per share, prices that translate to 91.38 and 96.00 bond points respectively.

This then, is how the put option is incorporated into the CB model. All that is required is a simple logical statement at the appropriate nodes. Figure 6.8 shows how the presence of a put option affects the price of a CB at various share prices. Not surprisingly, the put option has most influence at lower share prices. In practice the put option has the effect of reducing the life of the instrument but in a positive sense for the investor. If the share price is low the CB holder can exercise the put and receive the redemption proceeds sooner than later. Receiving cash today is

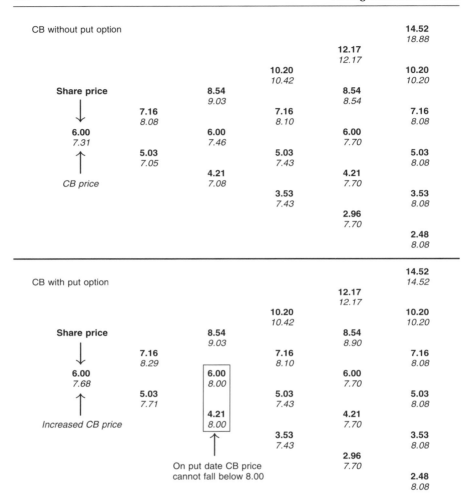

Figure 6.7 The effect of a put option on CBs

always better than receiving cash at some later date. So a put option is really useful, especially at low share prices.

The effects of the put option are also a function of interest rates, the coupon level and the volatility of the underlying share. High interest rates make CB put options worth more. High interest rates have the effect of increasing the discounting process and thus otherwise reducing CB prices. A put option essentially gives the holder the right to shorten the life of the instrument and thus reduce the discounting effects. CBs with high coupons have less valuable put options. Recall that exercising a put option tears up the future stream of coupons. If these coupons are

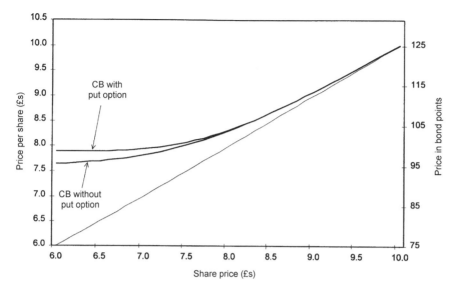

Figure 6.8   Influence of a put option on ABC Bank convertible bond

particularly large then it may not be worth while exercising the put — the put option becomes less valuable.

6.4   INTEREST RATE EFFECTS REVISITED

Up until this stage we have naïvely assumed that the CB model requires only one interest rate input and that this rate remains constant. In the real world of bond markets this is not appropriate. There are a number of interest rate issues to address and these are dealt with in the following sections.

6.4.1   The Term Structure of Interest Rates

Most CBs are issued with at least five years of life and many with ten or twenty years. The zero arbitrage model derived in Chapter 5 is built on the assumption that the portfolio of long one instrument and short another should return the risk-free rate dictated by, amongst other things, the value of the variable r. But what interest rate do we use? In most capital markets short-term rates are lower than long-term rates. Figure 6.9 could be a typical yield curve for government-backed debt. In this example the one-year rate is 6% but the ten-year rate is 9%. If a CB expires in ten years' time do we use 9% and if it expires in one year's time do we use 6%? The difference in pricing could be quite significant. What if the CB has ten years to

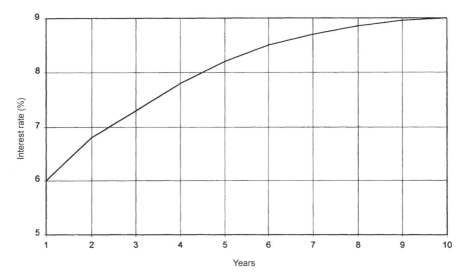

Figure 6.9 Typical yield curve

expire but the zero arbitrage (or hedged) portfolio is only in existence for one year. It may be that the CB is called or that the holder chooses to put it back to the corporation earlier than ten years. What if the hedged position is financed at short-term rates but the CB runs for 20 years? These and other aspects complicate the issue of what rate to use.

6.4.2   Default Risk and Credit Rating

In the straight (i.e., non-convertible) bond market, each bond will have a certain credit rating. Bonds that are issued by corporations that are deemed to be risky will have a lower credit rating than ones that are issued by blue-chip companies. And bonds issued by blue-chip corporations have credit ratings that are usually lower (though not much lower) than those backed by governments. There are a number of entities that rate corporations and they rank them from AAA+ (low risk) to BBB− (high risk). The risk being referred to here is the risk of default. When a straight bond is purchased there is in essence an agreement drawn up between the holder (the lender) and the issuer (the borrower). The buyer of the bond is lending the corporation a sum of money in exchange for a stream of coupons and a final cash lump sum. Simple arithmetic will give the yield to maturity implied in the purchase price, the coupons and the lump sum. If the corporation is deemed to be risky in the sense that they may not be able to pay one or more coupons, or worse still, not be there to pay the redemption proceeds, then the buyer will demand a higher yield.

This translates into the price of the bond being lower than it would otherwise be. Other things being equal, bonds with lower credit ratings will be priced lower and give higher yields to maturity. If ten-year government bonds are yielding 9% and a particular corporation's credit rating dictates that its debt should reflect an additional 1% then the bonds would be at such a price as to yield 10%. In the jargon of the market-place, the 'risk spread' would be 100 basis points over the curve.

CBs are issued on corporations that, by definition, have the risk of defaulting. The bond components of CBs will thus demand a higher yield to maturity than the corresponding government rate. This higher rate must be taken into account when modelling CBs.

6.4.3   Incorporating Two Interest Rates into the CB Model

The CB market is now dominated by hedgers. CB Hedgers are usually concerned with just two interest rates: the short-term financing rate and the rate corresponding to the maturity of the CB. This is because hedgers often borrow funds to put on trades and so their cost of carry is dictated by the short-term rate. At the other extreme, in the limit, CBs will trade at a price reflecting the appropriate long-term rate plus some adjustment. It is necessary therefore to model CBs incorporating these two interest rates.

In order to do this we must return to the one-period model outlined in Section 5.2. Recall the situation of the zero-risk arbitrage portfolio of long one CB and short h shares. The current share price is S and the CB fair value is CB_f. If the shares rise to Su by the end of the period, the CB will have risen to CB_u. If the shares fall to Sd, then the CB will have fallen to CB_d. The zero-risk arbitrage portfolio is specially constructed so that whatever happens (1) the final portfolio value is the same with the shares up or down and (2) the portfolio must return the risk-free rate. These two constraints produce the hedge ratio and the fair value. Applying the first constraint:

$$\text{value of portfolio with shares up} = \text{value of portfolio with shares down}$$
$$CB_u - h.S.u = CB_d - h.S.d$$

which rearranges to give the hedge ratio as

$$h = \frac{CB_u - CB_d}{S.u - S.d} \tag{6.1}$$

Applying the second constraint usually means that

Value of portfolio at beginning $\times$ interest rate factor = Value of portfolio at end

Now there are two interest rates to take into account. Consider the situation of a hedger borrowing money to set up this portfolio. The portfolio is long the CB and usually this will be a long-dated instrument. The CB also has an associated credit risk. A bank lending money to put this trade on will want at least the rate that someone long a CB gets. It is therefore appropriate to apply this higher rate which we designate r_{cb} to the CB side of the portfolio. The portfolio is short shares and the proceeds will usually be placed on deposit. The short shares thus produce a positive cash flow at a rate of r_s and this should be applied to the short side of the portfolio. Using these two interest rates in the second constraint equation gives

$$CB_f.r_{cb} - h.S.r_s = CB_u - h.S.u \qquad (6.2)$$

Solving (6.1) and (6.2) simultaneously gives

$$CB_f = \frac{pCB_u + qCB_d}{1 + r_{cb}} \qquad (6.3)$$

where $\quad p = \dfrac{1 + r_s - d}{u - d}, \quad$ and

$q = 1 - p$

The fair value is very similar to that derived in Section 5.2. The difference now is that one interest rate appears in the p and q expressions and another in the discounting expression. And this seems intuitively correct. Recall that the risk-neutral argument allows one to think of the p and q terms as being probabilities of up and down movements. Here the p and q terms are expressed in terms of the short-term risk-free rate. So the probability of the share price rising or falling in this formulation is identical to that in the previous one-interest-rate model — the long-run average share price change is the same. The long-run average final CB value will be given by the numerator of the CB_f term in expression (6.3). The difference is, however, that this average is now discounted by the new higher riskier rate r_{cb}.

It is instructive to see the effect of using the two interest rates instead of the one. Returning to the very first simple example of Section 5.2 in which $S = £7.80$, $S.u = £9.00$ and $S.d = £7.20$. The time period is one year, the CB has one share and the conversion price is £8.00. Initially, we assume that both interest rates are 3%. Substituting $r_s = r_{cb} = 0.03$ in (6.3) we get $CB_f = £8.22$ and a hedge ratio of 0.56. However, if we assume that the rate associated with the CB is much higher at 10% then we substitute $r_s = 0.03$ and $r_{cb} = 0.10$. We get $CB_f = £7.69$, a much lower value. This new value is so low that it is below the current share price and this cannot be. At this price the CB would be immediately converted into shares at £7.80 for a risk-free profit. So the CB must trade at least £7.80. But at this higher price, putting on the hedge trade would lock in a loss and it is left as an exercise for the reader to show this. So something must be wrong here? The CB cannot trade at a discount, but it cannot trade as high as £7.80. How can we arrive at a theoretical or fair value that makes sense? The answer is given in the next section.

6.4.4 Mixing Interest Rates in the CB Model — The George Philips Approach

An innovation derived by George Philips, an experienced practitioner in the CB market, cleverly incorporates all the complications associated with using the short-term rate, the long-term rate and the issue of credit risk. The approach looks afresh at the interest rate associated with the CB side of the portfolio and successfully solves the paradox of the model described in Section 6.4.3. The approach again uses the situation of the classical hedger — the individual long the CB and short the underlying shares and is best explained by considering two extreme cases.

1. If the share price is considerably lower than the conversion price, then the CB will be trading like a straight bond. At these levels, since the probability of conversion is so low, the instrument should be priced like a straight bond. The yield to maturity will be identical to a straight bond, i.e., the appropriate long-term government rate plus an additional amount to reflect the default risk. Note also that with the share price so low the sensitivity to further changes in the share price will be zero. This means that a classical hedger will have no short position against the CBs — the hedge ratio, $h = 0$.
2. If the share price is considerably higher than the conversion price, then the CB will be trading like straight equity — the hedge ratio, $h = 1$. The classical hedged portfolio will be long CBs and short 100% of the underlying shares. The total portfolio value will be independent of the further share price movements. Furthermore, in the event of a complete collapse of the corporation, the CB and the share will be priced at zero. Since the portfolio is 100% hedged there will be no loss (except possibly a small loss due to coupons). With such a riskless portfolio it does not make sense to use the same interest rate as in (1) above. With such a riskless portfolio the appropriate rate to use is the financing risk-free rate.

In situations when the share price is between the two extremes of (1) and (2) above, it makes sense to use an interest rate that is intermediate between the values. What George Philips suggests is that since in case (1) the hedge ratio is zero and that in case (2) the hedge ratio is 1, then the appropriate rate, r_{mix}, could be derived from a mixture of the two as follows:

$$r_{mix} = (\text{long rate} + \text{credit spread}).(1 - h) + \text{short rate}.h$$
$$r_{mix} = r_{cb}.(1 - h) + r_s.h \tag{6.4}$$

So in the one-period model given in Section 6.4.3

$$r_{mix} = (0.09 + 0.01)(1 - h) + 0.03h$$

or

$$r_{mix} = 0.10(1 - h) + 0.03h$$

In this way when the share price is very low and $h = 0$, then $r_{mix} = 0.10$, i.e., a rate of 10%. When the share price is very high and $h = 1$, then $r_{mix} = 0.03$, i.e., a rate of 3%. With the share price at the intermediate level of say $S = £7.80$ when $h = 0.56$ then $r_{mix} = 0.0608$ or 6.08%. Substituting these values into the new expression

$$CB_f = \frac{pCB_u + qCB_d}{1 + r_{mix}} \tag{6.5}$$

gives a new fair value of $CB_f = £7.98$. Figure 6.10 gives the CB price using the short-term rate, the long-term rate and the mixed rate. As suspected, at very low share prices the model value using the mixed rate is identical to that using the long rate and at very high share prices the model value is identical to that using the short rate. At intermediate share price levels the model value is in between the two extreme cases.

We can easily extend this approach to the general n-period model as follows.

1. From the current share price generate the share price tree with $n + 1$ final nodes using the p and q values derived only from the short rate r_s.
2. Consider the final share price values and see if the CB holder will convert or redeem.
3. Step back one period and calculate the hedge ratios, h, at each of the penultimate n nodes.

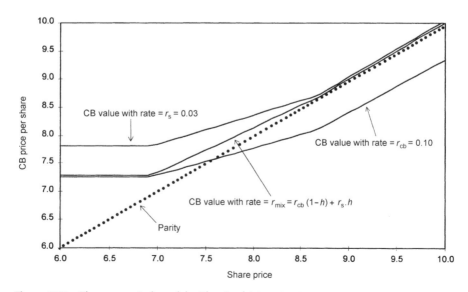

Figure 6.10 The one-period model with mixed interest rates

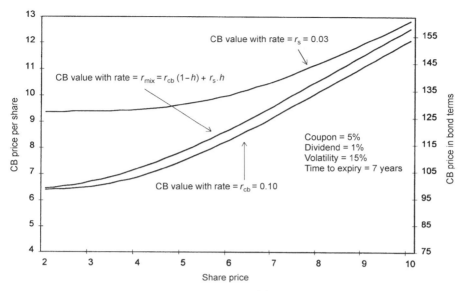

Figure 6.11 Using mixed rates with 50-period model

4. Use expression (6.4) to calculate the appropriate discounting mixed interest rate, r_{mix}, at each node.
5. Calculate the CB value using expression (6.5).
6. Step back one period and calculate the new hedge ratios using (6.4).
7. Calculate the new CB values using (6.5).

Repeat steps 6 and 7 until finished. Figure 6.11 illustrates how the price of a seven-year CB price varies with respect to the underlying share price.

6.4.5   Non-constant Interest Rates

In the above we have always assumed that interest rates (whether using one or two or a mixture) are constant. This is not so. In reality the short-term financing rate and the long-term bond rates vary over time and this will obviously have an impact on CB prices. The real problem is that the whole term structure of interest rates is non-constant. Currently there is no generally agreed method to model this multidimensional uncertainty. Consider the extreme examples given in Figure 6.12. In the upper panel we have two different yield curves and in the lower panel the associated different CB price profiles. Imagine following a particular CB when the yield curve changes from the normal form to the inverted form. Although we cannot model the curve change it is possible to hedge out the effects of interest rate changes using futures and swaps and we deal with this in the next chapter.

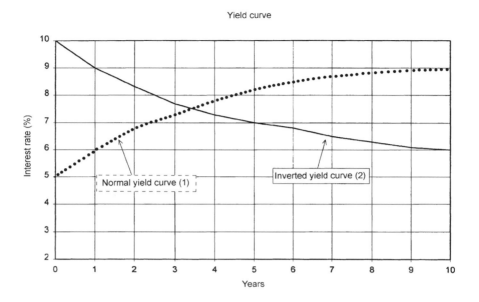

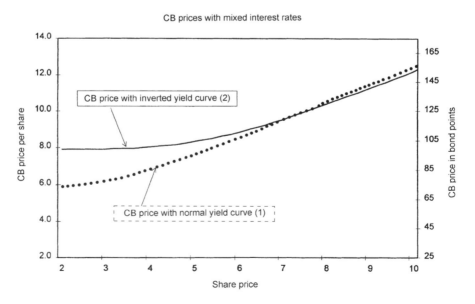

Figure 6.12 Changing yield curves

Another complication is the issue of interest rate changes/share price changes. It may be that interest rates and share prices are correlated in some way and this should also be incorporated in any model. It is, however, beyond the scope of this book to include the dual dynamics of interest rates and share prices.

6.5   NON-DOMESTIC CBs AND THE FOREIGN EXCHANGE COMPLICATION

There are many CBs that are issued in a non-domestic currency. An example would be a CB that is redeemable in, say, US dollars, but convertible into shares valued in pounds sterling. At the time of writing there are a number of CBs being issued by Asian corporations denominated in US dollars but convertible into local shares. These flotations are significant in that they allow foreigners to gain exposure to some equity markets for the first time. They also have allowed non-US corporations to raise funds in US dollars. The dual currency aspect, of course, introduces yet another source of complexity for the CB modeller. But before we consider the effects on CBs it is necessary to review the whole subject of investing in instruments that are priced in a different currency.

6.5.1   Foreign Currency Market Quotations

Spot and forward currency trades take place in what is probably the biggest market in the world. Each day, trillions of dollars worth of Yen, Pounds, Dollars, Marks, Francs and Lira are exchanged. The currencies can be traded forward (for future exchange) or spot (for immediate exchange). There are also well-established exchange-traded currency futures contracts. Most currencies are quoted in the press and the financial information services in relation to the US Dollar. At the time of writing the Swiss Franc is quoted on Reuters as 1.47. The market reads this as meaning 1US$ can be exchanged for 1.47 Swiss Francs. The German Mark rate quote is 1.71 meaning 1US$ can be exchanged for 1.71 Marks and the Japanese Yen quote is 114.0, so 1US$ can be exchanged for 114.0 Yen.

Unfortunately, the British Pound is quoted the other way round. At the time of writing the quoted rate is 1.67 and in this case this means that £1 can be exchanged for $1.67. For simplicity throughout this book we have dealt with CBs that are convertible into British shares quoted in sterling and so for continuity we will, as often as possible, convert everything into sterling terms. Later on we consider shares and CBs that are quoted in US Dollars and so will wish to convert everything into sterling. We will also be looking at buying and selling US Dollars as a hedging strategy. Accordingly, it is better to consider the Pound/US Dollar exchange rate quoted in the reverse sense, i.e., how many Pounds does 1 US Dollar cost? If the standard quoted rate is £1 equals $1.67 then £ (1/1.67) or £0.60 equals $1. An alternative way of thinking of this rate is to consider a US Dollar to be like a share.

How much does one of these shares cost? The answer is £ 0.60. So throughout the rest of this chapter we will talk about the reciprocal of the usual quoted price.

6.5.2 Investing in Foreign Equity

Before we consider CBs it is useful to look at the situation of an individual based in Britain (valuing everything in sterling) and investing in foreign equity. To make matters simpler we will restrict 'foreign' to meaning US Dollar investments. In the following examples we examine how the profit and loss of a foreign share can be significantly altered by movements in the exchange rate.

Say a British individual has £10,000 to invest. He decides to buy an American share priced initially at \$166.67. On the day of purchase, the US Dollar is priced at £ 0.60 (or £1 = \$1.6667) . He exchanges Pounds for Dollars and gets \$16,667. With this sum he can buy 100 shares. He can calculate the value of this portfolio in sterling using the simple expression

$$\text{Sterling value of portfolio} = \text{value of portfolio in dollars} \times \text{exchange rate}$$

or

$$\text{Sterling value of portfolio} = \text{no. of shares} \times \text{share price} \times \text{exchange rate} \quad (6.6)$$

Initially the portfolio value is therefore

$$\text{Sterling value of portfolio} = 100 \text{ shares} \times 166.67 \text{ \$} \times 0.60 \text{ £ per \$} = £10,000$$

Expression (6.6) tells us that the individual is now long of two investments — the US shares and the US dollar. If both increase in value then he will make a profit. If the share price increases to \$200 and the exchange rate increases to £0.70 then his portfolio value will increase to $100 \times 200 \times 0.70 = £14,000$. If both investments decrease in value then the portfolio will decrease in value. If the shares fall to \$130 and the dollar falls to \$0.50 then the portfolio value falls to $100 \times 130 \times 0.50 = £6,500$. If one price increases and the other falls the outcome depends on the relative magnitude of each movement. In certain circumstances the fall in one will cancel out the rise in the other. If the dollar share price rises in value by 10% but the dollar falls in value by 10%, then the portfolio value will remain unchanged.

Fluctuations in exchange rates can thus eliminate or reduce profits made in foreign shares. What confuses the issue is that it is difficult to separate out the effects of the share price changing and the effects of the exchange rate changing. We now show algebraically and graphically how this can be done. This will be particularly useful later when we look at currency hedging.

We begin by rewriting expression (6.6) algebraically. Let us assume that the number of shares is m, that the quoted dollar share price is S and that the exchange rate is F. The sterling value of the portfolio, V, is given by

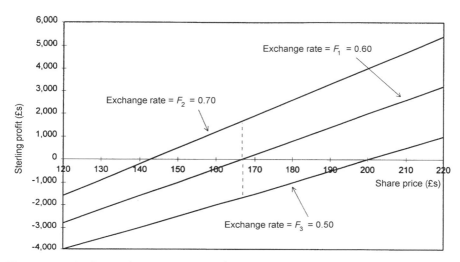

Figure 6.13   Sterling profit to investor in US$ equity

$$V = m.S.F \tag{6.7}$$

Say that the shares were initially bought when the dollar price was S_1 (= \$166.67) and the exchange rate was F_1 (= £0.60). The initial portfolio value is = $m. S_1. F_1$ = $100 \times 166.67 \times 0.60 = £10,000$. For the moment let us assume that the exchange rate stays constant at F_1 but that the share price varies. If the exchange rate stays fixed then the value of the portfolio will vary directly proportional to the share price. If the share price doubles or halves, so will the portfolio value. This is represented in Figure 6.13 by the straight line labelled 'Exchange rate = F_1 = 0.60'. Figure 6.13 shows the profits and losses to the portfolio by subtracting the initial £10,000 investment.

Now consider the situation of the share price remaining constant at S_1 but the exchange rate suddenly changing to F_2 = £0.70. The portfolio value has now increased to $m.S_1.F_2$ = $100 \times 166.67 \times 0.70 = £11,667$. This represents an increase in value of £1,667 and this is represented in Figure 6.13 by the vertical dashed line above the horizontal axis. Say the exchange rate were now to stay fixed at this higher level, but the share price start to move about. The portfolio value would again be directly proportional to the share price but the constant of proportionality would be higher and this is because each dollar change is worth more in sterling terms. This new profit and loss line is represented by the straight line labelled 'Exchange rate = F_2 = 0.70'. Note that the slope of this new line is steeper than the original one.

One can follow a similar argument for the case when the dollar weakens to F_3 = £0.50. With the dollar weaker there is an immediate loss represented by the vertical dashed line below the horizontal axis and the new profit and loss is given by the straight line labelled 'Exchange rate $= F_3 = 0.50$' which has a smaller gradient than the original.

Figure 6.13 clearly shows the separate effects of changing share price and exchange rates. Only three different exchange rates are shown but it is possible to imagine a set of 100 or so different lines each representing a different exchange rate. Each line radiates from the point corresponding to a share price of zero and a profit of £10,000 that is not shown. Each line corresponds to a different exchange rate. The higher the exchange rate the steeper the line. The separate effects of share price changes and exchange rate changes thus have a direct graphic interpretation.

1. The vertical distance between any two lines represents the immediate profit or loss due to the exchange rate changing from one value to another at any given fixed share price.
2. The straight lines represent the profit or loss due to share price changes at any fixed exchange rate.

We now show how it is possible to use foreign currency to hedge away some of these losses (and of course profits).

6.5.3 Hedging Foreign Equity Investments

When the sterling investor above buys US equity he will be aware that he has now exposed himself to two sources of risk — the share price and the price of the currency. He may or may not be happy with this situation. If he likes the share but is not sure about the direction of the currency, then he will need to take action to hedge out the foreign exchange rate risk. In the example given, to buy the shares he exchanged £10,000 and bought $16,667. He then used the dollars to buy 100 shares at $166.67 each. At this stage he is long of $16,667 worth of risk. If the share price collapses to zero he will lose $16,667; if the value of the dollar collapses to zero then he will also lose $16,667.

For the moment we leave aside the share price risk. Assume that the share price stays constant. How can he remove the risk of the dollar collapsing, or indeed weakening slightly? There are many ways of doing this, but by far the simplest is to *sell dollars forward*. Using forwards or futures contracts, it is possible to enter into a short position in dollars. Let us assume that the future $/£ exchange rate is the same as the current or spot rate at £0.60 per $1. The share portfolio is valued at $16,667 and so a short position of $16,667 is required for a perfect hedge. In the jargon of the market-place the investor sells forward $16,667 in exchange for £10,000. Now consider the situation under the following two exchange rate moves:

1. The dollar strengthens to $F_2 = £0.70$. The share value increases to $100 \times 166.67 \times 0.70 = £11,667$ — a profit of £1,667. However, the foreign exchange position has lost money. The dollar was shorted at £0.60 and at £0.70 represents

a loss of $0.1 \times 16{,}667 = £1{,}667$. The profit on the shares is exactly cancelled by the loss on the dollar position.

2. The dollar weakens to $F_3 = £0.50$. The share value decreases to $100 \times 166.67 \times 0.50 = £8{,}333$ — a loss of £1,667. However, the foreign exchange position has made money. The dollar was shorted at £0.60 and at £0.50 represents a gain of $0.1 \times 16{,}667 = £1{,}667$. The loss on the shares is exactly cancelled by the gain on the dollar position.

So the share position has been made immune to fluctuations in the price of the dollar — the sterling investor has hedged away his currency risk. The combined position of long US shares and short dollars is equivalent to being long the shares priced in pounds. And this works for any \$/£ exchange rate changes. We show this algebraically as follows. Using the above notation, the value V_1 of the portfolio at share price S and an exchange rate of F_1 is given by

$$V_1 = m.S.F_1$$

If the share price stays fixed at S but the exchange rate changes to F_2 then the new share value is

$$V_2 = m.S.F_2$$

The profit or loss on the share portfolio will be the difference:

$$
\begin{aligned}
\text{Profit on shares} &= V_2 - V_1 \\
&= m.S.(F_2 - F_1)
\end{aligned}
\tag{6.8}
$$

The profit or loss on the foreign exchange side is calculated as follows. The initial portfolio contained $m.S$ dollars and so $m.S$ dollars were sold short at F_1. At the new rate of F_2 the profit would be

$$\text{Profit on foreign exchange trade} = m.S.(F_1 - F_2) \tag{6.9}$$

The total overall profit is therefore

$$
\begin{aligned}
\text{Total profit} &= \text{Profit on shares} + \text{profit on foreign exchange trade} \\
&= m.S.(F_2 - F_1) + m.S.(F_1 - F_2) = 0
\end{aligned}
\tag{6.10}
$$

Expression (6.10) is valid for all values of F_1 and F_2 provided the share price, S, stays constant.

The interesting thing about this portfolio of dollar-denominated shares and a short position in the \$/£ exchange rate is that the total portfolio behaves as if the shares were denominated in pounds. It is as if the investor has converted his dollar shares into pound shares — he will be completely indifferent to the exchange rate.

There is a problem, however, if the share price *and* the foreign exchange rate change. Let the initial share price be denoted by S_1. As before, to hedge out the currency risk the investor sells $m.S_1.F_1$ dollars at a rate of F_1. If after some time the exchange rate has changed to F_2 and at the same time, the share price has changed to S_2, then the situation is different. The share portfolio values V_1 and V_2 are now given by the expressions

$$V_1 = m.S_1.F_1 \quad \text{and} \quad V_2 = m.S_2.F_2$$

so the profit on the share portfolio will now be

$$\text{Profit on shares} = V_2 - V_1$$
$$= m.S_2.F_2 - m.S_1.F_1$$

The profit on the currency trade is given by

$$\text{Profit on foreign exchange trade} = m.S_1.(F_1 - F_2)$$

So the total profit is as before, the sum of profits or losses on both components, i.e.,

$$\text{Total profit} = \text{Profit on shares} + \text{profit on foreign exchange trade}$$
$$= m.S_2.F_2 - m.S_1.F_1 + m.S_1.(F_1 - F_2)$$
$$= m.F_2.(S_2 - S_1) \tag{6.11}$$

If $S_2 > S_1$ a profit results and if $S_2 < S_1$ a loss results, the degree depending on the new exchange rate. The situation is depicted in Figure 6.14.

If $S_2 > S_1$ a profit results, whatever happens to the exchange rate. However, the higher F_2, the higher the profit. This is because at a higher share price the dollar value of the share portfolio is higher and although the currency changes have been hedged, the hedge was for a lower amount. If the share price increases the investor gets lucky in that he only hedged out his original dollar amount. We can follow a similar argument for the case of the new exchange rate being lower. Figure 6.14 illustrates clearly that the currency exchange trade hedges out the currency risk perfectly at only one share price — the original share price. Once the underlying share price changes the portfolio is no longer hedged and if the investor wished to stay currency neutral he would have to carry out additional exchange rate trades.

In our example the investor starts with £10,000 ($16,667) worth of shares. The perfect hedge would be to sell forward $16,667. Say the share price were to increase from $166.67 to $166.70. The portfolio value is now $16,670 and so the currency hedge would have to be increased by selling a further $16,670 - 16,667 = $3. This procedure could be carried out each time the share price moved. As the share price increases, the currency hedge would be increased. As the share price decreases, the currency hedge would be decreased. In this way the portfolio would change in value reflecting only the dollar change in share price. As before, it would be as if the investor were involved in shares quoted in pounds.

There are two problems with the above exposition. First, when dealing in currency forwards or futures it is not possible to deal in small amounts. Small share

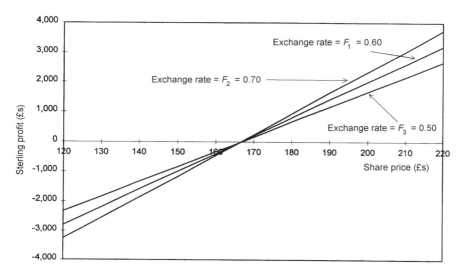

Figure 6.14   Sterling profits to investor in US$ equity with fixed currency hedge

price changes causing small valuation changes could not be hedged out. There would be some minimum price change below which one could not hedge. Secondly, the above argument conveniently assumes that the share price moves and then the currency price moves. This is of course not so. In reality both prices are moving constantly. And this means that there will be occasions when profits enjoyed by an unhedged dollar investor will not be enjoyed by the sterling investor.

To illustrate we consider an extreme example. Say the initial share price is $100 and the initial exchange rate is £0.60. If the share price increases from $100 to $105 the dollar investor makes a profit of 5%. Say the $/£ exchange rate were to simultaneously fall from £0.60 to £0.54 — a drop of 10%. It is left as an exercise for the reader to show that the hedged sterling investor makes a profit of 4.5%, not the 5% enjoyed by the dollar investor. There of course will be occasions when the opposite occurs, i.e., the sterling investor enjoying more profits than the dollar investor. If the share price movements and the currency movements are completely uncorrelated, then in the long run, the two effects should cancel out.

Figure 6.15 shows the outcome of one set of simulations to illustrate what happens over time to a foreign share portfolio that is continually dynamically hedged against currency moves. The upper panel shows the two price series on the same chart. The share price starts at $100 and after 300 different up and down movements finishes at $187. The currency rate starts at £0.50 and after 300 different up and down movements finishes at £0.43. The lower panel of Figure 6.15 plots the value of the dollar share price and the share portfolio dynamically hedged at each of the different 300 time points, rebased to 100. Note that the two plots do not coincide perfectly. There are times when the hedged portfolio is worth more

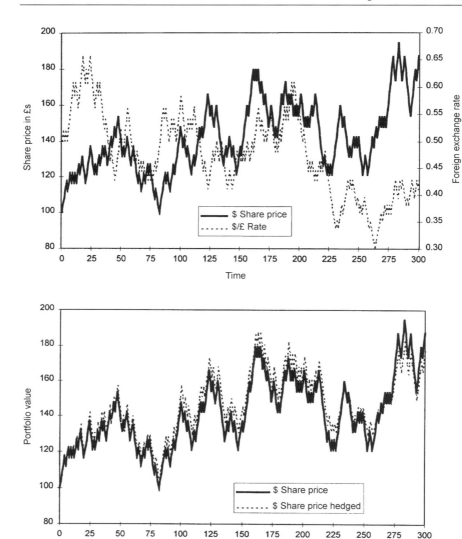

Figure 6.15 Joint share prices and currency price simulations

than the unhedged portfolio and times when the reverse is the case. The hedged portfolio ends up with an 80% profit compared to the 87% profit enjoyed by the dollar investor. The two charts are different but not by much.

There is one final point to make in relation to hedging out currency risks; that it is associated with interest rates will come as no surprise. In the above, when talking about establishing a short position in dollars, we conveniently assumed that the future or forward rate was always equal to the spot or current rate. This is often not the case. In fact there is a direct relationship between future rates, spot rates and interest rates. This has to be the case, otherwise zero risk arbitrage profits could be made. Consider the following imaginary example.

Let us assume that today the spot and the one-year forward $/£ rates are 0.50. Let us also assume that the one-year interest rates are 20% in dollars and 5% in sterling. We have £100 on deposit which will earn interest of £5 in one year's time. We see that the dollar rates are far higher so we exchange £100 for $200 and earn interest of 20% or $40 in one year's time. The problem is that although the dollars earn a higher interest rate there is the risk that the currency will weaken and we could lose far more than the $40 made in interest. To remove this currency risk we establish a short position in the forward $/£ market. On day one we would simultaneously exchange £100 for $200 at the spot rate of £0.50 and sell $240 forward at the forward rate of £0.50. It is left as an exercise for the reader to show that whatever happens to the spot rate in one year's time, the original sum of £100 will be turned into £120. The sterling investor has been able to get a risk-free return of 20%. If this situation existed in reality an investor could borrow £s at 5% and make 20%. The excess return of 15% could be geared up 20 or 30 times to produce risk-free returns in excess of 100%. So something must be wrong. It is. If dollar interest rates are 20% and sterling interest rates are 5% the forward exchange rate and the spot exchange rate cannot be the same. With dollar rates higher than sterling rates the forward exchange rate must be lower than the spot rate. Indeed for no arbitrage, the forward rate will be given by the following expression:

$$\text{forward rate} = \text{spot rate} \times \frac{1 + \text{domestic interest rate}}{1 + \text{foreign interest rate}}$$

Using this expression with the spot rate = 0.50 and interest rates at 5% and 20% we get a forward rate of 0.4375. It is left as an exercise for the reader to show that using this forward rate no arbitrage profit will be available. Exchanging £100 for $200 today and hedging by selling dollars forward will result in a sterling return of 5%. The portfolio of long real dollars earning 20% and short dollars forward result in a return identical to that of staying long sterling. The difference in the dollar and sterling interest rates will always be reflected in the forward rate. This fact is important when we go on to consider non-domestic CBs. When hedging non-domestic CBs we will be shorting shares in sterling and hedging out the currency risk using futures or forwards.

6.5.4 Introducing the Foreign Exchange Rate Complication on the Day of Expiry

We now show how, using the above hedging techniques, it is possible to begin to include the foreign exchange rate complication in the binomial CB model. As always we use ABC Bank as an example. Up until this stage in the book we have always assumed that the nominal value of the CB has been £5,000. Let us now assume that the bank issues a CB that is denominated in US dollars but convertible into ABC Bank shares quoted in sterling. On the day of issue the share price was £8.00 and the exchange rate was £0.50 (or £1 = $2). If the bond is to be converted into 625 shares then the nominal value will be = 625 × 8 = £5,000 or $10,000. This would be the typical nominal value of a US dollar-denominated CB. As with all CBs, the market would quote such an instrument as a percentage of the nominal value in bond points. So if the bond were trading at, say, 95 points, then the actual price paid would be 95% of $10,000 or $9,500. As before, it is useful to break down the CB into a per share basis. The nominal value of the bond is $10,000 or 10,000/625 = $16 per share.

The interesting thing about this and all non-domestic CBs is that the terms are fixed on the issue date. The foreign exchange rate used to determine the conversion ratio and the conversion price are really only valid for that one day. Once issued the conversion price is continually changing — the value depending on the current exchange rate. We illustrate by considering what will happen on the expiry date under three different scenarios and look at the CB on a per share basis.

1. *Expiring exchange rate = £0.50*   On expiry the holder of the CB must decide what to do. Does he convert or redeem? Converting will result in the delivery of one share. Redeeming will result in the payment of $16. With the exchange rate at £0.50 the pivotal price would be £8. At prices above £8 the optimal strategy would be to convert. Say the expiring share price were £10, then 10 / 0.50 = $20 is greater than the redemption value of $16. If the expiring share price were £7, then 7 / 0.50 = $14 is lower than the redemption value. If the exchange rate on expiry equals that on issue then the pivotal price equals the conversion price in the issue document.

2. *Expiring exchange rate = £0.60*   At this exchange rate the pivotal price would be 16 × 0.60 = £9.60. If the share price were £9 then the dollar price would be 9 / 0.6 = $15.00. So in this case, because the dollar is so strong, even with the share price as high as £9, it still makes sense to redeem rather than convert. At all prices higher than £9.60 it makes sense to convert. If the exchange rate on expiry is higher than that on issue then the pivotal price is greater than the conversion price in the issue document. The real conversion price is higher than that originally set.

3. *Expiring exchange rate = £0.40*   At this exchange rate the pivotal price would be 16 × 0.40 = £6.40. If the share price were £7 then the dollar price would be 7 / 0.4 = $17.50. So in this case because the dollar is so weak, even with the share price as low as £7, it makes sense to convert rather than redeem. At all prices higher than £6.40 it makes sense to convert. If the exchange rate on expiry is lower than that on issue then the pivotal price is lower than the conversion price in the issue document. The real conversion price is lower than that originally set.

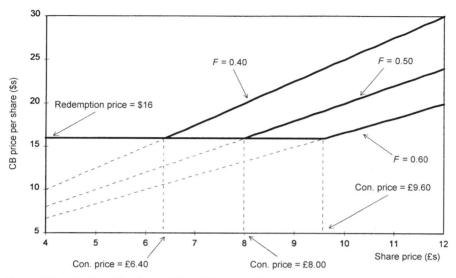

Figure 6.16   Expiring CB price in ($s) at different exchange rates

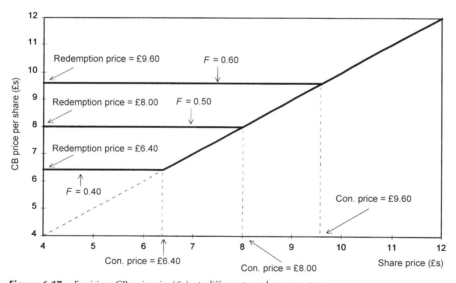

Figure 6.17   Expiring CB price in (£s) at different exchange rates

So although on issue the conversion price was set to £8, because the CB redeems into dollars the real conversion price depends on the expiring exchange rate. This is illustrated in Figure 6.16 which shows the expiring price profile under the above three scenarios. An alternative way of looking at this instrument is plotting the CB

Share price move	Currency price move	Share price ($)	Redeem or convert?

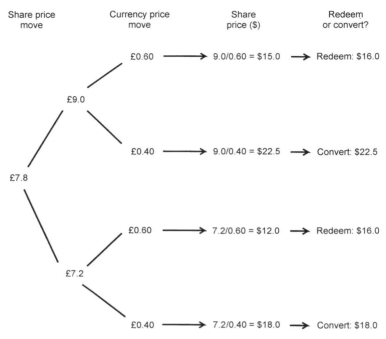

Figure 6.18   The one-period non-domestic CB model; redemption price = $16

price expressed in pounds against the sterling share price. This is given in Figure 6.17.

6.5.5   The One-period CB Model with Currency Complication — A Problem

We return to the very simplest CB model considered at the beginning of Chapter 5. In this model the initial share price is £7.8 and can either rise to £9.0 or fall to £7.2. With the conversion price set at £8.0 the decision process on expiry is simple. With the share price at £9.0 we convert into shares, sell and pocket £9.0. With the share price at £7.2 we redeem and get to keep £8.0. In Section 5.2 we showed using the two-way bet argument that the fair price for this CB was £8.33 per share. We now introduce the currency complication. As above, let the CB have a redemption value of $16. If the currency rate stays fixed at £0.50 per $1, the redemption value and hence conversion price will be £8.0. Now let the currency rate also change to one of two values: up to £0.60 or down to £0.40. The situation is depicted in Figure 6.18. With two different final share prices and two different final currency rates there are four different final outcomes. In order to decide whether to convert or redeem we must choose the route that maximises the expiring CB's value. Since the redemption price is in dollars we must compare this with the share price expressed in dollars. Figure 6.18 shows that the four different expiring dollar share prices are $15.0, $22.5, $12.0 and $18.0. The optimal strategy is to pick the maximum of these values and $16. So the four expiring CB values would be: $16.0, $22.5, $16.0 and $18.0 respectively.

Although the optimal strategy is obvious after the event, it is not possible to construct a portfolio of shares, CBs and currency forwards that give a single fair value. And this is because we do not have a two-way bet situation. There are four different final outcomes, not two. Is it therefore not possible to solve the non-domestic CB problem? Well, yes and no.

Recall that throughout Chapter 5 it was stressed that the issue of chance never came into the modelling process. The p and q parameters used in the model were simple functions of the up and down multipliers, not probabilities. So whatever the probability of an up or down move, the CB fair value would always be the same. It was shown later that if the p and q values were assumed to be the probability of up and down moves, then the CB fair value could be thought of as an expected fair value and the two-way bet zero arbitrage value and the probabilistic or expected fair value turn out to be the same. And that is how we get around the problem of the non-domestic CB. We have to resort to a probabilistic argument. We have to assign probabilities to each of the four different outcomes listed in Figure 6.18. If these probabilities are known then one can derive the composition of a portfolio of shares, CBs and currency forwards that will (in the long run) yield the risk-free rate. The price of the CB in this portfolio will be the fair value.

The real problem is in the determination of the probabilities. We could, of course, fall back on the p and q values associated with the share price process in the standard binomial share price model. And we could similarly construct p and q values for a binomial currency price process. But what about the joint movement of share and currency price? Up until now we have conveniently ignored the possibility that there could be a link between share price and currency. If there is, then how would it be specified? This topic is beyond the scope of this book. However, we continue by approaching the problem from a slightly different angle.

6.5.6   The n-Period CB Model with Currency Complication: A Dynamic Hedging Approach

If we assume that the share and currency processes are uncorrelated there is a simple solution. Recall the situation of the sterling investor buying dollar-denominated stock. By selling dollars forward and continually adjusting the hedge we showed that, in the long run, the profit or loss on his portfolio would exactly match that experienced by a dollar investor. The same approach could be used by a dollar investor involved in a share price quoted in sterling. He would sell forward the equivalent sterling amount and continually rehedge. The net result would be the same as if the dollar investor was long a dollar-denominated share.

Consider now our non-domestic CB with four or five years to go before expiry. Since the redemption value is in dollars and is fixed, it makes sense to convert the sterling share price into dollars by selling pounds forward. If the currency hedge is continually adjusted, the total value of the shares and forward contracts would exactly match that of a dollar-denominated share. If initially the currency rate was £0.50 per $1, then the short position in shares used to adjust the CB is essentially converted into dollars. It will be as if the dollar CB is convertible into dollar shares, with everything fixed at a rate of £0.5 per $1. If the initial currency rate was £0.6 per $1 then the continual currency rehedging essentially turns the problem into one with the exchange rate fixed at £0.60 per $1. So the CB price profile before expiry can be made independent of currency considerations by continually adjusting the hedge. The situation is depicted in Figure 6.19 for a 50-period model.

The fascinating aspect of this approach is that the interest rate considerations are automatically taken into account. With the standard CB hedged with short shares there are two interests to consider; one associated with the long CB and one associated with the short share proceeds. With the non-domestic CB, the interest rate associated with the long side will of course be the credit-adjusted dollar rate corresponding to the appropriate time horizon. The short shares produce a positive sterling cash flow. With no currency hedge these cash proceeds would yield the short-term sterling interest rate. By simultaneously selling pounds forward the sterling share price is converted into a dollar share price *and at the same time* the sterling interest rate is converted into a dollar interest rate. Hedging out the currency risk transfers the modelling process completely into one involving dollars.

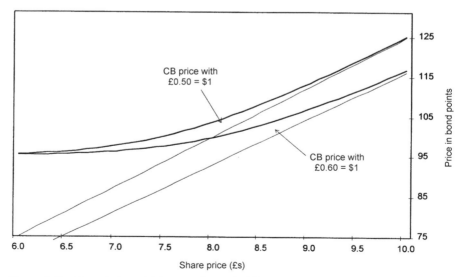

Figure 6.19   50-period model for non-domestic CB

7
Convertible bond sensitivities

Almost as important as pricing CBs is the estimation of the price sensitivities. Sensitivities are measures of the way CB prices vary when the value of some underlying variable varies. Some of these sensitivities can be thought of as slopes of lines or curves. Others can be thought of as absolute shifts in lines or curves. Many sensitivities are given a Greek symbol and the study of sensitivities is often referred to as studying the Greeks. The usual sensitivities are of the first-order type — measuring the change in price with respect to the change in something else. We will also discuss second-order sensitivities — the change in a first-order sensitivity when something else changes. These characteristics are important to hedgers, speculators and fund managers.

7.1 CALCULATION OF CB SENSITIVITIES

If the CB price curve were in a closed form such as an algebraic equation then one could simply resort to differential calculus. Unfortunately, as we have seen in Chapters 5 and 6, all the extra complications associated with CBs mean that a non-closed form binomial model is usually necessary. Therefore the most straightforward way of finding a given sensitivity is to alter the value of the underlying variable and generate a new binomial tree. This is time consuming and there are extra complications associated with choosing the appropriate number of periods in the tree. However, the sensitivity of a CB price with respect to movements in the underlying share price — the delta, lends itself to a particularly simple solution that does not require recalculation through a binomial tree. For consistency throughout this chapter we will use various versions of the ABC Bank CB to illustrate numerical examples. And for simplicity in this chapter we will make the following assumptions about the CB: the underlying share pays no dividends; the CB pays no coupons; there is no short call provision and there is no put.

7.2 THE DELTA OR HEDGE RATIO — SENSITIVITY TO THE UNDERLYING SHARE PRICE

Probably the most important CB sensitivity measure is the 'delta'. We came across this measure earlier on in Chapter 5 when we referred to it as the 'hedge ratio'. The hedge ratio is important because it tells the hedger what ratio of shares to sell against a long position in CBs, but we show below that it can be also used as a measure of CB sensitivity to share price change. Recall that the calculation of the CB fair value for the one-period model given in Chapter 5 is:

$$CB_f = \frac{pCB_u + qCB_d}{1 + r}$$

Where CB_u and CB_d are the CB prices corresponding to the two different expiring share prices $S.u$ and $S.d$ respectively and are given by:

$$CB_u = \text{Max}\ \{S.u,\ E\} \quad \text{and} \quad CB_d = \text{Max}\ \{S.d,\ E\}$$

For the example in which $S = 7.8$, $S.u = 9.0$, $S.d = 7.2$, $E = 8$, $r = 0.05$ and the time period was one year, the fair value reduced to three sets of linear equations

(a) $CB_f = S$, if $8.67 < S$
(b) $CB_f = 0.60\ S + 3.43$, if $6.93 < S < 8.67$
(c) $CB_f = 7.62$, if $S < 6.93$

The graphical representation of these appears in the upper panel of Figure 7.1.
   Recall also that the hedge ratio is given by the expression

$$h = \frac{CB_u - CB_d}{S.u - S.d}$$

Following the same argument we note that the CB_u and CB_d expressions are either a constant or a linear function of S (depending on the value of S) and that the hedge ratio reduces to three sets of equations:

(a) $h = 1$, if $8.67 < S$
(b) $h = 5 - 34.67\ /\ S$, if $6.93 < S < 8.67$
(c) $h = 0$, if $S < 6.93$

The lower panel in Figure 7.1 illustrates graphically the relationship between the hedge ratio and the underlying share price. At very low share prices the hedge ratio is zero. At very high share prices the hedge ratio is 1. At intermediate share prices the hedge ratio is somewhere between these two extremes.
   The one-period model has only *two* different final share prices and this results in the model price and the hedge ratio being given by *three* different sets of disjoint equations. In the case of the CB prices, the equations are linear in S and so appear

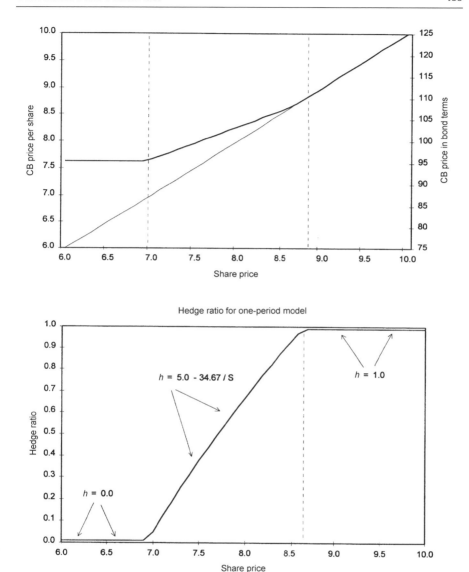

Figure 7.1   One-period model CB price

as straight lines. The hedge ratio equation is a function of the inverse of S and so appears as a slightly curved line.

We now extend the hedge ratio calculation to the two-period case. Following a similar approach to that used in modelling the price, the two-period hedge ratio expression is:

$$h = \frac{CB_u - CB_d}{S.u - S.d}$$

$$= \frac{p.CB_{uu} - (p - q).CB_{ud} - q.CB_{dd}}{(1 + r).S.(u - d)}$$

To convert this into an expression involving the share price, we must express the final CB values in the usual way, i.e., $CB_{uu} = \text{Max}\{S.u^2, 8\}$, $CB_{ud} = \text{Max}\{S.u.d, 8\}$ and $CB_{dd} = \text{Max}\{S.d^2, 8\}$. Substituting the appropriate values of u, d, p, q and r we get

(a) $h = 1$, if $8.67 < S$
(b) $h = 5.60 - 38.81/S$, if $7.75 < S < 8.67$
(c) $h = 4.47 - 30.04/S$, if $6.93 < S < 7.75$
(d) $h = 0$, if $S < 6.93$

With the two-period model there are three different possible final share prices and hence four different sets of disjoint equations. As with the one-period model, the equations express the hedge ratio as a function of the inverse of S and are hence curved. Figure 7.2 shows the price and hedge ratio of the CB in question.

We can extend the above process to the general n-period model. As n increases, so does the number of final share prices and so does the number of separate equations. It is easy to see that each equation will be of the form

$$h = a - b/S$$

where a and b are certain constants. With $n = 50$ there will be 52 different equations. Figure 7.3 shows the 50-period model price and hedge ratio of the ABC Bank CB with volatility set to 15%, the interest rate set to 5% and the time to expiry set to one year. To the eye both curves look smooth, but they are in fact 52 different sets of curves and lines.

Until now we have referred to the hedge ratio as being a number that tells the hedger the correct number of shares to short against a CB position. If the hedge ratio is 0.40 and a CB is convertible into 625 shares then one CB should be hedged by selling $0.40 \times 625 = 250$ shares. But if the model used has a sufficient number of periods, then the hedge ratio also tells us something else — it is the price sensitivity of the CB to movements in the share price. To see why this is the case consider the example in Figure 7.3. With the share price at £7.30 the CB is priced at £7.92 per share (or 99 bond points) and the hedge ratio is 0.40. A hedger long one CB will need to sell 250 shares. If the share price increases by a small amount, say £0.10 to £7.40, then the CB price increases from £7.92 to £7.96 per share — a change of £0.04. The profit on the long CB side is $£0.04 \times 625 = £25.00$ and the loss on the short share side is $£0.10 \times 250 = £25.00$. The profits are cancelled by the losses. This is what we would expect. The portfolio is hedged so we would not expect to make a profit or loss. If the share price were to fall £0.10 from £7.30 to

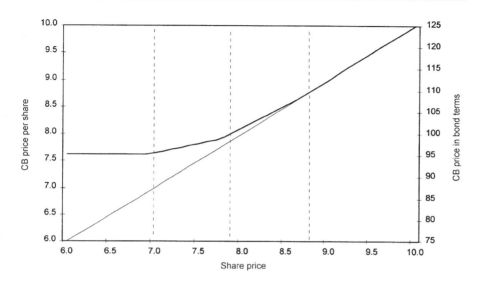

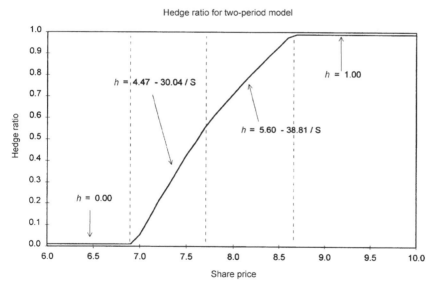

Figure 7.2 Two-period model CB price

£7.20 then the CB price would fall £0.04 from £7.92 to £7.88 per share. In this case the losses on the CB side are completely cancelled by the profits on the short share side. So the portfolio is immune to profits and losses for small share price movements.

Now consider a speculator or fund manager who is not interested in a hedged

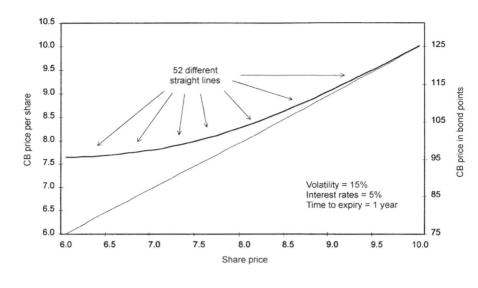

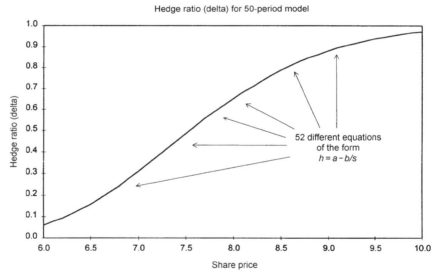

Figure 7.3 50-period model, ABC bank

position, but is interested in taking a bullish positive view on the share and CB price. This individual, though not interested in the hedge ratio as a means to remove risk, can use the number as a way of forecasting the future movements of the CB if the underlying share price moves. Look again at the above example. If the share price rises (falls) £0.10 then the hedge ratio tells us that the CB price must rise (fall) by £0.04. The hedge ratio of 0.40 tells us that the CB price will move by a factor of 40% of the underlying share price. When used in this sense the hedge ratio is usually referred to as the delta. The delta of any derivative product is a number that gives the sensitivity to changes to prices in whatever underlies the instrument.

We see from Figure 7.3 that the delta of a CB depends on the price of the share. When the share price is low the delta is low. At low share prices the instrument behaves more like a bond than equity and so is insensitive to price movements. In the limit, at very low share prices the delta approaches zero. At very low share prices CBs are completely unconnected to the underlying share price.

At high share prices the delta is high. From Figure 7.3 we see that when the share price is at £8.80 the delta is 0.85. At this level the CB price will catch 85% of the share price change. At very high share prices the delta approaches the limiting value of 1.0. In this example at any share price above £9.80 the delta is 1.0. At these very high prices a CB behaves exactly like the underlying share.

One final point is worth noting on the interpretation of the delta. Since it is the price sensitivity of the CB with respect to the share price we can see that it therefore must be the slope or gradient of the CB price curve. At low share prices the curve is flat and horizontal — the delta is zero. At high share prices the curve becomes a straight line that is parallel to the parity line. The parity line by definition has a slope of 1.00 — at high share prices the delta is 1.00.

7.3 THETA — TIME DECAY

Most derivative instruments involving an option component suffer time decay. The time decay or rate at which the price changes from day to day or week to week is usually referred to as 'theta'. The most straightforward way to calculate the time decay of a CB is to use the binomial model to calculate the price today, then alter the time parameter by a given amount and then recalculate the price. The theta is the change in price. As an example with one year (52 weeks) to expiry, a volatility of 15%, interest rates at 5% and a share price of £8.00, the ABC Bank CB is priced at £8.2984. With 51 weeks to expiry the CB is priced at £8.2970, a drop of £0.0014 per share. This small change would translate into a fall in price of 0.0175 bond points. In this example we used a week as the unit of time change. This was because with a year to go the instrument price does not change much over time. With exchange-traded options with only months of life, the theta is often measured over a period of one day.

Figure 7.4 illustrates how the theta of a CB varies with the underlying share price and is produced by carrying out the above procedure at many different share price levels. Since the theta values are very small it is necessary to use a very large number of periods. Smooth plots like that in Figure 7.4 need models with more than 1,000 periods.

Note that at low share prices the theta is actually positive, i.e., the instrument price increases as time passes. At very high share prices the theta is almost zero and

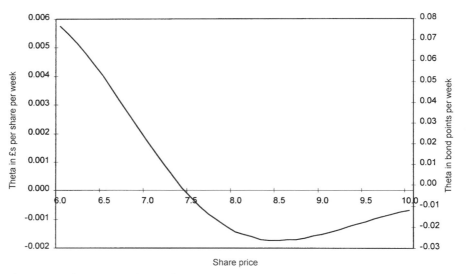

Figure 7.4   Theta – time decay of a CB

with the share price around £8.00, the time decay is maximum. This behaviour can be explained if we think of a CB as a mixture of a bond (zero coupon in this case) and an equity call option. At very low share prices the call option component will be almost worthless and so will have virtually no time decay. So at very low share prices the CB behaves purely like a zero coupon bond redeemable at £8.00. With one year to expiry the bond will be priced to reflect the discounted value of £8.00. As time passes the sum of £8.00 is getting nearer and nearer and so the discounting effect will be less and less. As time passes such zero coupon bonds obviously increase in value and this is what we are witnessing.

As one considers higher share prices, the equity call option component begins to have an effect. Equity options always suffer time decay and this will reduce the positive theta effects of the bond. As one considers higher and higher share prices there comes a point when the positive theta effects of the bond components are completely cancelled by the negative theta effects of the call option component. In this example this happens at a share price of £7.40.

At even higher share prices the option component has most effect, resulting in a maximum negative theta effect of −£0.002 per share per week. At very high share prices the time decay of the option begins to diminish and in the limit the two opposing effects eventually completely cancel one another out. At very high share prices CBs suffer no time decay — they behave just like straight equity.

This time decay behaviour is unusual in the field of derivatives. A CB has positive time decay at one share price and negative at another. We will return to this property in Chapter 8 when we revisit a simple CB modelled as a package of a bond plus equity call option.

7.4 VEGA — VOLATILITY SENSITIVITY

Equity call option prices depend on, amongst other things, the volatility of the underlying share price. It should not be surprising therefore that CBs are also sensitive to volatility. The industry standard measure of volatility sensitivity is 'vega'. Vega is usually defined as the change in price caused by volatility increasing by 1% point. With one year to expiry, a volatility of 15%, interest rates at 5% and the underlying share price at £8.00, the ABC Bank CB is priced at £8.2984. If we change the volatility to 16% the price increases to £8.3278. This increase of £0.0294 per share or 0.3675 bond points is the vega at this price level.

Figure 7.5 illustrates how the vega of a CB varies with the underlying share price and is produced by carrying out the above differencing calculation at many different share price levels. As with the theta calculations, since the values are very small it is necessary to use a very large number of periods.

Note that the volatility sensitivity is maximum with the share price at £7.50. At this level a change in volatility from 15% to 16% results in an increase in price of £0.0299 per share or 0.3730 points per bond. At share prices higher and lower than this value the vega decreases in a non-linear or curved manner. This reflects perfectly the characteristics of the embedded equity call option. Both types of derivative are most sensitive to volatility changes when the share price is near the exercise or conversion price.

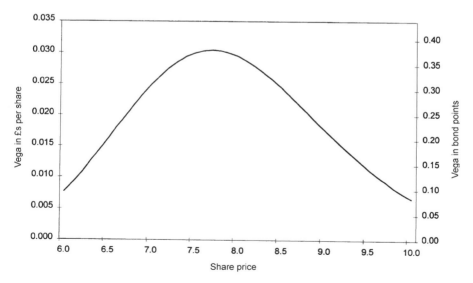

Figure 7.5 Vega – the volatility sensitivity of a CB

7.4.1   What Volatility to Use in Pricing CBs

It is instructive at this point to address the question of what volatility to input into the CB model. Many practitioners use the calculated historic volatility as outlined in Chapter 3. But what time period do we use and what frequency of observations is appropriate? Individuals involved in exchange traded equity call options with expiry cycles of 3, 6 and 9 months, typically use short-dated volatility estimates. The last 30 or 60 days' closing prices could be used to estimate the likely future volatility for such options. But CBs are long-dated instruments, some with lives of up to 20 years and using such short-dated estimates does not really make sense. The real problem is that short-dated volatility is not constant. In the jargon of the market place — the volatility is volatile. A particular share price might go through long periods when the underlying volatility is low (at, say, 10%) and then suddenly experience periods of rapid price movements with volatilities as high as 40%. Most empirical research shows that volatility changes over time but generally tends to return to some mean level. This reversion to the mean is the subject of much academic research and is beyond the scope of this book.

Many studies also show that longer-dated volatility values are lower than shorter-dated volatility values. This may imply that the underlying share price generating process is not completely random. If there is a tendency for prices to reverse then volatility estimates calculated over long time periods will be smaller than those calculated over shorter time periods. This topic was addressed in Chapter 4 where models with extreme share price reversalling were discussed. Whether the underlying process is non-random or not, the classical hedger needs to know when to rehedge his portfolio. If the long-term volatility estimate is 20% and the short-term estimate is 30%, it makes more sense to use the more conservative (i.e., lower) value of 20%.

7.4.2   The Implied Volatility of a CB — A Measure of Relative Value

Probably the most common volatility term referred to in the CB market (or indeed in any derivative product market) is the 'implied volatility'. The binomial CB model requires a number of inputs: the share price, the conversion price, the coupon details, the dividend details, the expiry time, the number of periods, the (two) interest rates and an estimate of the future volatility of the share price. Most of these inputs are directly observable, measurable and not subject to question — the volatility, however, is not. Say two individual market participants have differing views on the future share price volatility. As an extreme example, say one individual thinks the future volatility will be 20% and the other thinks it will be 45%. Substituting these two values into our ABC Bank CB model gives prices of 107.1 and 124.1 bond points respectively. Say a third individual is convinced the volatility will be 25%; his model price will be 110.5 bond points. In fact it is possible to think of the problem as one just involving the volatility input and the model price. Figure 7.6 is a plot of different CB model prices versus the different volatility inputs (all other parameters being kept constant). This diagram (or the appropriate Excel function) could be used to translate an individual's volatility estimate directly into a CB price.

This is all very well, but what if in this example, the actual market price of the CB is 115.0 bond points? What is the market price telling us? We can use Figure 7.6 in a reverse sense to work back and find out what volatility would give a model value exactly equal to 115.0 bond points. In this case the answer is 32%. If we use a volatility input of 32%, then the model price matches the market price. In the market jargon we say that the actual price of 115.0 bond points is 'implying' a volatility of 32%. Put more simply we say that the 'implied volatility' of the CB is 32%. So although one individual thinks the volatility should be 20% and another thinks it should be 45%, the market is saying it will probably be 32%.

For hedgers trading long volatility, the implied volatility of a CB is the most important measure of value. Other things being equal, CBs with low implied volatilities are better value than ones with high implied volatilities. If a hedger buys a CB on an implied volatility of 10%, convinced that the underlying share will exhibit a volatility of 20%, then he will make a profit whatever direction the share price takes. The implied volatility is also a much better measure of value than the naïve break-even or premium measures. The implied volatility has all the complications associated with the CB embedded in one number.

But how do we calculate the implied volatility of any CB? It does not make sense to draw graphs like the one in Figure 7.6. One way would be to try many different

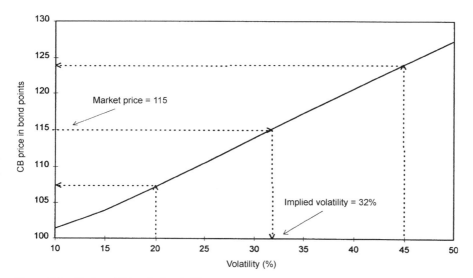

Figure 7.6 Finding CB implied volatility

volatility values and see which one gives a model price that matches the market price. But this could take forever. Remember each n-period model evaluation involves a considerable number of calculations. Another solution is to use a well-known iterative technique known as the 'Newton-Raphson Procedure'. This technique begins with an initial guess at the implied volatility. If this volatility is wrong then a second guess is made and then a third guess and so on. Successive guesses are arrived at using differential calculus and often a solution is found within four or five tries. Fortunately, however, Microsoft Excel provides a very simple solution in the form of the 'Goal Seek' function. The Goal Seek function is a procedure that is perfectly suited to finding the implied volatility. This function was mentioned in Chapter 2 and its use to find the implied volatility is shown in the Appendix.

7.5   RHO — INTEREST RATE SENSITIVITY

Regular straight bonds are obviously sensitive to interest rate changes. Other things being equal, if interest rates increase, bond prices fall. The bond market uses a number of measures of interest rate sensitivity one of which is the 'duration'. In the derivative product industry the standard measure of interest rate sensitivity is 'rho'. Rho is usually defined as the change in price caused by interest rates increasing by 1%. With one year to expiry, a volatility of 15%, interest rates at 5% and the underlying share price at £8.00, the ABC Bank CB is priced at £8.2984. If we change the interest rate to 6% the price decreases to £8.2681. This decrease of £0.0303 per share or 0.3787 bond points is the rho at this price level.

Figure 7.7 illustrates how the rho of a CB varies with the underlying share price and is produced by carrying out the above differencing calculation at many different share price levels. At very low share prices, when the instrument is behaving like a straight bond, the rho is maximum at about 1.000 bond points per 1% increase in interest rates. At very high share prices, when the instrument is behaving like straight equity, the rho tends to zero.

7.5.1   Hedging out Interest Rate Risk

For hedgers the rho estimate can be almost as important as the delta. The classical hedged portfolio is long CBs and short shares. Such a position should be immune to share price changes. But what about interest rate changes? The reader is no doubt aware that there have been periods when interest volatility was higher than share price volatility. What would happen to the above portfolio if the interest rates were to suddenly increase? If the share price were £8.00 and interest rates went from 5% to 6% then the CB portion of the portfolio would drop approximately 0.38 bond points or 0.38 × £5,000/100 = £19 per bond. If the portfolio contained 1,000 CBs,

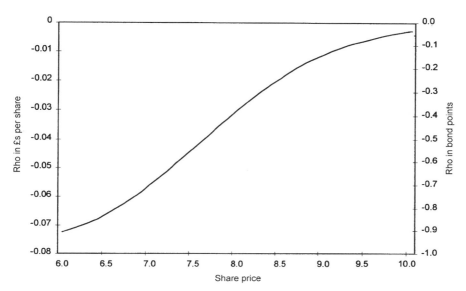

Figure 7.7   Rho – the interest rate sensitivity of a CB

this would represent an immediate loss of £19,000 with no offsetting profit. The CB portion of this portfolio was hedged against a fall in share prices but not a rise in interest rates.

Fortunately, there are other derivatives that can be used to hedge out the interest rate risk. The simplest route would be to use an interest rate future. These instruments decrease (increase) in price when interest rates increase (decrease). All that is required is to establish a short position in the relevant interest rate future. Another route would be to use interest rate put options. Interest rate puts increase (decrease) in price when rates increase (decrease). The appropriate course of action would therefore be to buy interest rate puts.

There is an additional source of interest rate risk than cannot be hedged out with exchange traded derivatives. All CBs are issued by corporations and so by definition have a credit risk component. It may be that the relevant straight bond rate is 4% with an additional 1% for the credit risk. The hedger would thus use 4% + 1% = 5% in his model to price the CB. It is possible to hedge out interest rate increases using futures or options, but how does he hedge out the risk of the credit rating decreasing? If the next day the market re-rates this particular issue at a new credit risk of 2%, then the CB price will drop to reflect the new total interest rate of 4% + 2% = 6%. Futures and options will be of no use.

There are two ways to hedge out this credit rating change. One is to use over-the-counter credit derivative products and the other is to short an existing straight bond. Both of these topics are beyond the scope of this book and so will not be discussed here.

7.6   THE EFFECT OF TIME ON CB SENSITIVITIES — SECOND-ORDER SENSITIVITIES

The delta, the theta, the vega and rho are all standard derivative product sensitivities that are relatively easy to estimate. Their meanings are intuitive and their importance to the hedger is obvious. The outright long CB player can also use these measures as a guide to how his position will alter if the share price increases or volatility changes or a month passes, etc. Unfortunately these measures change over time and we need to know how they change. A lot can be gleaned by simply looking at how the CB price changes over time. Figure 7.8 shows how our standard ABC Bank CB price changes starting from a point four years prior to expiry.

The illustration tells us straight away that this particular CB increases in value as time passes if the share price is low and that this is more marked the lower the share price. The way the delta changes can also be seen from Figure 7.8. At low share prices with four years to expiry, the CB price curve has a moderate positive slope — the delta is positive. As time passes, the instrument increases in value and at the same time the curve becomes more horizontal. At low share prices, as time passes, the delta must therefore decrease. Both these effects can be illustrated more clearly by calculating explicitly the theta and delta of this CB at various share prices. The results are shown in Figure 7.9.

In a similar fashion, Figure 7.10 shows how the passage of time affects the other two sensitivity measures of this CB. The upper panel shows the vega and we see that longer-dated CBs are far more sensitive to volatility inputs than short-dated ones. Misspecifying a volatility at 20% when it should really be only 15% has a far greater

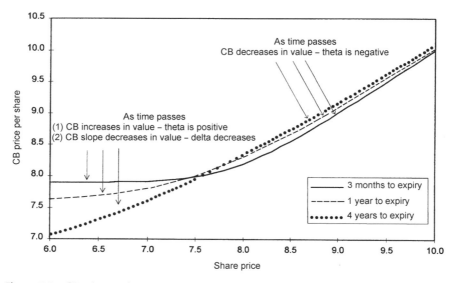

Figure 7.8   CB price as time passes

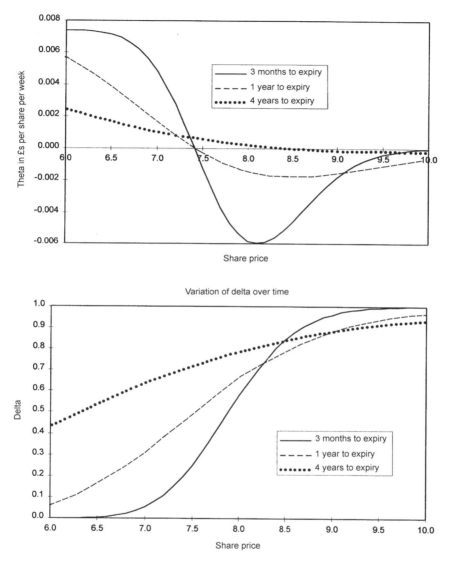

Figure 7.9 Theta – the time decay of CB at various times to expiry

effect on a four-year CB than on a three-month one. The lower panel shows how the rho changes over time and we see that longer-dated CBs are more susceptible to interest rate risk. A four-year CB is more at risk to interest rates rising than a three-month one and this effect is more pronounced the lower the share price.

All the examples above are related to one example — the ABC Bank CB. The figures are just illustrations of how this particular CB price and price sensitivities

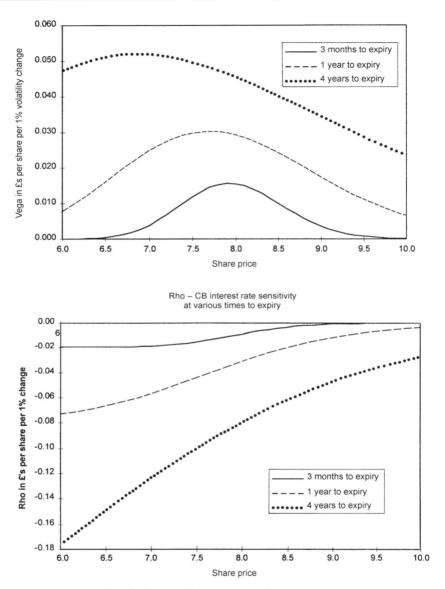

Figure 7.10   Vega – CB volatility sensitivity at various times to expiry

behave. What would the pictures look like if we changed the instrument to one
paying a coupon or one on a share-paying dividend? There are eight inputs to a
given CB model: (1) the share price, (2) the conversion price, (3) the interest
rate(s), (4) the volatility, (5) the time to expiry, (6) the size and frequency of the

coupon, (7) the share dividend flow and (8) the credit spread. In an attempt to display how changing one or more of these variables affects the price or price sensitivity we would need an enormous number of diagrams. Assuming we restrict ourselves to two-dimensional representations like Figures 7.9 and 7.10, in which three variables are represented, we would need 280 different diagrams and this is not including the addition of the short-call feature, the possibility of a put or the complication associated with foreign exchange rates. The reader can be in no doubt that CBs are complicated instruments and that each one will be different from the next. The only way to discover how interest rates or volatility or whatever, affects CBs is to look at each one individually.

7.7 CONTOUR DIAGRAMS

The most complicated chart that investors usually study is the classic time series diagram. These are simple historical records of the price of the underlying share. The vertical axis is usually the share price and the horizontal axis, time. It is possible to gain further insight into the way price sensitivities alter over time by looking at fixed sensitivity contours in the same framework. An example is given in Figure 7.11 which shows the delta contours of our ABC Bank CB starting at one year prior to expiry. Each contour maps out all the points that have a given delta. The 11 contours correspond to deltas starting at 0.0 and increasing in equal units of 0.1 until 1.0. Along the lowest contour, the delta is 0.0; along the second lowest

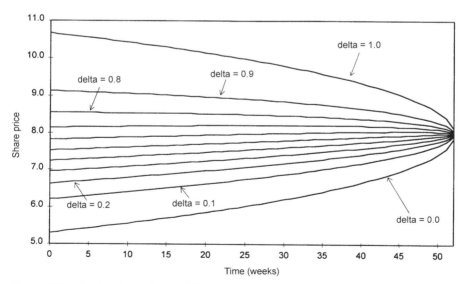

Figure 7.11 Fixed delta contours of CB

contour, the delta is 0.1 and so on. The highest contour corresponds to a delta of 1.0.

There are a number of ways of looking at this diagram. Consider a straight horizontal line drawn through the £7.50 share price level. This represents the situation of the underlying share price remaining constant at £7.50 until expiry. At the start (time = 0) with one year to go we can see that the CB has a delta of between 0.4 and 0.5. So with one year to expiry this CB will respond to changes in the underlying share prices to the tune of 40% to 50% — the instrument will catch almost half the underlying share price movement. As time passes, if the share price stays constant, the straight line enters lower and lower delta territory until after approximately 50 weeks the line cuts into the 0.0 delta zone. As time passes the delta of this CB has decreased until eventually, with only two weeks to expiry, it ends up being completely insensitive to share price changes. By considering a straight line drawn through the £8.50 share price level one can see that exactly the opposite occurs. The line cuts through higher and higher delta contours eventually to enter the delta = 1.0 zone. As time passes, the delta of this CB increases. As time passes with the share price near the £8.50 level, this CB will respond more and more to share price changes until eventually it will mimic it perfectly. This reinforces the observations from the CB price curves and Figure 7.9.

Contour plots such as these can demonstrate the way in which a classical hedger alters his portfolio as expiry approaches. If we plot the usual time series representation of the share price on the same contour map, as in Figure 7.12, we can see what happens to the hedged portfolio. As the share price moves over time, the

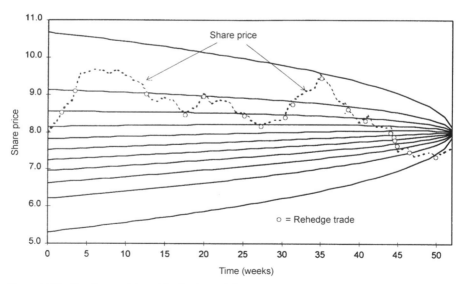

Figure 7.12   Trading activity of hedged portfolio

contours give a direct indication of the state of the portfolio. In this example the initial share price is £8.00 and the delta is 0.60 — the CB would have a hedge of 60% in place. After instigation we note that the share price begins to increase with a resultant increase in delta. As the share price crosses higher and higher delta contours the portfolio would become increasingly unbalanced on the long side. There will be a point, depending on the rehedging strategy, at which rebalancing should take place. One can, in fact, use the contours to dictate when to rehedge. If the hedger makes an arbitrary rule that he only adjusts the portfolio each time the delta changes by 0.10, then each time the share price crosses one of the fixed contours, a rehedge would be required. It is thus possible to see on a traditional share price versus time chart when a rehedging trade occurs.

With one year to go the distance between the rehedging contours (in share price terms) is large and there may be little activity. As time passes, the contours converge and provided the share price stays fairly near the conversion price of £8.00, the rehedging activity would increase. With one year to expiry a share price move from £7.60 to £8.10 would cross two contours. The same move with only three weeks to expiry would cross seven contours.

Contour diagrams like Figures 7.11 and 7.12 assume (often incorrectly) that all other characteristics affecting the CB remain fixed. The only variables changing in these two figures is time (which is gradually evolving) and the underlying share price. However, it is unlikely that parameters such as the underlying volatility and interest rates would remain fixed for a period as long as a year. It is possible to extend the scope of these sorts of diagrams to illustrate how changes in a number of inputs would affect sensitivities. Figure 7.13 shows how the delta of this CB would change if, half-way through the year, volatility were to increase from 15% to 20%. Figure 7.14 shows how the delta of this CB would change if, half-way through the year, interest rates were to increase from 5% to 10%. It is possible to construct diagrams like Figures 7.13 and 7.14 for all the other CB sensitivities such as theta, vega and rho.

7.8 CONCLUDING REMARKS ON CB SENSITIVITIES

Because CBs are so complex they have to be priced using the iterative binomial method. This means that the calculation of the sensitivities usually has to be done using a crude differencing method. Because the differencing method is highly sensitive to small changes in the inputs, it is necessary to use a large number of iterations. In this chapter we illustrated how a particular CB would be affected by changes in share price, interest rates, volatility and time. However, with certain CBs, there is a much quicker and neater way at arriving at these values. The method can be applied only to very special cases and relies on considering CBs as the sum of two separately tradable instruments, a bond and an equity warrant. This will be dealt with in the next chapter.

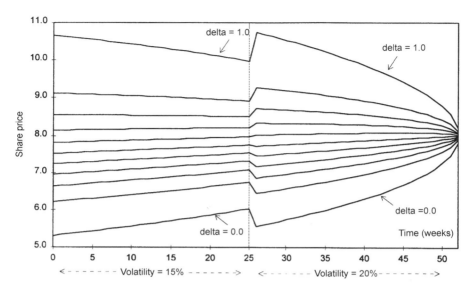

Figure 7.13 Effect of increasing volatility on delta contours

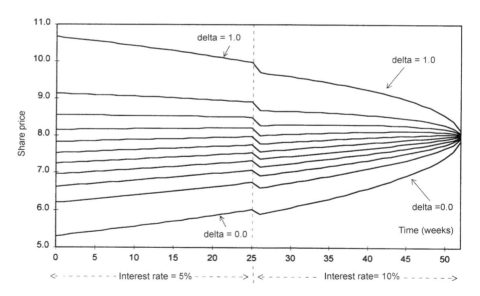

Figure 7.14 Effect of increasing interest rates on delta contours

8
Using equity warrant models to price CBs

Some market participants like to think of a CB as a package of two instruments — an equity warrant and a regular straight bond. The justification of this way of thinking is that in certain circumstances a CB behaves like a bond and in others it behaves like a warrant. Many equity derivative sales units still promote the instruments in this way. Early workers in the field used this idea to price the instruments. These individuals priced the two separate components and simply added the results together. The problem is that with a CB, the two components are inextricably tied together and in many cases this method of valuation will produce erroneous results. The complications caused by the issuer's call and the presence of a put, often means that one cannot simply sum the price of a warrant and a bond together.

There are, however, certain CBs that can be priced using this technique. The real advantage of using this method of valuation is that a closed form exists — no need for the countless iterations required by the binomial model. It is possible to use a standard option model to value the warrant component and a straightforward bond calculator to value the bond component. Another advantage of this approach is that all the sensitivities — delta, vega, theta and rho are all expressible in a simple closed form. This method produces CB prices and price sensitivities very quickly and can be extremely useful when running a large portfolio. This chapter deals exclusively with this method of valuation.

8.1 EQUITY WARRANTS

In order to understand why a CB can be viewed as a combination of an equity warrant plus bond, we first outline what an equity warrant is and how it is priced. Warrants are issued by corporations and, like CBs, come to the market with a number of fixed characteristics. Most warrants are issued with four or more years of life, after which they expire. Each warrant gives the holder the right, but not the obligation, to buy a given number of shares at a given price. The given price is referred to as the 'exercise price' and when and if the holder chooses to exercise his right to buy shares, the additional exercise price is paid to the corporation. When a warrant is exercised the additional exercise proceeds are received by the corporation and in return they issue the fixed number of shares. So equity warrants are very much like equity call options and we illustrate by considering a warrant on ABC Bank shares.

ABC Bank warrant
Shares per warrant: 625
Exercise price: £8.00
Present price of the underlying share: £7.80
Maturity: 1 year

The ABC Bank warrant is exercisable into 625 shares and the exercise price is £8.00. This example has been deliberately concocted to resemble the ABC Bank CB used throughout this book. Let us see now what happens to an investor buying one of these warrants. (For the moment we leave aside the issue of what price was paid.)

Buying one of these warrants places the investor in the position of being able to buy shares at £8.00. Clearly, if after buying this warrant the underlying share price rises rapidly to, say, £20.00, then the warrant must be worth a considerable sum. If the share price were £20.00, then the warrant investor could exercise his right to take up shares from the corporation at £8.00. In exercising he must pay up the additional £8.00 per share (or 625 × 8.00 = £5,000.00 per warrant) to the company and take delivery of the shares. He then could sell his shares at £20.00 each and thus make a profit of £12.00 per share (or 625 × 12.00 = £7,500 per warrant). The total profit would be slightly less than this because we must take into account the original warrant investment. But it is easy to see that at £20.00 the warrants must be worth at least £12.00. In the jargon of the market-place, the 'intrinsic value' or 'parity' of the warrants is £12.00 per share.

The similarity between a warrant and a CB is obvious. In our simple examples both instruments involve 625 shares, both involve a given price, £8.00, and both will have fixed lives. Also, when either is transformed into shares, the corporation must issue new stock with the resultant dilution affecting existing shareholdings. But there is a crucial difference between a warrant and a CB and it is all to do with the £8.00 price. When a warrant is 'exercised' the investor pays up the exercise price of £8.00 per share and the warrant then becomes shares. When a CB is 'converted' into shares no extra funds are required from the investor. When an investor buys a CB he is in a way already paying up front the full amount — he does not need to pay the extra £8.00 per share. This simple difference makes the instruments behave completely differently. We already know how a CB price varies. We now develop a warrant pricing model.

8.2 MODEL FOR WARRANT PRICES

The similarity between a CB and a warrant allows us to use an almost identical procedure to arrive at a warrant-pricing model. In Chapter 5 we started by considering a one-period CB model. At the end of the period the CB investor would choose to optimise his wealth by either redeeming or converting. If the final share price were below the conversion price of £8.00 then he would redeem and take the lump sum of £8.00. If the final share price were above £8.00 then he would convert into shares and sell in the market. We derive a one-period warrant model using exactly the same logic.

8.2.1 The One-period Warrant Model

As with CBs, rather than look at a warrant that is exercisable into 625 shares, it is far easier to understand what is going on if we convert everything into a per-share basis and consider instead a new type of warrant. This new warrant can be exercised into one share on or before maturity. For the purposes of this simple model we assume that the underlying shares pay no dividend and that interest rates are zero. Also for simplicity we assume that in one year's time (on expiry) the share price will be either £9.00 or £7.20.

What will the holder of the warrant do on expiry? He can exercise, pay up the extra £8.00 and take delivery of one share valued at whatever the then current share price is, or he can choose to let the warrant expire by doing nothing. What should he do?

Clearly, if the share price is up at £9.00 he will exercise, pay the additional £8.00, take the shares and sell immediately with a final payoff of £1.00. The final payoff is equal to the warrant's intrinsic value. If the share price is down at £7.20 it does not make sense to exercise. Why exercise and pay £8.00 per share, when the price in the market is lower at £7.20? If the share price is down below £8.00 it makes sense to let the warrant expire worthless. If the share price is below £8.00 the final payoff is zero.

This illustrates the difference between a CB and a warrant. With a CB you end up with either the share price or the redemption value. With a warrant you end up with either the intrinsic value or zero. And this can be expressed more neatly using the Max { } function. The final value of a warrant is given by:

Expiring warrant value = Max {(Expiring share price − Exercise price), 0}

So we can illustrate the situation in the same way as we did when considering the standard two-way bet and this is shown in Figure 8.1.

We therefore have an identical situation to that encountered with the one-period model CB. We have two instruments that are perfectly correlated in the sense that

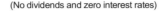

Figure 8.1   The one-period binomial warrant model

the final outcome of one (the warrant) depends on the final outcome of the other (the share). It should be easy to see that, as with the CB model, we can construct a hedged portfolio of long one instrument and short the other that should be riskless. Using the same simple two-way bet logic of Section 5.1.1 and the mathematical expression (5.5) we calculate the hedge ratio as

$$h = \frac{1.00 - 0.00}{9.00 - 7.20} = 5/9 = 55.5\%$$

and use expression (5.6) to calculate the warrant fair value, W_f, as

$$W_f = \frac{1.00(7.80 - 7.20) + 0.00(9.00 - 7.80)}{(9.00 - 7.20)} = £0.33$$

So in this very unrealistic situation, if the warrant were priced significantly below £0.33 per share, then one could go long the warrant and short the underlying in the ratio of 55.5% and make a risk-free return. Similarly if the warrant were priced significantly higher than £0.33 per share, one could short the warrant and go long the underlying in the same ratio and still make a risk-free return. We say that £0.33 per share is the warrant fair value.

It should come as no surprise to the reader that the hedge ratio for this warrant at 55.5% is exactly the same as the hedge ratio for the one-period model CB discussed in Section 5.3. A hedge ratio is simply a ratio of differences. The numerator of a hedge ratio is the difference between the final upper and lower CB or warrant value. In the case of the CB, the difference is: £9.00 − £8.00 = £1.00 and in the case of the warrant the difference of £1.00 − £.00 = £1.00 is the same. Also, it will be no surprise that the fair warrant price at £0.33 is £8.00 lower than the CB fair price of £8.33. The difference between a CB and a warrant is all about the difference between converting and exercising.

8.2.2 The General One-period Warrant Model with Different Stock Prices

The argument above shows that the fair value of the warrant is £0.33 per share if the current share price is £7.80. But what if the current share price were £7.85 or £7.90 or in fact any other value? As with CBs it is easy to construct a general formula giving the warrant price in terms of the current share price. By following the same formulation if we let the share price today be S and the up and down multipliers be u and d then the general form of the problem is shown in Figure 8.2.

W_u and W_d are the values of the warrant corresponding to the share price being up at $S.u$ or down at $S.d$. As in the particular case we can use expression (5.5) to calculate the hedge ratio as

$$h = \frac{W_u - W_d}{S.u - S.d}$$

and use (5.6) to calculate the warrant fair value as

$$W_f = pW_u + qW_d \qquad (8.1)$$

where $\quad p = \dfrac{(1-d)}{(u-d)}, \quad$ and

$$q = \frac{(u-1)}{(u-d)} = 1 - p$$

Note the striking similarity between expressions (8.1) and (5.8). All the terms on the right-hand side are known. We just substitute for S, u, d, W_u and W_d and out falls the warrant value.

Expression (8.1) shows us that the warrant fair value is a simple weighted average of the upper expiring value, W_u, and the lower expiring value, W_d, with the weights given by the parameters p and q. Here $u = 1.1538$ and $d = 0.9231$ and so the weights p and q are 0.33 and 0.667 respectively. This gives the fair value of the warrant as

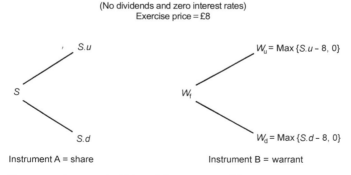

Figure 8.2   The general one-period binomial warrant model

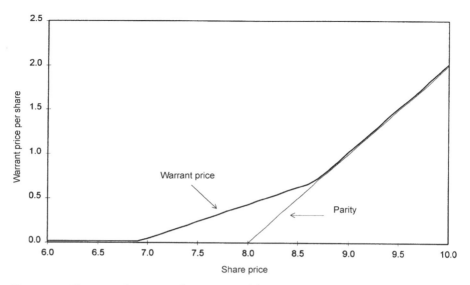

Figure 8.3 The general one-period warrant model

$$W_f = 0.33 \ W_u + 0.67 \ W_d$$

So whatever the initial share price, the warrant value is always a mixture of one-third of the upper value and two-thirds the lower value. In Figure 8.1 the upper value is £1, the lower value is £0 and so the answer is $0.33 \times 1 + 0.67 \times 0 = £0.33$.

The general expression that gives the warrant value in terms of the initial share price, S is obtained by substituting for W_u and W_d as follows.

$$W_f = 0.33\text{Max}\{(1.1538S - 8), 0\} + 0.67\text{Max}\{(0.9231S - 8), 0\} \qquad (8.2)$$

Figure 8.3 shows how W_f varies with respect to the underlying share price.

The picture is very much like the one-period CB model given in Figure 5.5. The warrant fair value is given by one of three straight lines. And the reason for the three straight lines is the same for the CB model: the two Max { } functions in expression (8.2) have the effect of splitting up the share price range into three separate areas. Following the same logic of Section 5.2.1 we can rewrite expression (8.2) as

(a) $W_f = 0.333 \ (1.1538 \ S - 8) + 0.667 \ (0.9231 \ S - 8)$
     i.e., $W_f = S - 8$, if $S > 8.67$
(b) $W_f = 0.333 \ (1.1538 \ S - 8) + 0.667(0)$
     i.e,. $W_f = 0.38 \ S - 2.66$, if $6.93 < S < 8.67$
(c) $W_f = 0.333 \ (0 \ ) + 0.667 \ (0)$
     i.e, $W_f = 0$, if $S < 6.93$

8.2.3   Expressing a CB as Warrant Plus Cash

Before we proceed to consider more periods it is instructive to look in more detail at the similarity between the CB and the warrant model. The above three warrant equations are identical to the three CB equations given in Section 5.2.1 except in one respect — the number 8. To emphasise this point we express one derivative in terms of the other for each section.

(a) $W_f = S - 8$
     $CB_f = S$
     $\therefore CB_f = W_f + 8$ $\Big\}$ If $S > 8.67$

(b) $W_f = 0.38\ S - 2.66$
     $CB_f = 0.38\ S + 5.34$ $\Big\}$ If $6.93 < S < 8.67$
     $\therefore CB_f = W_f + 8$

(c) $W_f = 0$
     $CB_f = 8$ $\Big\}$ If $S < 6.93$
     $\therefore CB_f = W_f + 8$

So at all share prices we could have modelled this CB in terms of the warrant by simply adding the exercise price or conversion price of £8.00. This fact can be illustrated graphically by adding the warrant price profile shown in Figure 8.3 on top of a horizontal value of £8.00 and this is shown in Figure 8.4. Figure 8.4 and Figure 5.5 are identical.

We could have arrived at this conclusion much quicker using a little algebra. The only difference between the CB and the warrant models is that in the former we have the expressions like Max $\{S.u,\ 8\}$ and in the latter we have expressions like Max $\{(S.u - 8),\ 0\}$. We need to be able to express one in terms of the other. It is very easy to show that

$$\text{Max}\{a, b\} = \text{Max}\{(a - b), 0\} + b \tag{8.3}$$

so this means that

$$\text{Max}\{S.u, 8\} = \text{Max}\{(S.u - 8), 0\} + 8$$

and

$$\text{Max}\{S.d, 8\} = \text{Max}\{(S.d - 8), 0\} + 8$$

We can thus write the general one-period CB model in terms of the general one-period warrant model. From Section 5.2.1 we have

$$CB_f = 0.333\text{Max}\{S.u, 8\} + 0.667\text{Max}\{S.d, 8\}$$

or more generally

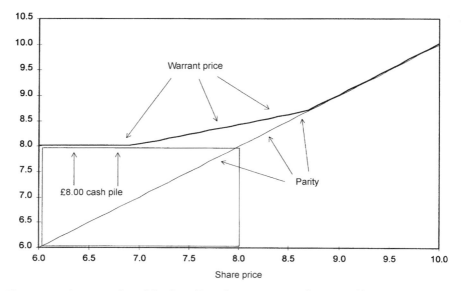

Figure 8.4 One-period model values (CB value = warrant value + cash)

$$CB_f = p\text{Max}\{S.u, E\} + q\text{Max}\{S.d, E\}$$
$$= p[\text{Max}\{(S.u - E), 0\} + E] + q[\text{Max}\{(S.d - E), 0\} + E]$$
$$= p\text{Max}\{(S.u - E), 0\} + p.E + q\text{Max}\{(S.d - E), 0\} + q.E$$
$$= p\text{Max}\{(S.u - E), 0\} + q\text{Max}\{(S.d - E), 0\} + E(p + q)$$
$$CB_f = W_f + E$$

8.2.4 The General *n*-period Warrant Model

As with the binomial CB model, we can extend the warrant model to have more periods. Using a similar argument, the two-period warrant model is

$$W_f = p^2.W_{uu} + 2p.q.W_{ud} + q^2.W_{dd}$$
$$= p^2.\text{Max}\{(S.u^2 - E), 0\} + 2p.q.\text{Max}\{(S.u.d - E), 0\}$$
$$+ q^2.\text{Max}\{(S.d^2 - E), 0\}$$

and using identical algebra to that above it is possible to show that for the two-period model

$$CB_f = W_f + E \qquad (8.4)$$

With the two-period model there are three final share prices and four final linear equations. We can continue to increase the number of periods and it is possible to show that expression (8.4) is always valid. As the number of periods increases, the number of different disjoint equations increases. If $n = 50$, there are 51 different final share prices and 52 different warrant equations. But remember that the whole point in considering modelling warrant prices is to try to find a quicker and neater way of pricing CBs. We now know that (under certain circumstances) we can model a CB as a warrant plus cash. But what is the point of using a 50-period warrant model when we might as well use a 50-period CB model? The number of iterations will be the same and the problems caused by the lumpiness of the general binomial technique will be the same.

8.2.5   A Closed Form Solution — The Black and Scholes Warrant Model

In 1973 two pioneers, Myron Scholes and Fisher Black, derived an options model that is in a 'closed form' and that can be applied to warrants. Their model allows us to value warrants and their sensitivities very quickly. The model is as follows:

If S = share price
E = exercise price
r = interest rate
t = time to expiry in years
σ = volatility

then the warrant price is given by

$$W_f = S.N(d_1) - E.e^{-r.t}.N(d_2) \qquad (8.5)$$

where $d_1 = \dfrac{\ln(S/E) + (r + 0.5\sigma^2)t}{\sigma\sqrt{t}}$

$d_2 = d_1 - \sigma\sqrt{t}$
$N(\, . \,)$ = cumulative normal density function

Although this expression looks formidable, the process of arriving at the warrant fair price is very straightforward. As an example, say $S = £7.80$, $E = £8.00$, interest rates are zero ($r = 0.00$), time to expiry is one year ($t = 1$) and share price volatility is 15% ($\sigma = 0.15$). Substituting these values in the above equation we get $d_1 = -0.0938$ and $d_2 = -0.2438$. To get the value for the cumulative normal density function one can use tables or if using Excel simply call the NORMDIST { } function. Either way we get $N(d_1) = -0.09379$ and $N(d_2) = -0.24379$. Substituting these values into expression (8.5) gives $W_f = 0.38$. The Black and Scholes warrant fair value is £0.38 per share.

What is the link between the binomial warrant model and the Black and Scholes model? It is beyond the scope of this book but it is possible to show that as one considers binomial models with one period, then two periods, then three periods and

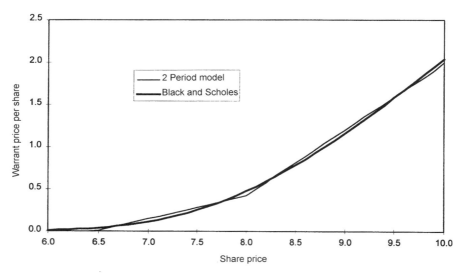

Figure 8.5   Binomial model vs. Black and Scholes model

so on, that in the limit we approach the Black and Scholes value. So we can think of expression (8.5) as being equivalent to a binomial model with an infinite number of periods and the amazing thing is that the solution can be arrived at in an instant.

Figure 8.5 shows the two-period warrant model values along with the Black and Scholes values. There are areas where the two-period model undervalues the warrant and other areas where it overvalues the warrant, but the difference really is not that great. The more periods one uses the nearer the true (i.e., Black and Scholes) value we get. More periods produce more straight lines but each one gets nearer and nearer the true curve. Figure 8.6 is a plot of the difference between the two models at the share price of £8.00 as a function of the number of periods. At $n = 1$ the difference is high at £0.120 per share. As n increases the difference oscillates between positive and negative values, but the difference decreases gradually with increasing n. When $n = 20$ the difference is as small as + or −£0.006.

8.2.6   Using the Black and Scholes Model to Price CBs

The algebraic trick that allows us to express a CB in terms of a warrant is all to do with the Max { } function relation (8.3). We used this to express a one-period CB in terms of a one-period warrant. We also used this for a two-period example. It is possible to show that it works for any value of n and indeed for the Black and Scholes warrant value. So we now can very quickly arrive at a CB valuation using

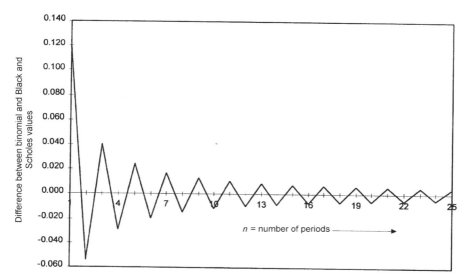

Figure 8.6   Binomial values approach Black and Scholes values

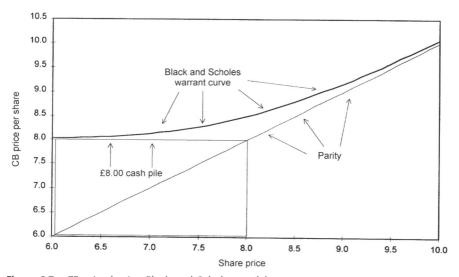

Figure 8.7   CB priced using Black and Scholes model

$$CB \text{ value} = \text{Black and Scholes warrant value} + \text{cash}$$

where the cash value is the conversion price of the CB or the exercise price of the warrant. Figure 8.7 illustrates how our example CB can be modelled using this approach.

If one were to draw on the same chart as Figure 8.7, the 50-period binomial CB model, the human eye would not be able to detect the differences. If there are no coupons, no dividends, no short-call provision and no bond put, the two procedures produce near identical results. The 50-period model involves 1,275 different calculations per share price, whereas the Black and Scholes model plus cash requires only five. It is easy to see the attractiveness of the latter technique.

8.2.7   Interest Rate Effects on Warrants — The One-period Model and the Discounted Parity Line

In all the above we conveniently assumed that interest rates were zero. This has the effect of allowing us to value to the £8.00 exercise price (or conversion price in the case of a CB) always as £8.00. With zero interest rates, time does not affect the value of money. With zero interest rates, the £8.00 conversion value embedded in a CB will be independent of time. Unfortunately, in the real world, interest rates are non-zero and we now include this fact in the modelling of our warrant.

Including interest rates into the two-way bet approach to modelling warrants is again almost identical to that when modelling CBs. The only difference is that now the risk-free arbitrage portfolio must return the (non-zero) risk-free rate. One can use an identical approach to that used in the one-period CB model to show that the fair warrant price is given by

$$W_f = \frac{pW_u + qW_d}{1 + r}$$

where $p = \dfrac{1 + r - d}{u - d}$,   and

$q = 1 - p$

These expressions are very similar to those used to derive the one-period CB model with interest rates. Figure 8.8 illustrates the effects interest rates have on warrant prices and we see that unlike CBs, interest rates increase rather than decrease the value of warrants. Furthermore, above a certain share price the difference between the zero interest warrant price and the 5% warrant price is constant. In this example, above $S = £8.67$, all Max { } functions return the parity values. It is left as an exercise for the reader to show that the two upper warrant equations reduce to

$W_f = S - 8$ with rate = 0% and $S > £8.67$

and

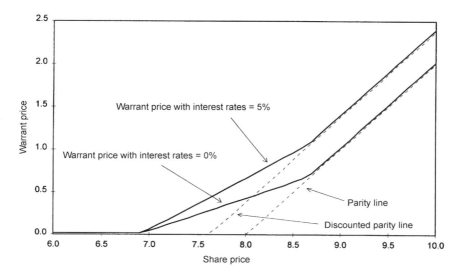

Figure 8.8 One-period warrant model with different interest rates

$$W_{\mathrm{f}} = S - 8/1.05 = S - 8 + 0.38 \quad \text{with rate} = 5\% \text{ and } S > £8.67$$

Above $S = £8.67$ the warrant in a 5% interest rate environment will always be £0.38 per share more expensive than the one in a zero rate environment. Above this special share price, the two warrant prices run on parallel lines a fixed distance of £0.38 apart.

The parity or intrinsic value of a warrant is always given by Max {(Share price − Exercise price), 0}. In a zero interest rate environment the upper warrant equation is exactly the same as the parity line and the general expression is

$$W_{\mathrm{f}} = S - E$$

In a non-zero interest rate environment the upper warrant line sits above the parity line and this is given by the general expression

$$W_{\mathrm{f}} = S - E/(1 + r)$$

The difference between these two lines is $E[1 - 1/(1 + r)]$ and represents the discounting effect interests rates have on the exercise price, E. In our example the difference is £0.38 and this is the difference between £8.00 and £8.00 discounted at 5% a year. We say that the warrant in a non-zero interest rate environment sits on a 'discounted parity line'.

The discounted parity line concept is particularly useful in that it enables us to spot warrant arbitrage opportunities without the use of a complex model. If warrants trade below their discounted parity line, then a zero risk arbitrage profit can be made and the hedge ratio is always 1. In these very special situations the profits made are really associated with interest rate considerations. As an example, suppose in the 5% interest rate environment the underlying share price was £12.00 and the warrant was offered at £4.10 per share. The exercise price is £8.00 so the parity is 12.00 − 8.00 = £4.00; the warrant is sitting above the parity line. However, the discounted parity value is 12.00 − 8.00/1.05 = £4.38. The risk-free portfolio would be long one warrant at £4.10 and short one share at £12.00. It is left as an exercise for the reader to show that the absolute minimum profit that the portfolio will return will be £0.295 per share. Of course, if interest rates were higher, for example, 10%, then the discounted parity line would be even higher and the profit even higher.

8.2.8   The Discounted Warrant Parity Line is the CB Parity Line

But can one model a CB as a warrant plus cash in a non-zero interest rate environment? The answer is yes but we have to treat the cash sum differently. Recall the one-period CB model with interest rates.

$$CB_f = \frac{p\text{Max}\{S.u, E\} + q\text{Max}\{S.d, E\}}{(1 + r)}$$

$$= \frac{p[\text{Max}\{(S.u - E), 0\} + E] + q[\text{Max}\{(S.d - E), 0\} + E]}{(1 + r)}$$

$$= \frac{p\text{Max}\{(S.u - E), 0\} + p.E + q\text{Max}\{(S.d - E), 0\} + q.E}{(1 + r)}$$

$$= \frac{p\text{Max}\{(S.u - E), 0\} + q\text{Max}\{(S.d - E), 0\}}{(1 + r)} + \frac{E(p + q)}{(1 + r)}$$

$$CB_f = W_f + \frac{E}{(1 + r)}$$

So in a non-zero interest environment a CB can be modelled as a warrant *plus the discounted conversion price*. This can be seen graphically in Figure 8.9 in which the one-period warrant model is placed on top of a cash sum of £7.62, i.e., the £8.00 exercise price discounted by 5%. The total values of warrant plus discounted cash shown in Figure 8.9 and those corresponding to the one-period CB model in Figure 5.7 are identical. What is also apparent from these Figures is that *the CB parity line is the same as the discounted warrant parity line*.

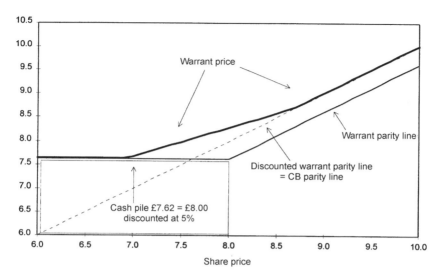

Figure 8.9   One-period model values: CB value = warrant value + discounted cash

This has interesting implications for the differences between warrants and CBs. Recall the above simple example in which the warrant was offered at £4.10 with the share price at £12.00. It was possible to set up a risk-free arbitrage portfolio and make a return just based on interest rate effects because the warrant was below its discounted parity line. Translating this warrant into CB terms we add £4.10 to £7.62 to get £11.72. But the parity of the CB, the value if immediately converted, is £12.00. If the CB were priced at £11.72 we would immediately convert into shares and make a profit of £0.28. This sum of £0.28 invested at 5% per annum would grow into a sum of £0.295 — exactly the same profit made in the warrant example. So a warrant offered at a price lower than the discounted parity line is equivalent to a CB offered lower than parity. In reality the former situation does occasionally present itself but never the latter. The reason is that to extract the warrant profit we have to set up a portfolio of long and short instruments and we have to wait (maybe) for a year. If a CB trades at a discount to parity all one has to do is to buy it, convert it and then sell the shares. With a CB the profit is immediate, whereas with a warrant the delay can make the trade unattractive.

8.2.9   Interest Rate Effects on Warrants: The *n*-period Model

As with CBs one can extend the warrant model including interest rates to one with two periods.

$$W_f = \frac{p^2.W_{uu} + 2p.q.W_{ud} + q^2.W_{dd}}{(1+r)^2}$$
$$= \frac{p^2.\text{Max}\{(S.u^2 - E), 0\} + 2p.q.\text{Max}\{(S.u.d - E), 0\} + q^2.\text{Max}\{(S.d_2 - E), 0\}}{(1+r)^2}$$

and using identical algebra to that above it is possible to show that for the two-period model.

$$CB_f = W_f + \frac{E}{(1+r)^2}$$

The two-period CB model therefore equals the two-period warrant model plus the discounted exercise price. It is easy to show that this works for any number of periods and it is all due to the fact that the E terms in the CB model can be brought outside the Max { } function terms and with rearranging we always get

CB value = Warrant value + discounted conversion price

8.2.10   Interest Rate Effects on Warrants — The Black and Scholes CB Model

It is possible to show that this process of separating out the E terms also works as the number of periods tends to infinity. In the limit of course, the warrant model becomes the closed-form Black and Scholes model and so we finally have

CB value = Black and Scholes warrant value + discounted cash   (8.6)

i.e.,

$$CB_f = S.N(d_1) - E.e^{-r.t}.N(d_2) + E.e^{-r.t}$$

or

$$CB_f = S.N(d_1) - E.e^{-r.t}(N(d_2) - 1)$$ (8.7)

where d_1 and d_2 are defined above. Figure 8.10 shows the Black and Scholes warrant curve placed on top of the discounted conversion value ($E.e^{-r.t}$). If the CB has no short-call feature, no bond put and the underlying share pays no dividends, the values produced by expression (8.7) would be equal to those produced by a 200-period binomial model.

8.2.11   Introducing Coupons to the Black and Scholes CB Model

It turns out that expression (8.6) is also valid (with a slight adjustment) when coupons are introduced. And this is again to do with the ability to manipulate the

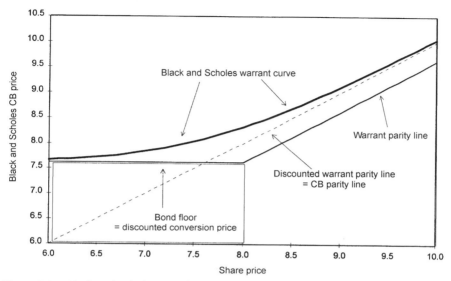

Figure 8.10   Black and Scholes CB value

Max { } functions. We begin with a one-period model. Assume that the CB has a coupon of £c per share, payable on redemption (but not on conversion). If the share price is up a $S.u$ then the final CB value corresponding to an up move is

$$CB_u = \text{Max}\{S.u, E + c\}$$
$$= \text{Max}\{S.u - (E + c), 0\} + E + c$$
$$= W_u + E + c$$

where, W_u, is the expiring upper value of a warrant with an exercise price of $(E + c)$. The CB value corresponding to a fall in the share price is

$$CB_d = \text{Max}\{S.d, E + c\}$$
$$= \text{Max}\{S.d - (E + c), 0\} + E + c$$
$$= W_d + E + c$$

where W_d is the expiring lower value of a warrant with an exercise price of $(E + c)$. Substituting these terms into the usual one-period CB model we have

$$CB_f = \frac{pCB_u + qCB_d}{(1 + r)}$$

$$CB_f = \frac{pW_u + qW_d}{(1 + r)} + \frac{E + c}{(1 + r)}$$

or

$$CB_f = W_f + \frac{E + c}{(1 + r)} \qquad (8.8)$$

where W_f is the one-period warrant model with the slightly higher exercise price of $(E + c)$. Expression (8.8) tells us that the one-period CB model is equivalent to the sum of a warrant plus discounted cash. The discounted cash is now the redemption proceeds and the final coupon.

We now extend the process to a two-period model and assume that there is a coupon at the end of both periods. The one-period result in expression (8.8) can be used to find the values of CB_u and CB_d at the end of the first period as follows.

$$CB_u = \frac{pCB_{uu} + qCB_{ud}}{1 + r}$$

$$= \frac{p\text{Max}\{S.u^2, E + c\} + q\text{Max}\{S.u.d, E + c\}}{(1 + r)}$$

$$= \frac{p\text{Max}\{S.u^2 - (E + c), 0\} + q\text{Max}\{S.u.d - (E + c), 0\}}{(1 + r)} + \frac{E + c}{(1 + r)}$$

$$CB_u = W_u + \frac{E + c}{(1 + r)}$$

Similarly

$$CB_d = W_d + \frac{E + c}{(1 + r)}$$

Working back to the beginning it is possible to show that since there is a coupon also paid at the end of the first period then

$$CB_f = \frac{pCB_u + qCB_d}{(1 + r)} + \frac{c}{(1 + r)}$$

$$CB_f = W_f + \frac{E + c}{(1 + r)^2} + \frac{c}{(1 + r)} \qquad (8.9)$$

The first term, W_f, is the two-period warrant model with an exercise price of $(E + c)$. The last term is the value of the first coupon discounted back over the first period and the middle term is the last coupon plus the conversion proceeds discounted back over the entire period. The last two terms in expression (8.9) are in fact the value of a bond paying just two coupons. So a CB can still be valued as a warrant plus cash. The difference now is that the warrant has a slightly higher exercise price and the cash is all the cash flows discounted by the appropriate amounts.

It should be obvious that by extending the process to n periods and then eventually to the Black and Scholes model, that a CB with coupons can be valued as a warrant plus all the discounted cash flows. All the discounted cash flows of course amount to the value of the instrument if it were valued as a straight bond.

$$\text{CB value} = \text{Warrant value} + \text{Bond value} \quad (8.10)$$

8.3 A COMMON ERROR IN USING THE BLACK AND SCHOLES MODEL TO VALUE CBs

The technique of valuing CBs as the sum of a warrant and a bond is often used, but usually with the wrong inputs. Early attempts at CB modelling were based on a flawed argument that resulted in using the wrong inputs. Some workers still use this technique and consistently get the wrong results. The flawed argument is as follows. Consider a CB as an equity warrant plus a sum of cash. When the share price is very low the warrant portion will be worthless and so the cash sum will reflect the discounted value of all of the coupons and the final redemption proceeds, i.e., the straight bond value. So a CB can be priced by adding a warrant price to the price of the straight bond as in expression (8.10). And this is valid so far. Now comes the mistake that many workers (including the author at one stage) make. In determining the price of the equity warrant we need to know, amongst other things, the exercise price. Rather than use the conversion price, most workers used the following logic to arrive at the wrong exercise price.

If the CB is converted today, then the bond portion is being torn up and thrown away. So by converting today we are forgoing a sum of money equal to the bond price. Compare this to exercising a straight warrant. If we were to buy a warrant today and exercise, we would have to pay up an additional sum — the exercise price. The two actions, (1) buying a CB and converting and (2) buying a warrant, exercising and paying up the exercise price, end up with the same result; some money is spent and some shares are delivered. Surely the exercise price of the warrant embedded within the CB must be equal to the bond value that is being lost by converting? If this is so, then a CB is a truly fascinating instrument. As time passes and/or interest rates change, bond prices change and so the exercise price of this instrument changes. At any one time, in order to value the warrant portion of a CB, we must input the *bond value as the exercise price*. This of course is completely wrong but it is easy to see how compelling the argument is.

As an exercise, consider our ABC Bank CB with no coupons, no dividends, one year to expiry and a share price volatility of 15%. Assuming interest rates are 5%, then the bond portion would be priced at £8.00 discounted by 5%, i.e., £7.62. Figure 8.11 illustrates how to value the CB using two different warrant models. One way (the correct way) is to let the warrant exercise price be £8.00. The other way is to assume the exercise price is lower at the bond value of £7.62. Both warrants are then placed on top of the bond value of £7.62. It is obvious that the warrant with the lower exercise price of £7.62 is more in the money than the one

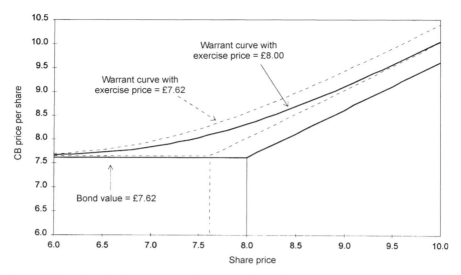

Figure 8.11 Using the bond value as the conversion price

with an exercise price of £8.00 and so will always price the CB higher. Using the bond value incorrectly as the exercise price will always overprice CBs. And this procedure was used to price CBs for years.

8.4 THE DILUTION ISSUE

Until now we have conveniently ignored a major source of contention with both CBs and warrants. The binomial and the Black and Scholes models were really devised for exchange traded options. There is a problem when these models are applied to corporate derivatives and this is associated with the issue of dilution. To see why this is so, consider two otherwise identical instruments: an exchange traded ABC Bank call option and our ABC Bank warrant. Let us assume that both instruments have an exercise price of £8 and that both expire in one year's time. Let us also assume that both are run to expiry and that on the expiry date, the price of the underlying shares is £10. It obviously makes sense for the holders of both the option and the warrant to exercise.

For every long call option position there will be a short call option position. When the holder of the long call option position gives notice to exercise, he pays up the £8 per share. The party that is short to him receives the £8 and then goes into the market-place and buys shares. (In this instance of course he has to pay £10, so unfortunately he has lost £2 per share.) The shares are then delivered to the individual that originally owned the option. So exercising an equity call option involves the transfer of existing shares from one party to another. The ABC Bank corporation is completely unaffected by the process. All that has happened is that ownership of some existing shares has changed.

The exercising of a warrant is different. When the holder of the warrant gives notice to exercise, he gives notice to the ABC Bank corporation. He pays up the £8 and waits delivery of shares. On receiving this notice (and the £8 per share) the corporation issues *new shares*. This is the difference between a call option and a warrant. With the former, the number of shares in circulation is unchanged. With the latter, the number of shares increases, if exercise takes place.

Say there were 10 million shares already in existence and that the exercise of the warrants results in the generation of another 10 million shares. Surely this will affect the share price? Just prior to exercise, the corporation was valued at 10 million times £10 or £100 million. After exercise the corporation has received an extra 10 million lots of £8, i.e., £80 million, but now there are 20 million shares in issue. So the original market value of £100 million should be added to the new cash sum of £80 million to make a total of £180 million. But this new market value is now spread over 20 million shares. So should not the new share price be £180 million/20 million = £9 per share? Does not the exercising of the warrants and resultant dilution of share ownership reduce the share price? And if this were the case, surely the shares would not be trading up at £10 in the first place, but really £9? The market would know that the outstanding warrants were about to be exercised and reduce the share price accordingly.

But the issue is even more complex than this because we have not taken into account the possibility of the warrants not being exercised. If the share price on the expiry day were suddenly to fall below £8, then the warrants would not be exercised and share dilution would not take place. So how does the market value the shares when it is not certain whether there is going to be 10 million shares or 20 million shares in existence?

Things are made more complicated by the fact that no-one knows for sure what the corporation is going to do with the new money injected into it by the exercise process. If the new money is deployed into exactly the same projects that the corporation is already involved in, then presumably analysts would say that the risk profile of the corporation is unchanged. If, however, the new money is placed into riskier projects, the whole profile of the company will have changed.

There is another aspect of warrants and CBs that until now has not been mentioned and that is, what does the corporation do with the premium received on issue? Issuing warrants or CBs is essentially issuing delayed delivery shares at a premium (that is assuming they are exercised or converted). Presumably the corporation having obtained a better price for existing shares will use the funds to enhance shareholder value.

But to get back to the point of this section — the exercising of warrants or converting of CBs must affect the underlying share price and this has not yet been taken into account in the modelling process. A further complication is that a corporation may have more than one warrant or CB outstanding that 'overhang' the share price. The modelling of one warrant should really take into account the possible added dilution caused by other warrants or CBs. It is not uncommon in Japan for one company to have up to five warrants overhanging the share.

In an attempt to model these complications it is easier to think of an entity that only has shares and outstanding warrants. The entity could be a corporation with no debt and no other commitments and be involved in a very simple business that could be modelled just like a share. Such entities already exist — investment trusts with warrants. In the next section we derive a model for the warrants on investment trusts and show how they can be used to shed light on the corporate warrant and CB modelling problem.

Before we go on to the next section it should be noted that a dilution factor as high as that given in the above example (i.e., 100%) is unusual. Often dilution ratios are only in the order of say 10% to 20%, but these may still have an impact on the underlying share price.

8.5 MODELLING INVESTMENT TRUST WARRANTS

Investment trust warrants lend themselves to particularly easy modelling. This is due to the fact that the three components that comprise an investment trust can be viewed (and often traded) separately. Investment trusts are managed investment vehicles that are traded like shares on the stock market. These vehicles come to market in much the same way as a new issue. The funds raised are used to buy shares that correspond to the investment proposals of the trust. This may mean buying shares in a particular sector or could mean buying all the leading shares in a particular country's stock market. The rationale for private individuals getting involved in such vehicles is that of economy of scale, diversification and management expertise. A small private investor could never efficiently buy, say, 50 different shares.

It has become common practice for new investment trusts to be issued with *free warrants* usually in the ratio of one to five. Subscribing for five shares at issue will result in the gift of one warrant exercisable into one share of the investment trust. These warrants are just like regular equity warrants in that exercise results in the issue of new investment trust shares. The exercise price is usually set to the investment trust issue price. These warrants are of course not free, but are included as an inducement to buy the shares on issue. After issue the warrants are detachable and can be traded separately. The inclusion of these warrants has caused much confusion in the investment trust community. Many do not know how to value warrants and even if they did, they are not sure how they should be included in the net asset value calculations. If the warrants are exercised, then for every five shares originally issued, there would end up being six. If the warrants are never exercised then the number of shares remains unchanged.

We begin the modelling process by making four simplifying assumptions. The first is that the trust invests in a very specific sector of the market — in fact so specific that it only invests in one company's shares. The astute reader will have probably guessed that the trust buys only ABC Bank shares. (This is not that unreasonable even though a real investment trust would buy a mixture of shares. Later on we will be modelling the trust warrants in terms of the underlying investments and we might as well restrict it to one type of share since all we will really be interested in is the volatility of the investments.) The second assumption is that the underlying shares do not pay a dividend and that they have no outstanding warrants or CBs. The third assumption is that the trust managers draw no fees and the fourth is that the trust never trades at a premium or discount to the true net asset value. We will call this new vehicle 'the ABC Bank Investment Trust'. So there are now three separate tradable entities: ABC Bank shares, ABC Bank trust shares and warrants exercisable into ABC Bank trust shares.

For simplicity and to make the numbers more meaningful let us assume that the trust consists solely of 100 ABC Bank shares and no cash. This trust has in issue 100 shares and 50 (not 20) warrants exercisable into one share, each with an exercise price of £8. For the moment we forget about what price these shares were issued at and go straight to the warrant expiry day. We consider three scenarios.

1. *Underlying ABC Bank shares priced at £6* The trust contains 100 shares and so the net asset value is £600. What should the holders of the warrants do? Say they exercise. They will have to pay up £8 each which will inject $50 \times £8 = £400$ into the trust. The trust now contains £600 worth of shares and £400 cash, so the total net asset value is £1,000. The trust now of course consists of 150 shares and no warrants and so the shares would be worth $1000/150 = £6.67$ each. The warrant holders have paid out £8 to get something worth £6.67. It clearly does not make sense to exercise. With the underlying shares at £6, the warrants would expire worthless and the number of shares would stay at 100. With the underlying shares at £6, the trust share price would thus stay at $600/100 = £6$.

2. *Underlying ABC Bank shares priced at £10* The net asset value of the trust is £1,000. If the warrant holders exercise they, as in scenario 1, will have to pay up £8 each, which still injects £400. The trust now contains £1,000 worth of shares and £400 cash, so the total net asset value is £1,400. The 150 shares would each now be worth $1400 / 150 = £9.33$. The warrant holders would have paid out £8 to get something worth £9.33. It makes sense to exercise. With the underlying shares at £10, the warrants would all be exercised and the number of shares in issue would increase to 150. With the underlying shares up at £10, the trust share price would thus alter to $1400/150 = £9.33$. At this higher share price, the trust has been diluted 50% and although the fund has received cash receipts of £400, these do not compensate the existing shareholders for the higher underlying share price.

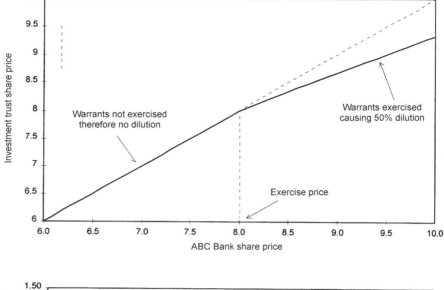

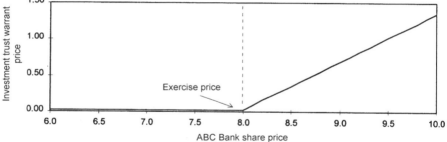

Figure 8.12   ABC Bank investment trust share price on warrant expiry day

3. *Underlying ABC Bank shares priced at £8*   The net asset value of the trust is £800. If the warrant holders exercise they inject £400 of cash. The trust now contains £800 worth of shares and £400 cash, so the total net asset value is £1,200. The 150 shares would each now be worth 1200/150 = £8.00. The warrant holders would have paid out £8 to get something worth £8.00. The warrant holders would be indifferent. It does not matter whether they exercise or not and so for simplicity we will assume that they would expire worthless.

So, as with a regular warrant, there is a key price — the exercise price. Below £8, the warrants would expire worthless and the number of shares would remain the same. Below £8, the trust price would be identical to the price of ABC Bank shares. Above £8, exercise would take place and although extra cash is taken in, the resultant dilution will mean that the trust share price will be lower than the ABC Bank share price. This is illustrated in Figure 8.12 which also shows the value of the warrant on expiry in terms of the underlying ABC Bank shares (not the investment trust shares).

We see that the shareholders in the trust are affected if the warrants are exercised. And this is exactly the point most workers make about corporate warrants. We can think of the similarity between the investment trust shareholders and regular shareholders. Shares in an investment trust give the holder ownership rights over ABC Bank shares. The existence of investment trust warrants introduces the possibility of that ownership being diluted. Shares in a regular corporation also give the holder ownership rights. The existence of outstanding warrants introduces the possibility of that ownership being diluted. In the case of the investment trust, the value is represented by the ABC Bank shares. These shares can rise or fall, pay a dividend or collapse. But the holder of the trust shares presumably is involved because he or she believes that in the long run, the underlying shares will produce a profit. The analogy with a regular share is clear. We hold individual shares because we believe that the underlying business is going to be profitable. The existence of warrants always introduces the possibility of the dilution of these profits.

8.5.1   A General One-period Investment Trust Warrant Model

Modelling an investment trust warrant is slightly more complex than modelling a regular call option, because the act of exercising alters the trust share price. And remember when exercised, the warrant produces trust shares, not the shares underlying the trust. We begin by modelling the investment trust shares and warrants in terms of the underlying ABC Bank shares. We use the following notation:

S = price of the ABC Bank share
s = price of the investment trust share
w = price of the investment trust warrant
E = exercise price of investment trust warrant (one share per warrant)
m = dilution factor

In the above example m was set to 0.5 so that 100 shares would be diluted to 100 (1 + m) = 150 shares. Now, for simplicity we assume the trust contains only one ABC Bank share but that fractional shares can be bought.

We can model s in terms of S on the warrant expiry day as follows. If $S < E$ then no exercise takes place and $s = S$. If $S > E$ then exercise takes place and proceeds equivalent to $m.E$ are injected into the trust. The trust now has in issue (1 + m) shares and so the new trust share price is $(S + m.E)/(1 + m)$.

$$s = \begin{cases} (S + m.E)/(1 + m) & \text{if } S > E \text{ (dilution)} \\ S & \text{if } S < E \text{ (no dilution)} \end{cases}$$

This can be expressed equivalently as

$$s = \text{Min}\{(S + m.E)/(1 + m), S\} \tag{8.11}$$

This is the situation depicted in Figure 8.12. On the expiry day the trust share price is represented by two disjoint straight line equations. The expiring warrant price w is given by

$$\begin{aligned} w &= \begin{cases} s - E & \text{if } S > E \\ 0 & \text{if } S < E \end{cases} \\ &= \begin{cases} (S + m.E)/(1 + m) - E & \text{if } S > E \\ 0 & \text{if } S < E \end{cases} \\ &= \begin{cases} (S - E)/(1 + m) & \text{if } S > E \\ 0 & \text{if } S < E \end{cases} \end{aligned}$$

or equivalently

$$w = \text{Max}\{(S - E)/(1 + m), 0\} \tag{8.12}$$

However, the expiring price, C, of a regular call option on ABC Bank shares is given by

$$C = \text{Max}\{(S - E), 0\}$$

So we can model the expiring investment trust warrant price in terms of an expiring call option on the shares underlying the trust as

$$w = C/(1 + m) \qquad \text{for all values of } S$$

and this is intuitively obvious. The expiring trust warrant prices will be equal to regular call option prices corrected for dilution effects (even if dilution does not take place).

We now consider what the situation is prior to expiry. We begin with a one-period model and try to express everything in terms of the ABC Bank share price. Assume that initially the ABC Bank shares are priced at S and that at the end of the period (the expiry day) the price could be up at $S.U$ or down at $S.D$. We express the expiring warrant prices in terms of the $S.U$ and $S.D$ using expression (8.12)

$$w_{\mathrm{u}} = \text{Max}\{(S.U - E)/(1 + m), 0\}$$

$$= \frac{\text{Max}\{(S.U - E), 0\}}{(1 + m)}$$

and similarly

$$w_d = \frac{\text{Max}\{(S.D - E), 0\}}{(1 + m)} \qquad (8.13)$$

The two-way bet argument can be used to construct a portfolio long of trust warrants and *short of ABC Bank shares.* The fair value of the warrants, w_f, will be given by

$$w_f = \frac{Pw_u + Qw_d}{1 + r}$$

where $P = \dfrac{1 + r - D}{U - D}$, and

$$Q = 1 - P$$

Substituting for w_u and w_d from expression (8.13) we have

$$w_f = \frac{P\text{Max}\{(S.U - E), 0\} + Q\text{Max}\{(S.D - E), 0\}}{(1 + m)(1 + r)}$$
$$= \frac{1}{(1 + m)} . C_f \qquad (8.14)$$

where C_f, is the one-period call option model fair value. So even before expiry, the investment trust warrant fair value can be expressed in terms of the fair value of a regular call option on the ABC Bank shares. The difference is again the dilution factor. We could now go on to the two-period model, then the three-period model and so on. With each model it transpires that the investment trust warrant price is always equal to the regular call option value divided by $(1 + m)$.

So why not leave it there? We can estimate the volatility, σ, of the ABC Bank shares and calculate $U = \exp(\sigma\sqrt{(t/n)})$ and $D = 1/U$. Substituting these into the n-period option model will give the call option value. Dividing this by the factor $(1 + m)$ will give the price of the investment trust warrant. Or even better, if appropriate, just simply use the Black and Scholes model and divide the result by $(1 + m)$.

The problem is that when we transfer the model back to the situation of a corporate warrant, the part played by the underlying ABC Bank shares is really the *company value.* In the above one-period model we used the two-way bet logic and constructed a portfolio of long the trust warrant and short ABC Bank shares. The U, D and σ parameters relate to the volatility of these shares. Translating this to the corporate warrant situation, the U, D and σ parameters relate to the volatility of the value of the company. Apart from the difficulty of conceiving this concept, it is not possible to trade in a company's value. We can only trade in the company's shares or warrants. So we need to express the price of the warrant not in terms of the underlying company value but in terms of the quoted shares. In terms of the investment trust model we need to express w_f in terms of s, and *not* in terms of S.

To do this we return to the one-period trust model. Expression (8.14) gives the price of the warrant prior to expiry in terms of S as w_f. Recall that one of the main assumptions is that the shares and the warrants together never trade at a discount or premium to the net asset value. So at the beginning of the period, i.e., prior to expiry, if the trust shares are priced at s then

$$s + m.w_f = S$$

we know w_f from expression (8.14) and so we can rearrange this expression and get

$$s = S - m.w_f \tag{8.15}$$

or

$$s = S - \frac{m.[\text{PMax}\{(S.U - E),0\} + Q\text{Max}\{(S.D - E),0\}]}{(1 + m)(1 + r)} \tag{8.16}$$

Before we continue it is interesting to see how graphically s and S are related and to get an idea we can revert to the example used throughout Chapter 5 in which $U = 1.1538$, $D = 0.9231$, $r = 0$, $P = 0.33$ and $Q = 0.67$. If $m = 0.5$ expression (8.16) reduces to

(a) $s = 0.67\ S + 2.67$, if $S > 8.67$
(b) $s = 0.87\ S + 0.89$, if $6.93 < S < 8.67$ $\hspace{2cm}$ (8.17)
(c) $s = S$, if $S < 6.93$

and this is illustrated in Figure 8.13.

Note that like the one-period warrant price, the trust price is also made up of three different straight lines. Substituting the U, D, P, Q, r and m values into expression (8.14) gives the warrant lines as

(a) $w_f = 0.67\ S - 5.33$, if $S > 8.67$
(b) $w_f = 0.26\ S - 1.78$, if $6.93 < S < 8.67$ $\hspace{2cm}$ (8.18)
(c) $w_f = 0$, if $S < 6.93$

Expressions (8.17) and (8.18) contain w_f, S and s. Eliminating S we get

(a) $w_f = 1.00\ s - 8.00$, if $S > 8.67$
(b) $w_f = 0.29\ s - 2.04$, if $6.93 < S < 8.67$ $\hspace{2cm}$ (8.19)
(c) $w_f = 0$, if $S < 6.93$

This is fair value of the warrant, w_f, expressed in terms of the investment trust share price, s.

There is another way of arriving at the warrant fair value. We could have arrived at this by constructing a portfolio long of warrants and *short investment trust shares*. The interesting point is that the investment trust shares move in a slightly different way from the underlying shares. We assume that the initial price of the

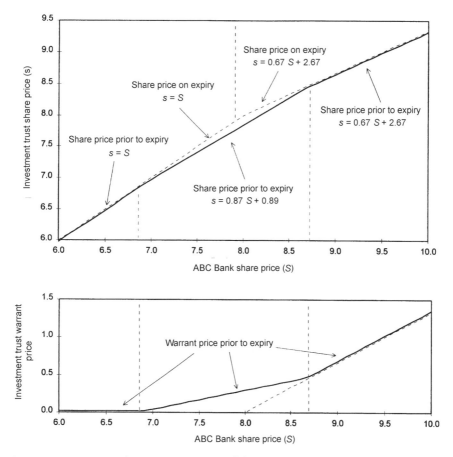

Figure 8.13   One-period investment trust model

trust shares and the ABC Bank shares are s and S respectively. If the underlying shares move up from S to $S.U$, then we assume that the trust shares move up from s to $s.u$, where the U and u factors are not necessarily the same. Similarly, if the underlying shares move down from S to $S.D$, then the trust shares move down from s to $s.d$, where the D and d factors are not necessarily the same. The situation is depicted in Figure 8.14.

Applying the two-way bet argument to the portfolio long of warrants and short trust shares we get the fair value as:

$$w_{\mathrm{f}} = \frac{pw_{\mathrm{u}} + qw_{\mathrm{d}}}{1 + r}$$

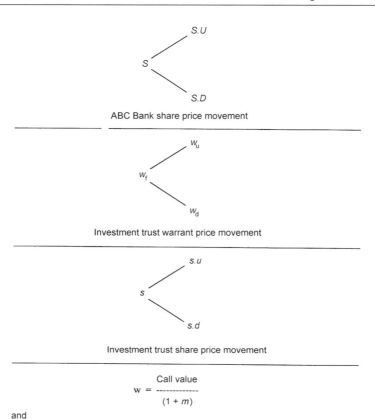

Figure 8.14 ABC Bank share, investment trust shares and investment trust warrants

where $p = \dfrac{1 + r - d}{u - d}$, and

$q = 1 - p$

$$w_{\mathrm{u}} = \mathrm{Max}\{(s.u - E), 0\} \text{ and } w_{\mathrm{d}} = \mathrm{Max}\{(s.d - E), 0\}$$

As before, this collapses to the three general equations:

(a) $w_{\mathrm{f}} = s - E$, if $S > E/D$
(b) $w_{\mathrm{f}} = (p.u.s - p.E)/(1+r)$, if $E/U < S < E/D$ (8.20)
(c) $w_{\mathrm{f}} = 0$, if $S < E/U$

Expressions (8.19) and (8.20) are identical and so it should be possible to find u, d, p and q — the parameters relating to the s process. This problem is solvable but very complex. The solution is complicated by the fact that u and d depend not only on U and D but also on the initial value of S. In our particular example with $U = 1.1538$, $D = 0.9231$, $r = 0$, $P = 0.33$, $Q = 0.67$ and $m = 0.5$, if $S = 2$ then $u = 1.1538 = U$ and $d = 0.9231 = D$. But if $S = 12$ then $u = 1.1154$ and $d = 0.9423$. So the degree to which the s price moves up or down depends on the original value of S. And this should be obvious. At very low S values the warrant will never be exercised on expiry and no dilution would take place. If no dilution takes place then the s price would mirror the S price. If the S price is high enough then dilution will take place and the up and down parameters affecting the s process will be different.

Remember that the point of this section is to try to include the possible dilution effects in a model for corporate CBs and warrants. The fact that the u and d parameters for the investment trust shares depend on the level of S, the underlying ABC Bank shares, has important implications. The up and down parameters define the extent to which something moves up or down and as such are related to volatility. The U and D values define the volatility of the ABC Bank shares and in our example are set at 1.1538 and 0.9231 respectively, whatever the value of S. The u and d parameters define the volatility of the investment trust shares, but these vary with S (and hence s). We explore this avenue more in the next section.

8.5.2 The *n*-period Investment Trust Warrant Model

We can clearly extend the one-period model to two-periods then three-periods and so on. As stated above, at all times, the investment trust warrant fair value is simply the value of a standard call option on the underlying ABC Bank shares divided by the $(1 + m)$ factor. However, what is of more interest is trying to value the warrant in terms of the s process rather than the S process. We also need to investigate how s depends on S.

To illustrate, let us use a standard five-period binomial model. We set the volatility of the ABC Bank shares at 25% and assume that the warrants have one year to expiry and that interest rates are zero. The S process is defined by the fixed up and down parameters $U = \exp(\sigma\sqrt{(t/n)}) = \exp(0.25\sqrt{(1/5)}) = 1.1183$ and $D = 1/U = 0.8942$. We assume that the share price is initially at £8. The ABC Bank share price tree and option price tree is shown in the top panel of Figure 8.15. The lower tree gives the investment trust warrant price (w) and share price (s) and is calculated as follows.

At each node the investment trust warrant price is calculated by dividing the corresponding call option price by $(1 + m)$ or 1.5. Once the warrant price is obtained, s is calculated using (8.15). In this example the call option price is worth £0.84 and so the investment trust warrant is worth $0.84/1.5 = £0.56$. This makes the investment trust share worth $8 - 0.5 \times 0.56 = £7.72$.

Compare the S and the s processes in the upper and lower panels of Figure 8.15 respectively. If the S process starts at £8 and follows the path up–down–up–down,

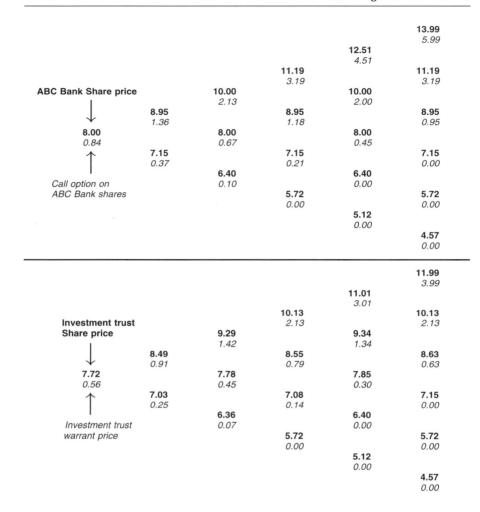

Figure 8.15   Five-period investment trust warrant model

the price always returns to the £8 level. The U and D values were specially constructed with $D = 1/U$ and so it is not surprising that up moves followed by down moves will result in identical S values. Now look at the corresponding s process. Starting at £7.72, an up followed by a down move gives $s = £7.78$. A further up and then down move results in $s = £7.85$. It seems that as time passes and with the underlying ABC Bank share price staying constant, the investment trust share price gradually increases. And this is because as time passes, the warrant is losing time value. If the net asset value of the trust remains constant (i.e., S stays at £8), then the warrants lose value and this value turns up in the trust share price. It is

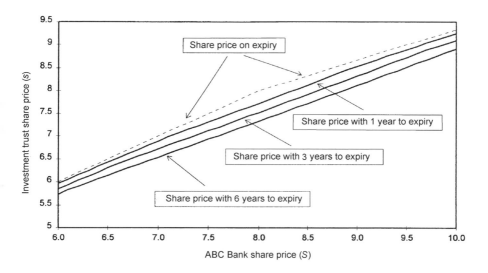

Figure 8.16   Five-period investment trust model

interesting to note that investors in investment trust shares benefit from the passage
of time at the expense of the warrant holders. The same can be said for corporate
shareholders and corporate warrant holders. The total value of a company is the
sum of all the shares and outstanding warrants. If the value of the underlying
business remains constant, the shares would gradually increase in value as the
outstanding warrants lose value.

This point is reinforced by Figure 8.16 which shows the investment trust share
price and warrant price variation at three different points in time: 6 years, 3 years
and 1 year to expiry. Other things being equal, as time passes, the warrant loses
value and the shares increase in value.

It is clear from Figure 8.16 that the relationship between the S process and the s
process alters over time and at different levels of S. Figure 8.15 shows us that if S

(a) The changing u and d parameters

u values				
				1.0896 / *0.9198*
			1.0871 / *0.9221*	
		1.0893 / *0.9201*		**1.0845** / *0.9245*
	1.0944 / *0.9156*		**1.0917** / *0.9180*	
1.1000 / *0.9106*		**1.0997** / *0.9108*		**1.0993** / *0.99112*
	1.1061 / *0.9051*		**1.1084** / *0.9031*	
d values		**1.1131** / *0.8989*		**1.1183** / *0.8942*
			1.1183 / *0.8942*	
				1.1183 / *0.8942*

(b) The volatility ratio = $(u-d)/(U-D)$

				0.76
			0.74	
		0.76		**0.71**
	0.80		**0.78**	
0.85		**0.84**		**0.84**
	0.90		**0.92**	
		0.96		**1.00**
			1.00	
				1.00

Figure 8.17   Five-period investment trust warrant model

moves up to $S.U$, then s moves up to $s.u$. The model is devised so that the U value is constant and set equal to $\exp(\sigma\sqrt{(t/n)})$. However, the u values are not constant and vary with S and time. As an example consider the first node in the s tree. If S moves up, then s moves up from $s = 7.72$ to $s.u = 8.49$ and so $u = 8.49\,/7.72 = 1.1000$. Similarly if S moves down, then s moves down from $s = 7.72$ to $s.d = 7.03$ and so $d = 0.9106$. It is possible to work through the s tree to calculate the u and d values corresponding to each node and these are illustrated in the top panel of Figure 8.17.

Note how at most nodes, the u values are smaller than the constant U value generating the S tree and that the d values are higher than the constant D value. In any binomial model, the up and down multipliers set the volatility of the process. If we have a process with smaller up multipliers (i.e., nearer to 1) and larger down multipliers (i.e., nearer to 1) then it must be that the volatility is lower. The s process therefore has a lower volatility and furthermore, since the u and d values change over time, this volatility is non-constant. It is possible to show that the ratio of the volatility of the s and the S process is given by the expression:

$$\text{ratio of volatilities} = \frac{\text{Vol}(s)}{\text{Vol}(S)} = \frac{(u-d)}{(U-D)}$$

The denominator of this ratio is fixed at all nodes but the numerator is constantly varying. The values of this ratio for the five-period model appear in the lower panel of Figure 8.17. At the first node the ratio is 0.85 and so with one year to expiry the investment trust shares will have a volatility equal to 85% of the volatility of the underlying ABC Bank shares (in this case 85% of 25% is 21.25%). At the end of the first period, i.e., after the passage of one-fifth of a year, there are two possibilities. If the share price rises then the volatility will fall to 80% of the underlying. If the share price falls then the volatility will increase to 90% of the underlying.

Tracing out the volatility ratio tree we see that generally, rising (falling) prices will be associated with a reduction (increase) in the volatility of the trust shares. This makes sense. The higher the share price the more likely it is that the warrants will be exercised. If the warrants are exercised there will be more shares plus some cash and this will have the effect of dampening down volatility. At lower share prices, warrant exercise is less likely. If the warrants are not exercised then share dilution does not take place and the trust share volatility will approach that of the ABC Bank shares.

This has a direct parallel to corporate warrants and CBs. The issuance of warrants should have a dampening effect on the volatility of the corporate's share price. If we assume that the volatility of the value of the corporation is a direct function of the volatility of the corporation's underlying business, then issuing a warrant has the effect of possibly diluting that volatility over more shareholders. And the higher the share price, the more likely that dilution will take place.

Figure 8.18 shows how this volatility ratio varies over time and at different possible dilution factors. The upper panel shows that, other things being equal, a trust with a short-dated warrant will have a lower volatility than one with a long-dated warrant. Also, although an increase in the value of S reduces the volatility of s, this effect diminishes and in the limit, the ratio approaches unity. At very high share prices the cash sum injected by exercise has a reduced effect. The lower panel illustrates that the higher the dilution factor the more marked the volatility reduction effect.

8.5.3 Using the Trust Share Price and Volatility to Value the Warrant

So far we have always calculated the warrant fair value from the dilution-adjusted call option price on the underlying share process. But what we really need is a way of calculating the warrant price from the investment trust share process. We could apply the one-period model and the associated two-way bet mathematics to each of the five sub-periods in the lower panel of Figure 8.15. At each node we would

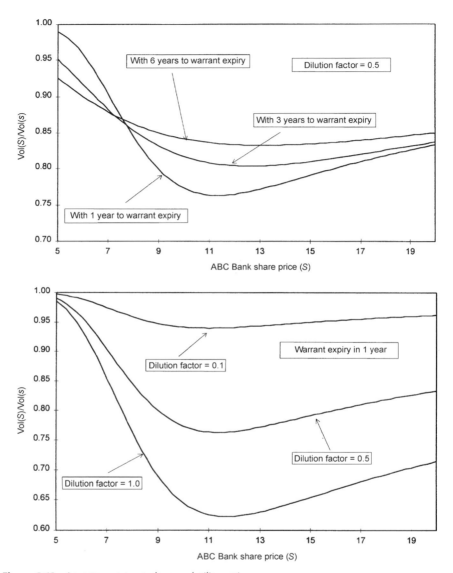

Figure 8.18   Investment trust share volatility ratio

employ the standard expression (8.1) to arrive at a warrant price. The problem is
that at each node, the u and d parameters change. At each node the u and d
parameters have to be calculated from an expression involving the S, U, D, m and
the previous warrant prices. It is solvable, but the resultant expressions are
enormously complex.

One attempt at getting around this problem is to try to price the warrant using the estimated volatility of the trust shares at each node. As an example consider the first nodes in Figure 8.15. We have:

ABC Bank
Share price = £8.00
Volatility = 25%
Call option price (with S = £8.00, vol = 25%) = £0.8360
Dilution-adjusted option price = £0.8360/(1 + 0.5) = £0.5573
The correct warrant price = £0.5573

Investment Trust
Share price = £7.72
Volatility = 21.25%
Call option price (with s = £7.72, vol = 21.25%) = £0.5555
The estimated warrant price = £0.5555

Rounded to two decimal places, the two methods arrive at the same answer of £0.56. Is this pure coincidence? Figure 8.19 shows that it is not. Figure 8.19 is a plot of the warrant prices arrived at by the two different methods, over a range of s prices. The model used has 50 periods and a dilution factor of 0.5. The two warrant values are almost identical at all s values. The author has investigated this feature at many different price levels, volatilities, times to expiry and dilution factors. The

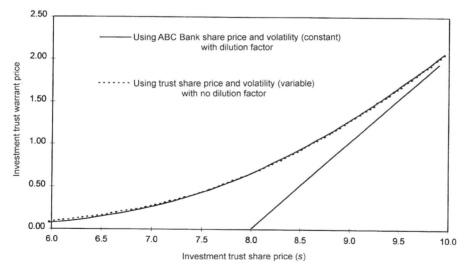

Figure 8.19 Two methods of calculating an investment trust warrant price

results are the same. The similarity between the two techniques is remarkable. And the similarity improves at lower dilution factors. With the dilution factors as low as 0.2, the maximum difference in the prices obtained by the two techniques is lower than 1%.

So one can arrive at a very good estimate of the true warrant value by using the investment trust share price and the (lower) investment trust share price volatility. And this is very useful in that in reality, it is often not possible to see or trade the underlying net asset value (in our case the ABC Bank shares). Often we can only participate in the trust's shares or warrants. So the only volatility we ever actually get to measure is that of the quoted trust's shares.

8.5.4   The Potential Dilution is Already in the Share Price

These results have important consequences for the valuation of corporate warrants and CBs. The standard argument against using techniques such as the binomial model or the Black and Scholes model to price warrants or CBs, is that of the dilution issue. Many workers believe that by ignoring dilution, these models overvalue corporate derivatives. But we can see that this is not the case.

Other things being equal, the correct fair price of a corporate warrant or CB can only be obtained if we can estimate the volatility of the value of the company. But this is never possible and it is never possible to trade in the total company's value — only its shares or warrants or CBs. However, we see from the modelling of investment trust warrants and shares, that an approximate solution exists. The very presence of a warrant or CB will have a dampening effect on the volatility of the quoted shares. Estimating the volatility of the quoted share price is a simple matter. And using this volatility in a standard model will produce a price that is very close to the correct fair price for the derivative.

Although outstanding warrants or CBs represent calls on the value of the corporation, they can be valued *without correction for dilution* by using the volatility of the quoted shares. We can say that the possible future dilution is already reflected in the share price. This possible future dilution manifests itself in the form of a lower share price and a lower volatility.

8.5.5   Final Remarks on the Dilution Issue

The above discussion on investment trust shares and warrants is an attempt to address the issue of dilution applied to corporate warrants. It is possible to apply the same type of argument to model that of a corporation with an outstanding CB. The basic idea is the same — the possibility of dilution changing the number of shares. But whether pricing warrants or CBs, there are still a number of complications associated with the model. We finish by making a brief note on each of these issues.

1. *Valuing derivatives with non-constant volatility*   If the volatility of the S process is constant, then the volatility of the s process varies. The binomial or the Black and Scholes model assumes that the variance of the underlying process is constant. The method of using the instantaneous volatility of the s process is only an approximation. Although it does seem to work well, it is only an approximation.

2. *Estimating a volatility that is constantly changing*   If the volatility of the s process is changing, how do we estimate it? The standard way of estimating volatility is to get the last n daily or weekly or monthly prices and use the procedures outlined in Chapter 3. But these procedures assume that the underlying volatility is constant. There are a number of techniques that can be applied if it is believed that the underlying volatility is variable and the most common one is to use some sort of time-weighted average. Say there were 20 weekly price changes, then the standard volatility expression could be altered so that most weight is placed on the most recent change, less weight on the next change and so on, until the last change has the least weight. The topic of non-constant volatility is the subject of much current research.

3. *The validity of the lognormal process*   If the U and D parameters are constant (and hence volatility constant) and the number of periods used increases, then in the limit, the S process follows what is known as the 'lognormal distribution'. The assumption that the underlying process follows a lognormal distribution is one of the basic assumptions of the Black and Scholes model. If S follows a lognormal distribution then, by definition, s cannot. The s process, just like the w process, is actually a derivative running on the top of the S process.

4. *Reversing the logic*   It is possible to change the model (of an investment trust or a corporation) to get around some of the above problems. Why not start off by assuming that the s process *drives* the S process. We could begin by modelling s as a fixed volatility process with the u and d parameters constant. The S process, which of course is the sum of the s and w processes, would thus have variable U and D parameters with a resultant variable volatility. In the limit, the s process would thus become lognormal and the S process non-lognormal.

5. *What happens to the exercise proceeds?*   In all the above we assume that the cash sum received on warrant exercise or on CB issue stays as cash. This, of course, is usually not the case. A corporation issues a CB or warrant to raise capital, usually for some project. If the project is going to be very much riskier than the company's existing business, then there is the possibility that issuing a corporate derivative will actually increase rather than decrease volatility of the share price. One could attempt to include this in our model by replacing the E term (corresponding to the exercise proceeds) with another risky term. This new risky term could be correlated to the existing share price s, or not. The resultant model would be more complex and will not be discussed here.

9
Refix clauses

CBs are very complex instruments and as a result quite difficult to model. In 1991 the level of complexity was stepped up one more notch with the introduction of refix clauses. These features, originally introduced to the Japanese warrant market, were an attempt by the issuers to make the instruments more attractive and have become increasingly common. A refix clause introduces the possibility of the terms of a CB being altered, usually in the holder's favour.

9.1 AN EXAMPLE

Consider a new type of CB issued by the ABC Bank. This one, like the one considered throughout this book, has a nominal value of £5,000. The conversion price is £8 and the number of shares per bond is 625 (625 × 8 = £5,000). This CB, however, has a refix clause that, subject to certain conditions, alters both the conversion price and the number of shares per bond on a certain day between issue and expiry. On the refix day, if the share price is below the conversion price, then the conversion price is reset to the share price and at the same time, the number of shares per bond is increased so that the nominal bond value remains constant.

For example, if on the refix day the share price is £7.50, then the conversion price is reset to £7.50 and the number of shares per bond is increased to 5000/7.50 = 667. If on the refix day the share price is £7.00, then the new characteristics are: conversion price = £7.00 and shares per bond = 5000/7.00 = 712. Refixes are usually limited to a maximum amount and a typical value would be 25%. So if the share price drops by 25% of the conversion price (to £6.00 in this example) then that is the maximum degree of refixing. If the share price is at £5.00 on the refixing day then the terms of the CB would be altered to: conversion price = £6.00 and shares per bond = 5000/6.00 = 833.

It is easy to see how the inclusion of a refix clause would make a CB more attractive. The clause acts in two ways. First, if the share price were to fall significantly between issue and refixing, then the lower conversion price and more shares per bond redefine the instrument at a new lower level. The refix clause acts as a sort of additional floor. Secondly, if the share price falls enough to get the maximum degree of refixing then it is always possible that a rally later on will drive the instrument deep in the money. In our example, if this happens, the CB will have 25% extra shares and so, other things being equal, will be worth 25% more than a CB without a refix clause. Both of these attributes make a CB with a refix more attractive than one without. And this should be reflected in the price. This additional feature should have to be paid for — the refix clause should make a CB more expensive. In this chapter we show how to include a refix clause in the CB model.

9.2   CB PRICE ON THE REFIX DAY

Before we get into the complexities of the modelling process, it is easy to deduce what the price profile will be on the refix day. We illustrate by continuing with the CB example given above. For simplicity we assume that there are no coupons, no dividends, that interest rates are zero and that the share price volatility is 25%. The CB has one year to expiry and we are at the refix date. We can use the Black and Scholes method to model two CBs, one with an unchanged conversion price of £8.00 and the other with the conversion price reduced by the maximum amount to £6.00.

Let us first assume that on the refix day the share price is £8.00. At this price the terms of the CB would not change. Using the Black and Scholes model with the above parameters the CB price would be £8.80 per share or $625 \times 8.80 = £5,500$ per bond. Now consider the situation if the share price is £7.50 on the refix day. The new conversion price is £7.50 and the model gives the new CB price as £8.25 per share. However, the instrument is now convertible into 667 shares and so the package value would be worth $667 \times 8.25 = £5,500$, i.e., the same. In bond terms or in terms of the original number of shares, the instrument value is unchanged. A little algebra shows that the CB price is constant for all share prices between £8.00 and £6.00. Above £8.00 the price follows the profile of a CB without a refix. Below £6.00 the price follows the profile of a CB that has had the maximum refixing. In between these two prices the price stays constant. This is illustrated in Figure 9.1.

9.3   CB PRICE PRIOR TO REFIX DAY

Figure 9.1 is the refix equivalent of the first step in modelling a standard CB. Recall that the first step is finding out what the value is on expiry. One then steps back through the binomial tree to the starting point. Unfortunately, there is an additional complication and it is that at the starting point we will not know what the final conversion price will be. If we do not know what the final conversion price is we cannot simply use backward induction.

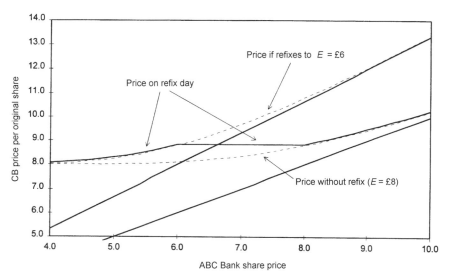

Figure 9.1 CB price on refix day

Recall that with an *n*-period model there are $(n + 1)$ different final share prices. If the initial share price is S and the up and down parameters are u and d respectively, then the final share prices, starting at the lowest are: $S.d^n$, $S.d^{n-1}.u$, ..., $S.u^n$. For any k, the number of different ways of ending up at $S.d^{n-k}.u^k$ is given by $n!$ $/(k! (n - k!))$. If $n = 5$ and $k = 2$ there are $5!/(2!(3!)) = 10$ different ways of ending up at $S.d^3.u^2$. If $n = 50$ and $k = 25$ the number of ways of ending up at $S.d^{25}.u^{25}$ is 126 trillion. Expiring CB prices are the maximum of the final share price and the conversion price. With a standard CB, all we need is the value of the final share price; it doesn't matter which way it was arrived at. But if there is a refix clause then the route to the final share price is important. Figure 9.2 illustrates the point.

In Figure 9.2 we consider in detail the situation of the final share price ending up at £10.00. Of the many ways of arriving at £10.00, we concentrate on just three: route 1, route 2 and route 3. These three routes are chosen to illustrate why the final CB price is dependent on the path taken by the share price.

Route 1   The share price on the refix day is above £8.00 and so the CB terms remain unaltered. On the expiry day the final share price is £10.00, so the holder would convert and the expiring CB price would be £10.00 per share or $625 \times 10 =$ £6,250.

Route 2   The share price on the refix day is £7.00 and so the conversion price is refixed at £7.00 and the shares per bond increased to 714. On the expiry day the CB holder would convert and the expiring CB price would be £10.00 per share or 714 $\times$ 10 = £7,140.

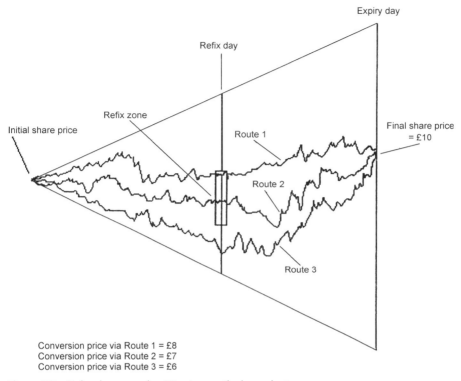

Conversion price via Route 1 = £8
Conversion price via Route 2 = £7
Conversion price via Route 3 = £6

Figure 9.2 Refix clauses make CB prices path dependent

Route 3 The share price on the refix day is £5.00 and so the conversion price is altered by the maximum amount to £6.00 and the shares per bond increased to 833. On the expiry day the CB holder would convert and the expiring CB price would be £10.00 per share or 833 × 10 = £8,333.

In this example the share price starts at £8.00 and ends up at £10.00, but the final CB value depends on which route was taken. *The final CB price is path dependent.* We need to devise a way of incorporating this path dependency into a model.

9.4 MODELLING REFIX CLAUSES — TWO-STAGE BINOMIAL TREES

One way to solve the problem of path dependency is to build two layers of binomial tree. This is illustrated schematically in Figure 9.3. We begin, as in the standard CB model, by starting with an initial share price S and map out the tree of prices using the up and down multipliers. When we reach the refix day we stop and branch out

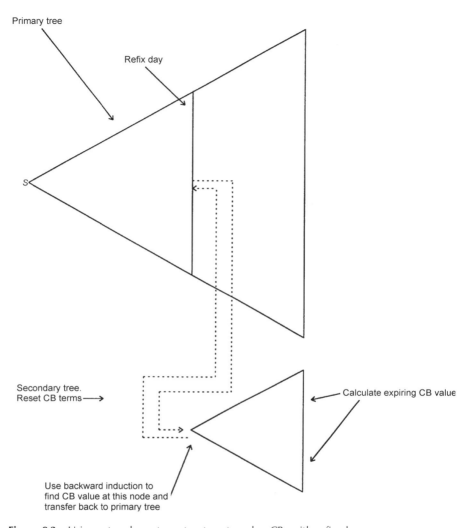

Primary tree

Refix day

S

Secondary tree.
Reset CB terms ⟶

Calculate expiring CB value

Use backward induction to
find CB value at this node and
transfer back to primary tree

Figure 9.3   Using a two-layer tree structure to value CBs with refix clauses

to a second set of binomial trees. For each node in the original tree we generate another tree. The initial share price in these new trees is set equal to the corresponding value on the refix day in the old tree. These initial share prices determine the CB terms for each new tree. The share price process is continued in the new trees until expiry day. On expiry the CB value is obtained in the usual way — the maximum of the share price or the conversion price. The difference now is that each of the new trees will have (possibly) a different conversion price.

Applying backward induction will produce a set of CB values at the origin of each of the new trees. These values are then transferred back to the original tree and backward induction will give the CB price required.

9.5   A FIVE-PERIOD REFIX MODEL EXAMPLE

To illustrate the two-layer binomial tree technique we use our ABC Bank CB example defined in Section 9.1. We assume no coupons, no dividends, no interest rates and a volatility of 25%. The CB has one year to expiry and the refix clause is two-fifths into the year. For an $n = 5$ period model these characteristics give the usual parameters as $u = 1.1183$, $d = 0.8942$, $p = 0.4721$ and $q = 0.5279$. Assume that the initial share price is $S = £7.00$. The solution is shown in Figure 9.4. On the refix day there are three possible share prices: £8.75, £7.00 and £5.60. There are three second-level share trees corresponding to each of these values.

With S = £8.75 on refix day   With the share price at £8.75, i.e., higher than £8.00, no refixing takes place. The conversion price and shares per bond are £8.00 and 625 respectively. Generating the second share tree results in four possible final share prices: £12.24, £9.79, £7.83 and £6.26. The CB values corresponding to these nodes are £12.24, £9.79, £8.00 and £8.00 respectively. Applying backward induction gives the *CB value as £9.06 per share*. This is then transferred back to the node corresponding to the appropriate share price in the original tree.

With S = £7.00 on refix day   With the share price at £7.00, i.e., lower than £8.00, refixing takes place. The conversion price and shares per bond are now £7.00 and 714 respectively. Generating the second share tree results in four possible final share prices: £9.79, £7.83, £6.26 and £5.01. The CB values corresponding to these nodes are £9.79, £7.00, £7.00 and £7.00 per share respectively. But the CB now has more shares and so to express these values in terms of the original shares we should multiply by the ratio $714/625 = 1.14$. So expressed in the original terms, the expiring CB prices are £11.19, £8.95, £8.00 and £8.00 respectively. Applying backward induction gives the *CB value as £8.67 per share*. This is then transferred back to the original tree.

With S = £5.60 on refix day   With the share price at £5.60, refixing takes place, but only to the maximum amount of £6.00 and 833 shares per bond. The second share tree results in four possible final share prices: £7.83, £6.26, £5.01 and £4.00. The CB values corresponding to these nodes are £7.83, £6.26, £6.00 and £6.00 per share respectively. Applying the new multiplier of $833/625 = 1.33$ to these values we get the expiring CB prices as £10.44, £8.35, £8.00 and £8.00 respectively. Applying backward induction gives the *CB value as £8.38 per share*. This is then transferred back to the original tree.

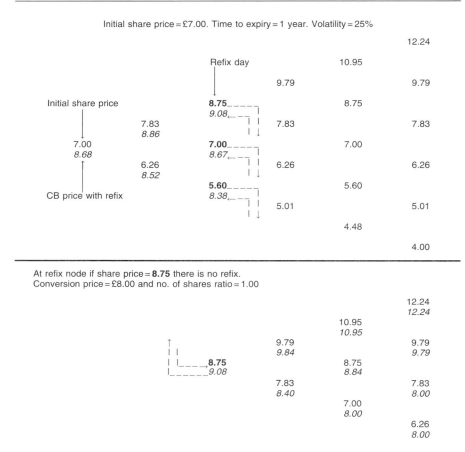

Initial share price = £7.00. Time to expiry = 1 year. Volatility = 25%

Figure 9.4   Five-period investment trust warrant model

Returning to the original tree we now proceed with the usual backward induction and arrive at a CB price of £8.68 per share. This compares with a price of £8.33 if the CB had no refix clause. So the refix clause does increase the fair value. In this example the difference is 4%.

9.6   INCREASING THE NUMBER OF PERIODS

With $n = 5$ periods the price profiles and price sensitivity profiles will be extremely lumpy. We need a model with at least $n = 50$. The problem is that the procedure for calculating CB prices with refixes involves many more iterations. In the above example, with $n = 5$, there are 6 nodes in the primary tree and 10 nodes in each of the three secondary trees. The refix model therefore requires the calculation of a

At refix node if share price = **7.00** refix takes place.
Conversion price = £7.00 and no. of shares ratio = 1.14

At refix node if share price = **5.60** maximum refix takes place.
Conversion price = £6.00 and no. of shares ratio = 1.33

Figure 9.4   Continued

total of 6 + 3 × 10 = 36 different nodes compared to 21 with no refix. Unfortunately, the number of node calculations required increases significantly with n. Table 9.1 gives a few examples. At $n = 50$ the standard binomial CB model requires the calculation of values at 1,326 different nodes. If there is a refix at the 17th period then this number increases eightfold to 10,881. Calculating the price and price sensitivities of a CB with a refix can be a time-consuming exercise. Rather than using spreadsheet type software like Excel it is more efficient to use a dedicated one-off program. The author has written a dedicated one-off routine called REFIX that can be called from Excel and this, although slow, is considerably faster than using the spreadsheet direct. (Note that REFIX is not on the disk supplied with this book.)

9.7   THE EFFECTS OF A REFIX CLAUSE ON CB PRICES

The program REFIX was used to create Figure 9.5 which gives the price of our example CB at various times before the refix day. The parameters used are: $n = 50$,

Table 9.1 Number of iterations involved in refix model

n = number of periods	No. of nodes in standard model	nr = period number of refix point	No. of nodes in refix model
5	21	2	36
		1	33
9	55	6	98
		3	122
50	1,326	40	3,567
		25	9,477
		17	10,881
200	20,301	180	58,282
		100	525,402
		67	617,406

vol = 25%, interest rate = 0, no coupons, no dividends, time to expiry = 1 year and a refix clause (up to a maximum of 20%) at the six-month point. Note that as time passes the price behaviour is different at different share prices. At high share prices the price behaviour is similar to a CB without a refix. The curved price profile collapses gradually towards the parity line corresponding to the unaltered CB. At low share prices the opposite happens. As time passes, the curved price profile rises towards the maximum refix parity line from below. At high share prices this instrument loses value over time, but at low share prices it gains value over time. With hindsight this behaviour is obvious. At high share prices, the likelihood of a refix is low and so the CB would behave like a regular CB, i.e., lose value over time. At low share prices, the likelihood of a refix is high and if this occurs the instrument must trade at a price at least equal to the new (higher) parity line. At share prices between the two extremes the price profile flattens out as refix approaches. And this is because between the two extremes, the reduction in the conversion price and the increase in the number of shares per bond exactly balance out. At these medium share prices the instrument would gradually become insensitive to price movements. The lower panel of Figure 9.5 shows in more detail the behaviour around the maximum refix point.

9.8 HOW MUCH IS A REFIX CLAUSE WORTH?

Figure 9.5 shows what happens as a given CB approaches its refix date. At certain points, the price rises and at others the price falls. But how much is a refix clause worth? We need to compare CBs with various different refix clauses with standard

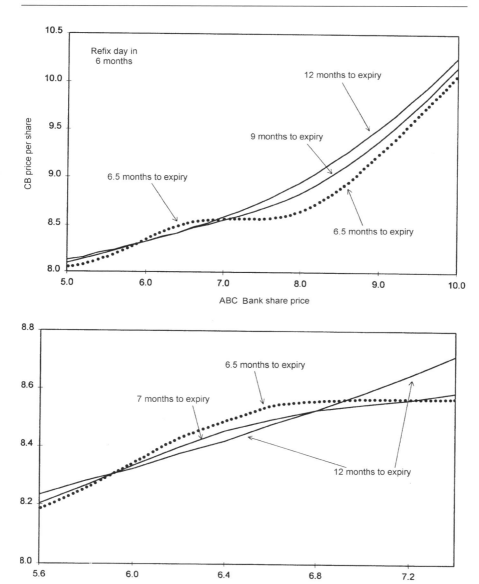

Figure 9.5   CB price as refix day approaches

CBs. Figure 9.6 illustrates four CBs with no coupons, no dividends, volatility set to 25%, interest rates set to 4% and all having five years to expiry. Three of the CBs have refix clauses that reset the terms to a maximum of 20%. The times to the refix clauses are: 3 months, 1 year and 2.5 years. The fourth CB has no refix clause.

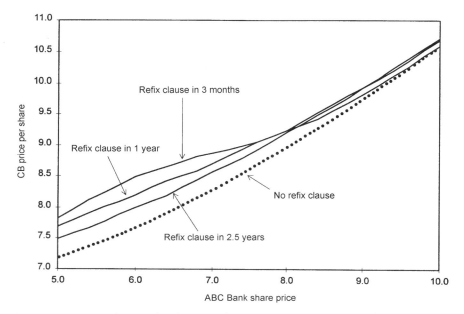

Figure 9.6   How much is a refix clause worth?

Note that at share prices lower than £8, the CB price is higher, the nearer the refix date. At a share price of £6.60, the difference between a straight CB and the instruments with refixes are £0.71, £0.48 and £0.29 per share for the 3 months, 1 year and 2.5 years cases respectively. These translate into 8.89, 6.00 and 3.63 bond points respectively. So refix clauses do make CBs more expensive and the nearer the refix, the more the feature is worth. Issuers then should (and often do) get higher prices for their CBs if they include these additional features.

9.9   UPSIDE AND DOWNSIDE REFIX CLAUSES

Most refix clauses reset the terms of a bond in favour of the bondholder. There are now some CBs that have refix clauses that alter the terms in a negative as well as a positive sense. As an example, consider a CB that refixes to a maximum degree of 20% on the upside as well as the downside. With the ABC Bank CB, the original conversion price and share per bond is £8.00 and 625 shares respectively. On the refix day we look at three different scenarios.

1.   *Share Price = £5.00*   The share price is below the maximum reset value and so the new CB terms are: new conversion price = £8 × 0.80 = £6.40 and new shares per bond = 5,000/6.40 = 781.

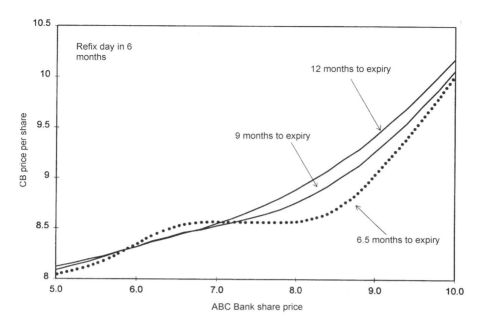

Figure 9.7 Upside and downside refix as refix day approaches

2. *Share Price* = *£9.00*   The share price is above the original conversion price so the instrument is reset to: new conversion price = £9.00 and new shares per bond = 5,000/9.00 = 556.

3. *Share Price* = *£11.00*   The share price is above the maximum reset value of £8 × 1.2 = £9.60 and so the new CB terms are: new conversion price = £9.60 and new shares per bond = 5,000/9.60 = 521

In this example the investor has the possibility of ending up with an instrument that is convertible into fewer shares as well as more shares than the original CB. These types of CBs should trade at lower prices than those with only favourable (i.e., downside) type refix clauses. Figure 9.7 gives the prices of the CB illustrated in Figure 9.5 but with the clause altered to include the possibility of an upside refix. The prices are lower but it is difficult to see from this illustration. The effect can be seen more clearly in Figure 9.8 which shows the difference between a CB with only a downside refix and one with both types. The difference is most marked just prior to the refix date and with the share price near the original conversion price.

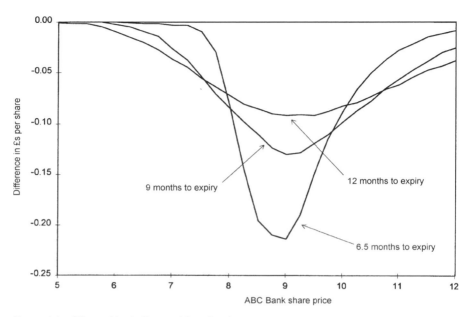

Figure 9.8   Effect of including upside refix clause

9.10   THE EFFECTS OF REFIX CLAUSES ON CB PRICE SENSITIVITIES

Refix clauses can drastically alter CB price sensitivities. It is possible to calculate and chart all the sensitivities mentioned in Chapter 7. However, some of the effects can be deduced simply by observing price charts such as Figure 9.5 and Figure 9.7.

The delta or rate of change of the CB price with respect to the underlying share price is the slope of the CB price curve. Note that if the refix day is far off, then the delta will be very much like that of a regular CB. As the refix day approaches, the price curve alters. Near the refix day the price curve flattens out over a certain range and so the delta will approach zero. Either side of this special range the delta will be positive. A hedger running delta neutral position into the refix period has an unusual rehedging strategy. If initially the share price is high, then the hedge will involve a short position in the shares of say 80%. If the share price were to gradually fall then this ratio would be decreased by buying back shares. A certain point will be reached when the delta is near zero and there will be no short position. If the share price continues to fall, the hedge ratio suddenly becomes significant again and a short position would have to be re-established.

The theta or time decay of a CB with a refix clause is even more complex than one without. In Figure 9.5 and Figure 9.7 we see that with the share price near the lower and upper maximum refix points, the theta effects are most marked. At the lower share price, the CB increases significantly as refix day approaches. This is because at a lower share price level there is a higher probability that the maximum refix will take place. A maximum refix has the possibility of making the CB worth much more. At the upper share price level, the opposite is true. At the higher share prices either the CB will not be refixed or if it is, then it will potentially reduce the future value.

9.11 MULTIPLE REFIX CLAUSES

It gets more complex. First came CBs with a single downside type refix clause. Then came instruments with both upside and downside refix clauses. And now there are CBs with more than one refix day. An example would be a five-year instrument with a refix clause at the end of year three and another one at the end of year four. It is easy to imagine the complications involved in valuing these CBs. In August 1995, Mitsubishi Bank issued a $2 billion, seven-year CB with a refix clause at the end of each and every year.

9.12 REFIX CLAUSES AND DILUTION

A refix clause clearly affects the future possible dilution. Downside refix clauses introduce the possibility of each bond being converted into more shares. If this refixing occurs then the total share dilution will be greater than that if the original bond terms are left unaltered. The question of the uncertain dilution factor may also have an impact on the modelling process.

APPENDIX
A guide to the software supplied on disk

This appendix is intended to assist those readers wishing to build their own CB models in a Microsoft Excel framework. All the models developed in this book are dealt with in more detail. Also, to save the reader the time and the problems associated with keying errors, most of the models are provided on the disc supplied with this book.

Note that when opening some of the files the RAND() function will generate a new set of random numbers, so the entries in those cells with the = RAND() statement will not correspond to those in the reported figures. Each time a file is opened, or a calculation is completed, or the F9 key is pressed, a new set of random numbers will be generated.

Wherever possible the equations written in cells contain named variables. Throughout this appendix named variables appear in *italics*. In Excel spreadsheets relating to models in Chapter 4 and onwards, the naming of variables follows an obvious convention. For example in the file Five.xls, the up parameter will be named u_1 in sheet Append_5_1, u_2 in sheet Append_5_2 and u_3 in Append_5_3.

CHAPTER 2: USING COMPUTER SPREADSHEETS

Chapter 2 already explains in full all the non-basic functions used in the CB and share price modelling process. All the programmes relating to this chapter are in the file Two.xls. Each model and each example is on a separate sheet within the file. The sheet names correspond to the examples outlined in Chapter 2.

CHAPTER 4: MODELLING THE SHARE PRICE PROCESS

The file Four.xls contains the models used to generate some of the Figures in Chapter 4.

The named variables *probup* and *move* represent the probability of an up move and the magnitude of the up move respectively. The simulations illustrated in Figure 4.1 are generated from the set of random numbers in the A column. Statements of the type:

$$\text{IF } (A5 < probup, move, -move)$$

translate the random numbers into up or down moves. The details are given in Figure A.1.

Figures 4.2 and 4.3 are generated using a similar process but with the *move* parameter set to a smaller value and with more periods.

In order to simulate a multiplicative model the *move* parameter is replaced by the parameters: *u* and *d* that represent the up and down multipliers respectively. In the multiplicative model if the random number is less than *probup* then the preceding price is multiplied by *u*. If the random number is greater than *probup* then the preceding price is multiplied by *d*. Figure A.2 illustrates how one of the multiplicative simulated series shown in Figure 4.4 is generated.

Non-independent time series are generated on sheet Append_4_3 and illustrated here in Figure A.3. The procedure works as follows.

The up and down multiplying parameters are named *up* and *down* respectively. Five different up probabilities are set as outlined in Section 4.4. If the preceding five moves are all up, then the probability of the next move being up is set to *pu5*. In the example given on the disc, *pu5* is set equal to 0.7. If four of the preceding five moves were up, then the probability of the next move being up is set to *pu4* = 0.6, etc. The random numbers are generated in the cells: B15 to B314. The probability of an up move is calculated and appears in the cells: A15 to A314. (More on this process below.) An up move is registered by a '1' appearing in the cells C15 to C314 and a down move is registered by a '0'. If the random number in column B is less than the appropriate probability in column A, then a '1' is placed in the C column using the statement:

$$= \text{IF } (B15 < A15, 1, 0)$$

If a '1' appears in column C, then the price in column E is set equal to the preceding price multiplied by *up*. If a '0' appears in column C, then the price in column E is set equal to the preceding price multiplied by *down*. In the example given the price series in column E starts at 100.00 and finishes at 46.67. For comparison purposes, column F contains a price series generated from the same set of random numbers but with the probability of an up move set to a constant value of 0.5. The price series in column E will exhibit price stickiness, whereas the price series in column F will be purely random.

The trick in generating the non-independent price series is in the method by which the probability of an up move is reset with every new move. This is

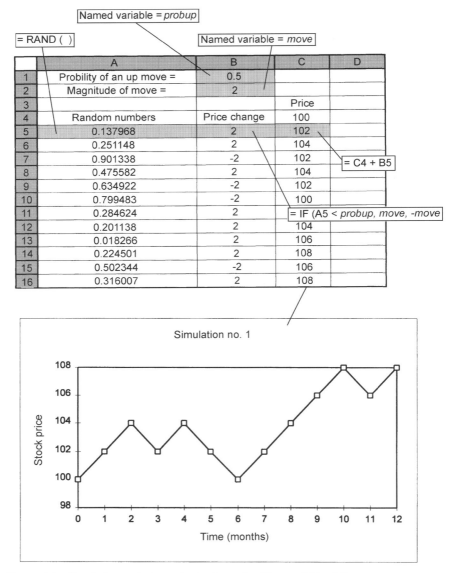

Figure A.1 Simulating an independent price series (Figures 4.1 to 4.3)

accomplished by keeping track of the number of up moves. The total number of up moves in the preceding five moves is calculated in the D column using a statement of the type:

$$= \text{SUM (C11:C15)}$$

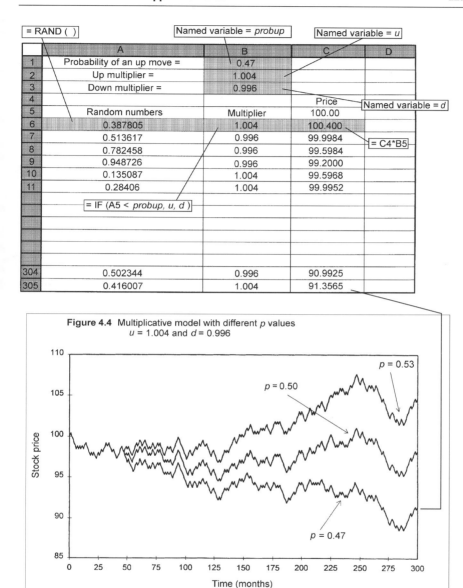

Figure A.2   Simulating a multiplicative independent price series (Figure 4.4)

The result of this calculation is obviously a number between 0 and 5 and this is used to reset the probability of an up move. In the example given in Figure A.3, the first total in cell D14 is equal to 4. Accordingly the new probability of an up move in cell A15 is set to 0.6. The statement that resets the probability in cell A15 is:

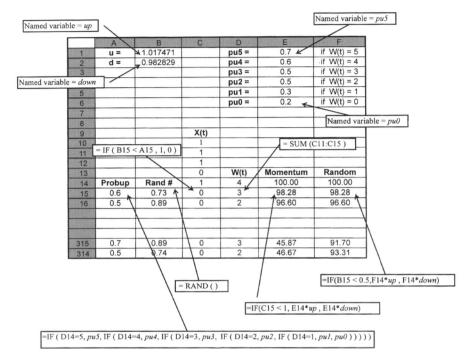

Figure A.3 Generating non-independent time series (Figures 4.7 to 4.8)

= IF (D14 = 5, *pu5*,

   IF (D14 = 4, *pu4*,

     IF (D14 = 3, *pu3*,

       IF (D14 = 2, *pu2*,

         IF (D14 = 1, *pu1*, *pu0*)))))

Although this looks very complex, it is simply a way of returning one of the values: *pu5, pu4, pu3, pu2, pu1* or *pu0*. (For a detailed explanation of how nested IF statements work, see Chapter 2.) The value returned depends on the number in the cell D14. In the example, D14 contains the value 4 and so the value of *pu4*, the probability of the next move being up given that four of the previous moves were up, is returned. So the cell A15 has the probability set to *pu4* = 0.6. Looking down the D column we note that the running total of the number of up moves varies. As this total varies so do the probabilities in the A column.

CHAPTER 5: THE BASIC CONVERTIBLE BOND MODEL

The file Five.xls contains the models used to generate some of the figures in Chapter 5 and has different sheets labelled Append_5_1 , Append_5_2 , etc. Progressive sheets deals with the ever more complex aspects of the binomial CB model.

The one-period model is dealt with on sheet Append_5_1. The up and down parameters are the named variables: u_1 and d_1. The interest rate parameter is the named variable r_1 and the conversion price is E_1. The details of this sheet along with all the named variables are shown in Figure A.4.

The one-period model is very simple and the mathematical expressions used are almost identical to those used throughout Chapter 5. The initial share price (named variable S_1) for the share price tree is in the cell B12. The two end share prices are obtained by multiplying this price by the up and down multipliers. So cells C11 and C13 contain the expressions:

$$= B12 * u\_1$$

and

$$= B12 * d\_1$$

respectively.

The CB tree is in the cell range: E11 to F13. The CB value corresponding to the upper share price in cell C11 appears in cell F11 and is given by the expression:

$$= \text{Max } \{C11 , E\_1\}$$

and similarly the CB value corresponding to the lower share price in cell C13 appears in cell F13 and is:

$$= \text{Max } \{C13 , E\_1\}$$

The CB fair price at the beginning of the tree is calculated in cell E12 using the expression:

$$= (p\_1 * F11 + q\_1 * F13) / (1 + r\_1)$$

which corresponds to equation (5.11)

$$CB_f = \frac{pCB_u + qCB_d}{1 + r}$$

With the share price at £7.80, the CB price becomes £8.33 with no interest rate and £8.14 with an interest rate of 5%. The 'Table' facility of Excel is used to

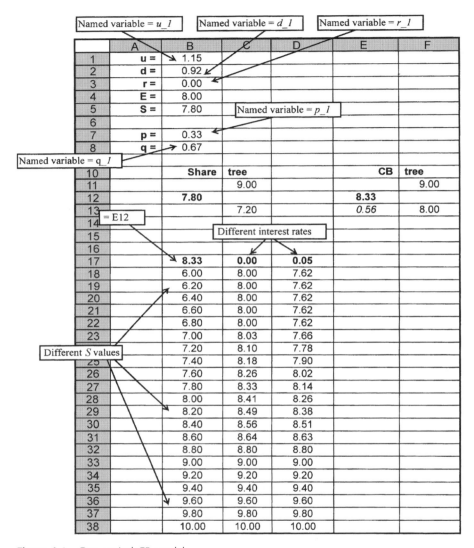

Figure A.4 One-period CB model

generate the list of different CB prices corresponding to the various share prices and two different interest rates. The results appear in the cell range B17 to D38. This table is generated by listing the different share prices of 6.00, 6.20, ...,10.00 in the cell range B18 to B38. The two different interest rates are placed in the cells C17 and D17. The general CB value appears in the cell E12 and so the expression = E12 is placed in the cell B17. When invoking the table command enter B3 (the

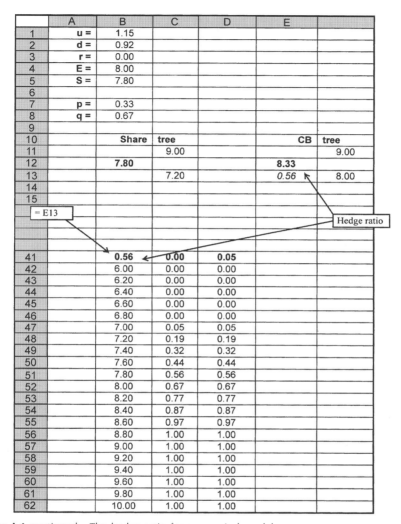

	A	B	C	D	E	
1	u =	1.15				
2	d =	0.92				
3	r =	0.00				
4	E =	8.00				
5	S =	7.80				
6						
7	p =	0.33				
8	q =	0.67				
9						
10		Share	tree		CB	tree
11			9.00			9.00
12		7.80			8.33	
13			7.20		0.56	8.00
14						
15						

= E13   Hedge ratio

	A	B	C	D	E	
41		0.56	0.00	0.05		
42		6.00	0.00	0.00		
43		6.20	0.00	0.00		
44		6.40	0.00	0.00		
45		6.60	0.00	0.00		
46		6.80	0.00	0.00		
47		7.00	0.05	0.05		
48		7.20	0.19	0.19		
49		7.40	0.32	0.32		
50		7.60	0.44	0.44		
51		7.80	0.56	0.56		
52		8.00	0.67	0.67		
53		8.20	0.77	0.77		
54		8.40	0.87	0.87		
55		8.60	0.97	0.97		
56		8.80	1.00	1.00		
57		9.00	1.00	1.00		
58		9.20	1.00	1.00		
59		9.40	1.00	1.00		
60		9.60	1.00	1.00		
61		9.80	1.00	1.00		
62		10.00	1.00	1.00		

Figure A.4 continued   The hedge ratio for one-period model

interest rate) in the row dialogue box and B5 (the share price) in the column dialogue box.

The hedge ratio is calculated in cell E13 and with a share price of £7.80 is equal to 0.56. The values of the hedge ratio at various share prices and interest rates is generated using the table facility and appear in the cell rage B42 to D62.

The two-period model on sheet Append_5_2 appears in Figure A.5. The formulation is very similar to that for the one-period model except that the up and down parameters and the interest rate parameters involve the square root function.

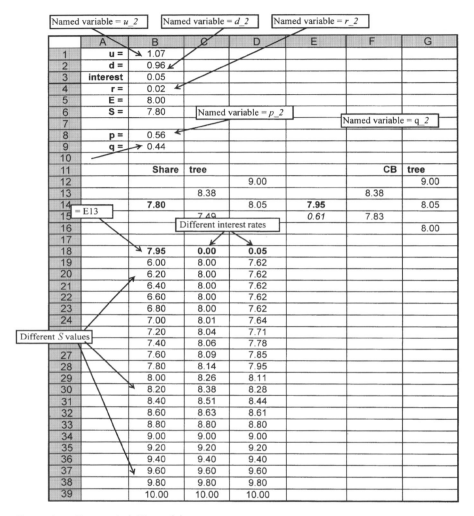

Figure A.5　Two-period CB model

The square root functions are necessary because the share and CB price movements take place over two periods.

The three-period model is on sheet Append_5_3 and is identical to Append_5_2 except that the cube roots of the appropriate parameters are used. The parameters are also named appropriately such as u_3, etc.

More realistic CB and share price trees are obtained using more periods. So a four-period model will give more meaningful results than a three-period model and a five-period model will give more meaningful results than a four-period model,

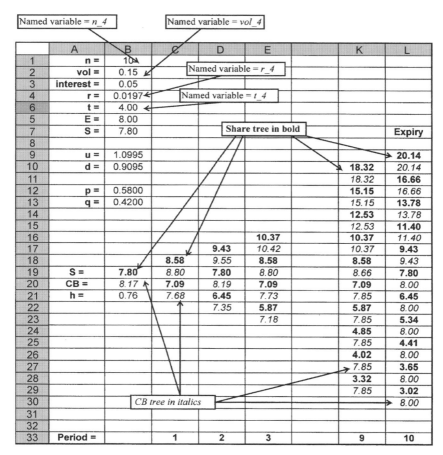

Figure A.6   The ten-period CB model

and so on. In Chapter 5, illustrations are generated using a 50-period model. Because of space restrictions we supply on sheet Append_5_4, a ten-period model. A section of this sheet is shown in Figure A.6. Following the procedures outlined in Chapter 5 the up and down parameters are given in terms of the volatility (vol_4), the time to expiry (t_4) and the number of periods (n_4). Accordingly the cell B9 contains the expression:

$$= \exp (vol\_4 * \mathrm{SQRT}(t\_4 / n\_4))$$

and this is set to the named variable: u_4. The d_4, p_4 and q_4 parameters are calculated as before. The initial share price (S_4) is in the cell B19. The share tree is generated using the up and down multipliers u_4 and d_4. A ten-period model gives eleven final share prices and these appear in the cells: L9, L11, ..., L29. In this representation of the ten-period model, the CB prices are placed directly underneath the corresponding share prices. The expiring CB values are calculated as the maximum of the expiring share price and the conversion price using expressions of the type:

$$= \text{Max } \{L9,\ E\_4)$$

All other CB values are calculated using expressions of the type:

$$= (p\_4 * L10 +\ q\_4 * L12)\ /\ (1 + r\_4)$$

With the volatility at 15%, interest rates at 5% and the share price at £7.80, a four-year CB would be priced at £8.17 per share with a hedge ratio of 0.76. Also on sheet Append_5_4 are tables showing how the CB price varies with interest rates and volatility. The interested reader can easily extend this to a 50-period model or indeed a 100-period model. It is simply a matter of extending the share and CB trees.

Coupons are introduced to the ten-period model on sheet Append_5_5 shown in Figure A.7. The coupon parameter is given the name c_5. The only difference between this model and the previous one is that a coupon is paid every other period. Accordingly the additional term: $+ c\_5$ has to be added at the appropriate points in the CB tree. In the model without coupons the expression:

$$= \text{Max } \{L9,\ E\_4)$$

is replaced by the expression:

$$= \text{Max } \{L9,\ E\_5 + c\_5)$$

and similarly, expressions of the type:

$$= (p\_4 * E16 +\ q\_4 * E18)\ /\ (1 + r\_4)$$

are replaced with the expression:

$$= (p\_5 * E16 +\ q\_5 * E18)\ /\ (1 + r\_5) + c\_5$$

With the volatility at 15%, interest rates at 5% and the share price at £7.80, a four-year CB paying £0.08 every six months would be priced at £8.57 per share. This can be compared to the otherwise identical CB paying no coupon priced at £8.17.

CHAPTER 6: INTRODUCING COMPLICATIONS

The file Six.xls contains the models used to generate some of the figures in Chapter 6 and has different sheets labelled Append_6_1, Append_6_2, etc.

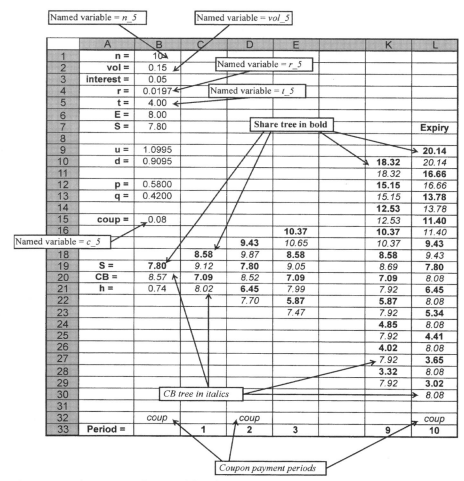

Figure A.7   The ten-period CB model with coupons

In sheet Append_6_1 the dividend complication is introduced into the two-period model using the multiplicative factor parameter *div_1*. This is set to equal to one minus the dividend yield. In the example given in Chapter 6, the dividend is set at 8% of the share price. Accordingly *div_1* is set to 0.92. Here the share goes ex-div at the first period and so the expression:

$$= B17 * d\_1$$

is replaced by:

$$= B17 * d\_1 * div\_1$$

The upper CB tree contains all the usual expressions to calculate the fair value at each node. However, the introduction of a dividend (particularly if it is large) introduces the possibility that the CB price will fall below parity. This cannot happen and in reality the calculated fair value would be overridden with the parity value. The American-style nature of a CB means that it will never trade below parity. Accordingly, the lower CB tree has an additional function that ensures that the reported CB value is always at least the parity value. The CB fair value appears in cell E26 and without the American-style feature would be:

$$= (p\_1 * F25 + q\_1 * F27) / (1 + r\_1)$$

But the parity value corresponding to this node is in cell B17. The above expression must therefore be replaced by:

$$= \text{Max } \{ B17, (p\_1 * F25 + q\_1 * F27) / (1 + r\_1) \}$$

In the example given, the CB values with and without the American-style feature are £7.80 and £7.70 respectively. The reason the latter price is so low is that the large dividend depresses the future share price. Append_6_1 appears in Figure A.8.

Append_6_2 has a ten-period CB model with dividends paid at periods 3, 6 and 9. The trees are integrated the same way as in sheet Append_5_4 with the share price above the CB price. Append_6_2 appears in Figure A.9. Note that the inclusion of three dividend payments of 2% reduces the CB price from £8.17 to £8.01.

Append_6_3 has a five-period model with a simple call feature. The example CB has 2.5 years to expiry and has a hard non-call period of one year. The additional restriction of the parity being above 130 is incorporated by defining the named variable call_3 and setting this to 130% of the conversion price. So in the example given call _3 is set to £10.4. The call restriction is included by the use of an = IF statement. The presence of the issuer's call means that the instrument cannot trade at a premium to parity if the share price is above call_3 and the time is right. The usual theoretical value in cell D36 would be calculated using the expression:

$$= (p\_3 * E35 + q\_3 * E37) / (1 + r\_3)$$

But since the cell D36 corresponds to the start of the call period there will always be the possibility that this theoretical value is greater than underlying parity or share price in cell D35. Accordingly, this expression is replaced with:

$$= \text{IF } \{ D35 > call\_3, D35, (p\_3 * E35 + q\_3 * E37) / (1 + r\_3) \}$$

In the example given, the share price in cell D35 is £11.11 which, in fact, is greater than £10.40 and so the theoretical value is overridden with the parity value of £11.11. All the CB cells after the second period contain this amended expression to

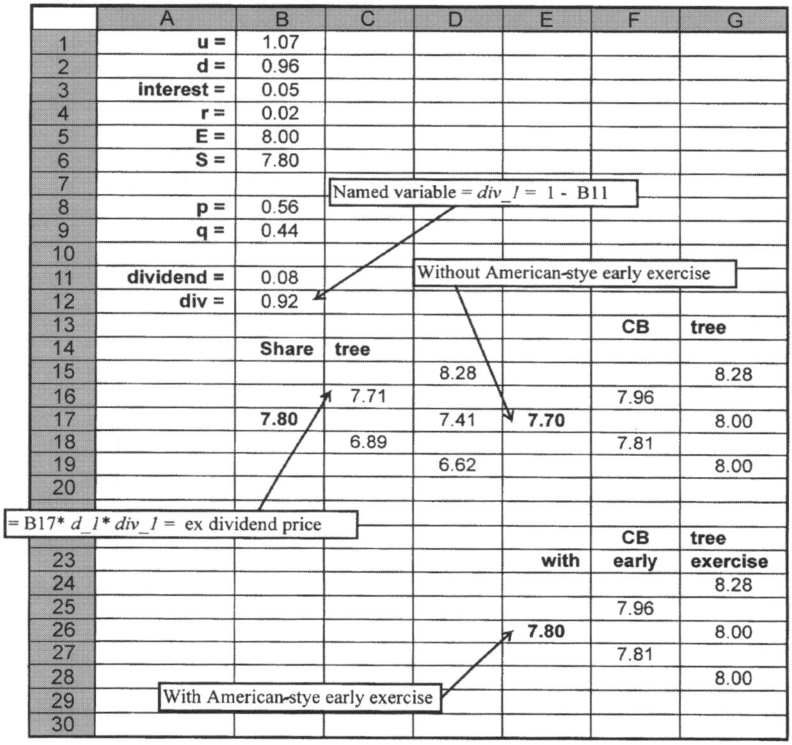

	A	B	C	D	E	F	G
1	u =	1.07					
2	d =	0.96					
3	interest =	0.05					
4	r =	0.02					
5	E =	8.00					
6	S =	7.80					
7				Named variable = div_1 = 1 - B11			
8	p =	0.56					
9	q =	0.44					
10							
11	dividend =	0.08		Without American-stye early exercise			
12	div =	0.92					
13						CB	tree
14		Share	tree				
15				8.28			8.28
16			7.71			7.96	
17		7.80		7.41	7.70		8.00
18			6.89			7.81	
19				6.62			8.00
20							

= B17* d_1* div_1 = ex dividend price

	A	B	C	D	E	F	G
						CB	tree
23					with	early	exercise
24							8.28
25						7.96	
26					7.80		8.00
27						7.81	
28							8.00
29		With American-stye early exercise					
30							

Figure A.8   Two-period CB model with dividends and early exercise feature

include the possibility of a call. Note that the CB with the call feature is priced at £9.46 compared to £9.61 with no call feature. Figure A.10 illustrates the five-period model in sheet Append_6_3. The sheet Append_6_4 has the extended ten-period model with the call feature at the halfway mark.

Append_6_5 has a five-period model with a put feature. The CB has 2.5 years to expiry and has a put option at the one year point (i.e., the second period). The put price is defined by named variable *put_5* and, as is usually the case, this is set to the conversion price (in this case *put_5* = 8). The put feature is included by the use of an = IF statement. The presence of the put at the second period means that the instrument cannot trade at a lower price than *put_5*. The usual theoretical value in cell D40 would be calculated using the expression:

$$= (p\_5 * E39 + q\_5 * E41) / (1 + r\_5)$$

But since the cell D40 corresponds to the put day there will always be the possibility that this theoretical value is lower than the put price. Accordingly this expression is replaced with:

	A	B	C	D	E		K	L
1	n =	10						
2	vol =	0.15						
3	interest =	0.05						
4	r =	0.0197						
5	t =	4.00						
6	E =	8.00						
7	S =	7.80						
8								
9	u =	1.0995						18.96
10	d =	0.9095					17.24	18.96
11			Named variable = div_2				17.24	15.68
12	p =	0.5800					14.26	15.68
13	q =	0.4200					14.26	12.97
14							11.80	12.97
15	dividend =	0.02					11.80	10.73
16	div =	0.98			10.16		9.76	10.73
17				9.43	10.17		9.76	8.88
18			8.58	9.43	8.40		8.07	8.88
19	S =	7.80	8.65	7.80	8.55		8.34	7.34
20	CB =	8.01	7.09	7.98	6.95		6.68	8.00
21	h =	0.77	7.52	6.45	7.55		7.85	6.07
22				7.23	5.75		5.52	8.00
23					7.12		7.85	5.02
24					↑		4.57	8.00
25							7.85	4.15
26							3.78	8.00
27							7.85	3.44
28							3.13	8.00
29							7.85	2.84
30							↑	8.00
31								
32					div		div	
33	Period =		1	2	3		9	10

Figure A.9 The ten-period CB model with dividends

$$= IF \{ (p\_5 * E39 + q\_5 * E41) / (1 + r\_5) < put\_5,$$

$$put\_5,$$

$$(p\_5 * E39 + q\_5 * E41) / (1 + r\_5) \}$$

In the example, the theoretical value without the put feature appears in the upper table as £7.08 and this is overridden with the put value of £8.00. All the CB cells in the second period contain this amended expression to include the possibility of putting the CB back to the issuer. Figure A.11 illustrates the five-period model. The sheet Append_6_6 has a ten-period model with the put feature at the halfway mark.

Append_6_7 has a one-period model with the two-interest-rate feature. The CB has one year to expiry and is identical to that given in Append_5_1 except that

	A	B	C	D	E	F	G	H
1	n =	5						
2	vol =	0.25						
3	interest =	0.05						
4	r =	0.0247						
5	t =	2.50						
6	E =	8.00						
7	S =	7.80						
8								
9	u =	1.1934						
10	d =	0.8380						
11			Five-period model with no call feature					
12	p =	0.5254						
13	q =	0.4746						
14							18.88	
15	coup =	0.4				15.82	18.88	
16					13.26	15.82	13.26	
17				11.11	13.66	11.11	13.26	
18			9.31	11.68	9.31	11.11	9.31	
19	S =	7.80	10.64	7.80	10.11	7.80	9.31	
20	CB =	9.61	6.54	9.18	6.54	8.66	6.54	
21	h =	0.61	8.96	5.48	8.64	5.48	8.40	
22				8.32	4.59	8.20	4.59	
23					8.40	3.85	8.40	
24						8.20	3.22	
25							8.40	
26								
27								
28			coupon		coupon		coupon	
29	Period =		1	2	3	4	5	
30								
31			Five-period model with call feature					
32	call =	130					18.88	
33		10.40				15.82	18.88	
					13.26	15.82	13.26	
				11.11	13.26	11.11	13.26	
36			9.31	11.11	9.31	11.11	9.31	
37	S =	7.80	10.35	7.80	10.11	7.80	9.31	
38	CB =	9.46	6.54	9.18	6.54	8.66	6.54	
39	h =	0.50	8.96	5.48	8.64	5.48	8.40	
40				8.32	4.59	8.20	4.59	
41					8.40	3.85	8.40	
42						8.20	3.22	
43							8.40	
44								
45								

Named variable = *call_3*

Call period begins here

Figure A.10 The effect of a call feature

there are now two interest rates. As explained in Section 6.4.4, the inclusion of two interest rates makes the modelling process more realistic. The two rates appear in the named variable cells *rs_7* (the short rate) and *rb_7* (the long or bond rate). In this model the two interest rates are mixed using the hedge ratio and so this first has

	A	B	C	D	E	F	G	H
1	n =	5						
2	vol =	0.25						
3	interest =	0.1						
4	r =	0.0488						
5	t =	2.50						
6	E =	8.00						
7	S =	6.00						
8								
9	u =	1.1934						
10	d =	0.8380						
11			Five-period model with no put feature					
12	p =	0.5933						
13	q =	0.4067						
14							14.52	
15	coup =	0.08				12.17	14.52	
16					10.20	12.17	10.20	
17				8.54	10.42	8.54	10.20	
18			7.16	9.03	7.16	8.90	7.16	
19	S =	6.00	8.08	6.00	8.10	6.00	8.08	
20	CB =	7.31	5.03	7.46	5.03	7.70	5.03	
21	h =	0.49	7.05	4.21	7.43	4.21	8.08	
22				7.08	3.53	7.70	3.53	
23					7.43	2.96	8.08	
24						7.70	2.48	
25							8.08	
26								
27								
28			coupon		coupon		coupon	
29	Period =		1	2	3	4	5	
30								
31			Five-period model with put feature					
32	put =	8.00					14.52	
33						12.17	14.52	
34					10.20	12.17	10.20	
35				8.54	10.42	8.54	10.20	
36			7.16	9.03	7.16	8.90	7.16	
37	S =	6.00	8.29	6.00	8.10	6.00	8.08	
38	CB =	7.68	5.03	8.00	5.03	7.70	5.03	
39	h =	0.27	7.71	4.21	7.43	4.21	8.08	
40				8.00	3.53	7.70	3.53	
41					7.43	2.96	8.08	
42						7.70	2.48	
43							8.08	
44								
45								

Named variable = put_5

Put date here

Figure A.11 The effect of a put feature

to be calculated and appears in the F14 cell as the named variable h_7. The hedge ratio is calculated in the usual way using the expression:

$$h = \frac{CB_u - CB_d}{S.u - S.d}$$

which in terms of the variables in sheet Append_6_7 is:

$$h\_7 = (G12 - G14) / (C12 - C14)$$

The interest rate mixing is done in the cell F15 and the result is the named variable *rmix_7* and is calculated using the expression:

$$= rs\_7 * h\_7 + rb\_7 * (1 - h\_7)$$

The CB price is then calculated in the standard way using the mixed interest rate *rmix_7* as follows:

$$= (p\_7 * G12 + q\_7 * G14) / (1 + rmix\_7)$$

Note that the *p* and *q* parameters are functions only of *rs_7*, not the mixed rate.

The sheet Append_6_8 has the much more complex ten-period CB model with mixed rates. Because the (mixed) interest rate used in the discounting process depends on the hedge ratio and the hedge ratio depends on the CB values, the process is quite complex and involves the calculation and presentation of the hedge ratio, the mixed interest rate and the CB value at each node. Figure A.12 is a snapshot of a small section of the spreadsheet Append_6_8. Here we briefly discuss the process of backward induction starting at the top of the share price tree.

Step 1 Calculate the expiring CB values. Cells L2 contains the usual expiring CB statement:

$$= Max \{L1, E\_8\}$$

This returns a value of 20.14. A similar expression in cell L6 returns a CB value of 16.66. At this stage, the two expiring CB values emanating from the previous share price value in cell L3 are now known.

Step 2 Calculate the hedge ratio and this is done in cell K5 using the expression:

$$= (L2 - L6) / (L1 - L5)$$

Step 3 Calculate the special interest rate that is a mixture of the short rate (*rs_8*) and the long rate (*rb _ 8*). This is done using the hedge ratio sitting in cell K5 as follows:

$$= rs\_8 * K5 + rb\_8 * (1 - K5)$$

The resulting mixed interest rate sits in cell K6. In this case, with the share price so

Named variable = rb_8		Named variable = rs_8				

	A	B	C	D		K	L
1	n =	10			Share price		20.14
2	vol =	0.15					20.14
3	rshort =	0.03			CB price	18.32	
4	rbond =	0.1				18.32	
5	rs =	0.0119			Hedge ratio	1.00	16.66
6	rb =	0.0389				0.0119	16.66
7	t =	4.00			Mixed rate =rmix_8	15.15	
8	E =	8.00				15.15	
9	S =	7.80				1.00	13.78
10						0.0119	13.78
11	u =	1.0995				12.53	
12	d =	0.9095				12.53	
13						1.00	11.40
14	p =	0.5389				0.0119	11.40
15	q =	0.4611				10.37	
16						10.37	
17				9.43		1.00	9.43
18				9.46		0.0119	9.43
19			8.58	0.97		8.58	
20			8.64	0.0128		8.64	
21	S =	7.80	0.94	7.80		0.88	7.80
22	CB =	7.91	0.0136	7.94		0.0152	8.00
23	h =	0.90	7.09	0.87		7.09	
24	rmix =	0.0147	7.31	0.0155		7.70	
25			0.80	6.45		0.00	6.45
26			0.0172	6.85		0.0389	8.00
27				0.65		5.87	
28				0.0214		7.70	
29							
30							
31							
32							
33							
34							
35							
36	Period		1	2		9	10

Figure A.12   The ten-period CB model with mixed interest rates

high, the hedge ratio is 1.00 and so the mixed interest rate will be the same as the short interest rate.

Step 4   Calculate the CB value using the p and q parameters, and the mixed interest rate. The result sits in the K4 cell and is given by the expression:

$$= (p\_8 * L2 + q\_8 * L6) / (1 + K6)$$

The process is repeated throughout the sheet. The resulting CB value (with short rates at 3% and long rates at 10%) is £7.91. The reader will find it interesting to vary the long and short rates and note the effects on the CB price and the hedge ratio.

A ten-period non-domestic CB is modelled in Append_6_9. Since the CB converts into dollars, the exercise price or redemption value (E_9) is set equal to $16. The foreign exchange rate variable (fx_9) is set to 0.60 The sterling share price tree is generated as before and appears in the usual cells, with the highest expiring price being £20.14 in cell L1. The dollar equivalent share price in the lower cell, L2, is calculated using the expression:

$$= L1 \: / \: fx\_9$$

On expiry the CB holder must choose the maximum of the dollar share price and the redemption value of $16. This is done with the expression:

$$= \text{Max} \: \{L2, \: E\_9\}$$

The rest is as before. In the example the CB fair value is $14.60 or £8.76. A subset of Append_6_9 is shown in Figure A.13

CHAPTER 9: REFIX CLAUSES

The file Nine.xls contains the models used to generate some of the figures in Chapter 9 and has sheets labelled Append_9_1 and Append_9_2.

Sheet Append_9_1 contains the five-period model with a refix at the second period illustrated in Figure 9.4. Figure A.14 shows the primary tree and one of the secondary trees. The maximum refix amount is in cell B15 and assigned the named variable sdn_1. In the example, this is set to 0.75 and so the maximum degree of resetting is 75% of the original conversion price. The minimum reset conversion price is therefore given by the expression:

$$= sdn\_1 \: * \: E\_1$$

This appears in cell B16 as the named variable $slow\_1$ and is equal to 6.00. The share price tree is generated as before and is labelled 'Primary tree'. In this example the refix day corresponds to the second period and so three secondary trees are generated. Each secondary tree corresponds to one of the nodes on the refix day. In Figure A.14 only the third secondary tree is shown and we now discuss this in more detail.

The initial share price in the third secondary tree is 5.60 and this sits in cell D49. The cell above this initial share price (cell D48) has the expression:

$$= \text{IF} \: (D49 < E\_1, \: \text{MAX} \: \{D49, \: slow\_1\}, \: E\_1\}$$

	A	B	C	D	E	K	L
1	n =	10					20.14
2	vol =	0.15		Share price in £'s			33.57
3	interest	0.05				18.32	33.57
4	r =	0.0197		Share price in $'s		30.53	
5	t =	4.00				30.53	16.66
6	E($) =	16.00		CB price in $'s			27.77
7	S =	7.80				15.15	27.77
8						25.26	
9	u =	1.0995				25.26	13.78
10	d =	0.9095					22.97
11						12.53	22.97
12	p =	0.5800	Named variable = fx_9			20.89	
13	q =	0.4200				20.89	11.40
14							19.00
15	FX =	0.60				10.37	19.00
16						17.28	
17				9.43		17.40	9.43
18				15.72			15.72
19			8.58	16.45		8.58	16.00
20			14.29			14.29	
21	S(£) =	7.80	15.43	7.80		15.69	7.80
22	S($) =	13.00		13.00			13.00
23	CB($) =	14.60	7.09	14.74		7.09	16.00
24	CB(£) =	8.76	11.82			11.82	
25			14.13	6.45		15.69	6.45
26				10.75			10.75
27				13.95			16.00
28							
29							
30							
31							
32							
33							
34							
35							
36	Period		1	2		9	10

Figure A.13 The ten-period non-domestic CB model

This returns the new amended conversion price using the following logic: If the share price (D49 = 5.60) on the refixing day is lower than the original conversion price (E_1 = 8.00) then refix the conversion price, otherwise leave it alone. If however, resetting does take place, reset it only to the maximum of the share price and the *slow_1* value. In this case the result of this statement is obviously 6.00. With the conversion price reduced, the number of shares per bond will increase and the increase will be in direct proportion to the decrease. Cell D47 contains the expression:

$$= E\_1 \ / \ D48$$

and this gives the increase in the number of shares per bond. In the example this

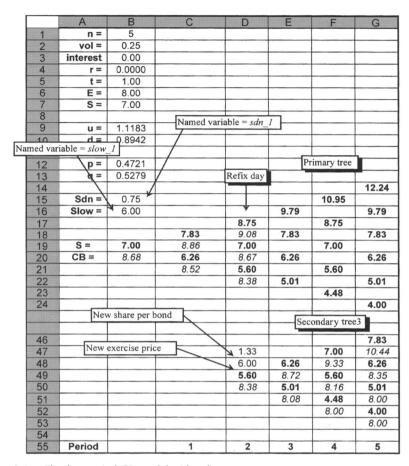

	A	B	C	D	E	F	G
1	n =	5					
2	vol =	0.25					
3	interest	0.00					
4	r =	0.0000					
5	t =	1.00					
6	E =	8.00					
7	S =	7.00					
8			Named variable = *sdn_1*				
9	u =	1.1183					
10	d =	0.8942					
Named variable = *slow_1*							
12	p =	0.4721				Primary tree	
13	q =	0.5279		Refix day			
14							12.24
15	Sdn =	0.75				10.95	
16	Slow =	6.00			9.79		9.79
17				8.75		8.75	
18			7.83	9.08	7.83		7.83
19	S =	7.00	8.86	7.00		7.00	
20	CB =	8.68	6.26	8.67	6.26		6.26
21			8.52	5.60		5.60	
22				8.38	5.01		5.01
23						4.48	
24							4.00
		New share per bond				Secondary tree3	
46							7.83
47		New exercise price		1.33		7.00	10.44
48				6.00	6.26	9.33	6.26
49				5.60	8.72	5.60	8.35
50				8.38	5.01	8.16	5.01
51					8.08	4.48	8.00
52						8.00	4.00
53							8.00
54							
55	Period		1	2	3	4	5

Figure A.14   The five-period CB model with refix

value is 1.33. With the share price down at 5.60 on the refix day the number of shares per bond increase by a factor of 1.33 and this value is used in the calculation of the expiring CB value. The new conversion price is in cell D48 and the expiring share price is in cell G46. The uppermost expiring CB cell G47 thus contains the expression:

$$= \$D\$47 * MAX \{G46, \$D\$48\}$$

The maximum function takes care of the fact that the holder will choose the highest of the redemption value and the share value. The multiplier D47 takes into account the fact that the CB now has more shares. In the example with the expiring share price up at 7.83 conversion would take place. The CB now has 1.33 shares and so the expiring value would be 7.83 × 1.33 = 10.44. The rest of the secondary tree is as before. The cell D50 (= 8.38) is therefore the value of the CB on the refixing day if the share price were 5.60. This value of D50 = 8.38 is then transferred back to the primary tree. The process is repeated for each of the other two secondary trees. Backward induction using identical procedures produces the theoretical CB value as £8.68 per share (compared to £8.33 without a refix). The sheet Append_9_2 has the more elaborate ten-period model with a refix.

Index

Accompanying disk

The disk included with this book contains the Excel workbooks referred to in the Appendix. The workbooks incorporate features only supported by Microsoft Excel 97. ATTEMPTING TO OPEN THE WORKBOOKS IN PREVIOUS VERSIONS OF EXCEL WILL CAUSE THE FUNCTIONS TO RETURN INCORRECT RESULTS.

A Microsoft viewer is freely available from the Microsoft website www.microsoft.com/excel/internet/viewer/. The viewer application is for Windows95/NT only.

The disk contains five workbooks named: two.xls, four.xls, five.xls, six.xls, nine.xls. Each workbook file refers to the corresponding chapter, e.g. two.xls contains all the programs relating to Chapter 2. Follow the steps below to copy the files to your hard disk into a directory called c:\CONNOLLY.

Windows 95: Copying Workbook Files to the Hard Disk

1. Place the disk into the floppy disk drive
2. From START/Run: type a:\Install
3. Click the OK button to copy files into directory CONNOLLY
4. After all workbook files have been extracted, close the MSDOS 'Finished–install' window
5. There should now be a directory called CONNOLLY on your hard disk (i.e. c:\CONNOLLY) containing all nine workbook files

If you have any further queries, please contact Wiley Customer Service, Technical Support Group:

E-mail: cs-electronic@wiley.co.uk
Fax: (+44) (0)1243 843315
Tel: (+44) (0)1243 843312

WILEY COPYRIGHT INFORMATION AND TERMS OF USE